THE RUSSIAN CHURCH UNDER
THE SOVIET REGIME,
1917-1982

VOLUME TWO

DIMITRY POSPIELOVSKY

THE RUSSIAN CHURCH UNDER THE SOVIET REGIME, 1917-1982

VOLUME TWO

ST. VLADIMIR'S SEMINARY PRESS
CRESTWOOD, NEW YORK 10707
1984

Library of Congress Cataloging in Publication Data

Pospielovsky, Dimitry, 1935-
     The Russian church under the Soviet regime,
1917-1982.

     Bibliography: p.
     Includes index.
     1. Russkaia pravoslavnaia tserkov—History—20th
century.   2. Orthodox Eastern Church—Soviet Union—
History—20th century.   3. Soviet Union—Church history—
1917-   I. Title.
BX492.P67   1984   281.9'3   84-5336
ISBN 0-88141-015-2 (v. 1)
ISBN 0-88141-016-0 (v. 2)
ISBN 0-88141-033-0 (set)

THE RUSSIAN CHURCH UNDER
THE SOVIET REGIME
1917-1982

© Copyright 1984

by

ST. VLADIMIR'S SEMINARY PRESS

ISBN 0-88141-015-2 (v. 1)
ISBN 0-88141-016-0 (v. 2)
ISBN 0-88141-033-0 (set)

PRINTED IN THE UNITED STATES OF AMERICA
BY
ATHENS PRINTING COMPANY
New York, NY 10018

Contents

VOLUME TWO

8 The Russian Churches in the Diaspora
   and the Mother Church 255

9 The Russian Orthodox Church during
   the First Postwar Decade 301
10 New Trials: Khrushchev's Attack on the Church 327

11 The Catacombs: The "True Orthodox" and Other Currents ... 365

12 The Russian Orthodox Church, 1965-1982 387

Conclusion 469

Appendix 1—Excerpts from Bishop Leonty of Chile's "Political
   Controls over the Orthodox Church in the Soviet Union" 473

Appendix 2—Excerpts from A.A. Valentinov's *The Black Book* ... 477

Appendix 3—Letter to the Priest P.F. 483

Appendix 4—The Administration of the Metropolia
   (Decisions of the 1937 New York Sobor) 489

Appendix 5—Address of Thanks to Adolph Hitler, Leader of
   the German People, from Metropolitan Anastasy of
   the Karlovci Synod 491

Appendix 6—The 1975 Amendments to the 1929 Legislation on
   Religious Associations 493

Bibliography 501

Index 517

CHAPTER 8

The Russian Churches in the Diaspora and the Mother Church

World War II ended with a complete reshuffling of the centers of gravity of the Russian emigration and with often unexpected reversals of loyalties in relation to the Soviet regime in general and the Moscow Patriarchate in particular. It was often the most right-wing, conservative elements, more often with military traditions of emotional patriotism rather than political understanding of the Soviet-Marxist system, who were overcome with emotion upon seeing the Soviet victory and who viewed the tsarist uniforms and ranks restored in the Soviet armed forces as "evidence" of a Russian national revival. The appearance of church delegations consisting of real bishops from Russia did the rest of the job. Thousands of Russian émigrés in France, China, Manchuria and elsewhere joined "Societies of Soviet Patriots," took Soviet passports and applied for repatriation. But the Soviets allowed only a small proportion to actually avail themselves of the right to return to the USSR. "Soviet patriots" were more useful as residents in the West, where they could demoralize the émigré community, sow discord in it and effect further church splits by creating and perpetuating parishes and dioceses of the Moscow Patriarchate in addition to those of the Karlovcians, the Evlogians and the Russian Orthodox Church of America and Canada.

Of the original Karlovci Synod of Bishops, only two European metropolitans, Anastasy and Serafim (Lade), survived the war as its members. Three other bishops died in the course of evacuation from Belgrade first to Karlsbad (western Czechoslovakia) and then to Munich, and one, Hermogen, had formed a puppet Croatian Orthodox Church[1] under the fascist Ustasi regime in Zagreb and was later executed by Tito's partisans. In China, even the staunch Karlovcian Archbishop Ioann (Maximovich) of Shanghai wavered for a long time, although there was no danger of Soviet troops or forced repatriations in Shanghai, "and for some time even tried to convince his flock to accept the Moscow administration."[2] As to the four other Karlovcian bishops in Soviet-occupied Manchuria and China (including Archbishop Dimitry, the father of the would-be ruling metropolitan of the neo-Karlovcian "Synod Abroad," Philaret), they all appealed, on July 26, 1945, to the Moscow Patriarch to accept them back into his fold. Moreover, on the occasion of the "Soviet victory over Japan," in September 1945, they addressed a laudatory telegram of congratulations to Stalin asking for God's blessings on the "dear Iosif Vissarionivich" Stalin.[3] In Europe, the extreme Karlovcian right wingers Archbishop Serafim of Bulgaria and Metropolitan Serafim (Lukyanov) of Paris likewise joined the Moscow Patriarchate—just like their predecessor and the very initiator of the idea of an all-émigré church administration, Venyamin (Fedchenkov), had done before the war. What saved the "Synod Abroad," newly reconstituted in Munich, was the huge new wave of wartime emigration from the Soviet Union

[1] Archbishop John (Ioann Shakhovskoi) thus described Hermogen's act: "This was a blow to the Serbian Orthodox Church, which suffered so greatly during the war and which had been such a generous protector of bishops and patron of the Synod in Karlovci." *Utverzhdenie pomestnoi tserkvi* (New York: Waldon Press, 1972) 16.

[2] See the brochure by Bishop Ieronim, a steadfast Karlovcian in the US, *Sovremennoe polozhenie russkoi tserkvi zagranitsei*, published in the US around late 1945 or early 1946. Likewise, the whole Karlovcian Lesna Convent in Serbia applied for Soviet citizenship and for repatriation to the USSR. See L.N. Pariisky, "Iz prebyvaniya moskovskoi delegatsii v Belgrade," *ZhMP*, no. 5 (1946) 42-3. This was probably the reason why after his quarrel with Moscow, Tito expelled all these nuns to Italy. Now the Lesna Convent is situated some sixty miles outside of Paris and is again under the post-Karlovci Synod.

[3] A text of the sycophantic telegram and of Stalin's answer is in the Archives of the Orthodox Church in America in Syosset, N.Y. The tattered state of the sheet on which it appears made it impossible to decipher the name or date of the newspaper or journal it came from. Their petition to be accepted into the fold of the Moscow Patriarchate is in *ZhMP*, no. 10 (1945) 5-6.

with its bishops of the wartime churches of Belorussia and the Ukraine (Autonomous), who joined Metropolitans Anastasy (Gribanovsky) and Serafim (Lade) to form the new Synod of Bishops in Munich in 1946. The heaviest setback to the Evlogian Church in Paris, although a brief one, was caused by Metropolitan Evlogy himself.[4]

In America the situation was quite different. Within five years of the end of the war the United States became also the seat of the Karlovci-Munich Synod, now in conflict with the traditional local Russian Orthodox Greek Catholic (Missionary) Church of America, which had been in existence since the end of the eighteenth century. But this situation warrants a separate discussion. For now, let us return to émigré church affairs as we left them in 1927.

Emigré Church Affairs from the 1930s to the Present

The parting of ways between Metropolitan Evlogy and the Karlovci Synod took place in January 1927, when a council of the Karlovci bishops "suspended" Evlogy and banned liturgical intercommunion with him. Officially, this was a punishment for Evlogy's demonstrative departure from the 1926 Council of Bishops, which had caused a schism. The latter act, however, was precipitated by the Karlovcians' attempt to wean the German deanery from Evlogy's archdiocese by granting de facto diocesan powers to his vicar-bishop for Germany, Tikhon, whom Evlogy, against his better judgment, had been forced by the Karlovcians to consecrate. Evlogy has consistently argued that, on the strength of Patriarch Tikhon's above-mentioned decrees, the Karlovcian bishops had no jurisdiction over this diocese and that it was simply out of his own good will that he participated in the sessions of the Karlovci Synod, not out of any sense of duty.[5] The canonical

[4]*Tserkovnaya letopis'*, ed. with introduction by Metropolitan Anastasy (Lausanne, December 1945) 16-7. Anastasy claims that Metropolitan Alexander (Inozemtsev), formerly of the Ukrainian wartime Autocephalist orientation, likewise applied to join Anastasy's Synod. If so, then his murder in West Germany (Heyer, 224, n. 99) should be seen as a further act of the Banderist terrorism. On Evlogy, see chapter 4 and below, pp. 260ff.

[5]Evlogy, *Put'*, 606-16. For the opposite interpretation see *Deyaniya vtorogo*

view on this dispute was expressed by the Ecumenical Patriarch, to whom Evlogy appealed as the supreme arbiter in disputes among Orthodox bishops: "the act of suspension against you, just like any other action of the so-called Episcopal Synod Abroad, is canonically invalid because the very existence of this self-styled assembly as an administrative organ is without canonical foundation." This decision of the See of Constantinople was endorsed by the Patriarch of Alexandria, the Church of Greece and the ruling archbishops of Lithuania, Latvia and Finland.[6]

The above statement by the ecumenical see must have acted as one of the incentives for Evlogy's second appeal to Constantinople at the end of 1930. Evlogy supported his action on the basis of canons allowing a bishop to turn for justice to an outside patriarch when in dispute with his own. But the canonist Sergei Troitsky points out that canon 17 of the Fourth Ecumenical Council mentions only the possibility of appealing to an outside patriarch *for arbitration*, and "the choice of the arbiter must be agreed upon by both sides." Hence, strictly speaking, the unilateral acts of both Evlogy and of Constantinople were uncanonical.

The subordination of his West European archdiocese to Constantinople was interpreted by the Karlovcians as a "sell-out to the Greeks." Their argument, however, that the canonical orthodoxy of the Ecumenical Patriarchate was itself suspect was not unfounded. They put forward the examples of the patriarchate's illegitimate interference into the dispute between Patriarch Tikhon and the Renovationists, its equally uncanonical recognition of the Renovationists as the Orthodox Church of Russia and its ecclesiastical-administrative persecution in 1923-1924 of Archbishop Anastasy, then residing in Constantinople, for elevating the name of Patriarch Tikhon at services and for criticizing Bolshevism in sermons.[7] However, these were the acts of Patriarch Grigorios

vsezarubezhnogo sobora russkoi pravoslavnoi tserkvi zagranitsei (Belgrade, 1939) 562-5. See also chapter 4 above. All Evlogy's statements regarding schisms with Karlovci and with Metropolitan Sergii correspond to the contemporary reports in the two Paris Russian dailies, *Vozrozhdenie* (popular-monarchist) and *Poslednie novosti* (republican-liberal), which we checked at the Syosset archives.

[6]Evlogy, *Put'*, 617; S. Troitsky, *Razmezhevanie ili raskol?* (Paris: YMCA Press, 1932) 102-3.

[7]*Deyaniya vtorogo sobora*, 566-7.

VII, who was hoping for Soviet support in his insecure position in Turkey in the wake of the Greek-Turkish War. Patriarch Vasilios III recognized Sergii and his Synod as the Church of Russia in 1927, as mentioned before, but, like his successor Photios II, he continued fraternal ecclesiastic relations with the Renovationists as well. This ambivalent policy of the ecumenical see was the main reason for Sergii's refusal to participate in the Prosynod—i.e., the preparatory commission for a future Orthodox ecumenical council originally planned by the Patriarchate of Constantinople for June 1932, to which the latter had invited both the Patriarchal and the Renovationist Russian Churches. Following the Russian refusal to participate, the Romanians, Serbs, Cypriots and the Church of Athens likewise declined, and the whole idea fell through.[8] But this uncanonical behavior of the Ecumenical Patriarchate itself made Evlogy's subordination to it vulnerable to attack on canonical grounds. Constantinople's creation of the proto-Karlovcian autonomous Higher Church Administration for the Russian émigrés in 1920 was also canonically questionable, but this question the Karlovcians prefer to ignore.[9]

At least some of the members of the Karlovci Synod, however, particularly Metropolitan Antony, paid little attention to their own bans and attacks. A perfect illustration of this was the aged metropolitan's 1934 private letter to Evlogy inviting him to come to Belgrade and patch up their differences, "even under the prevailing present conditions"—i.e., recognizing the status quo of Evlogy's subordination to Constantinople. This was followed by a telegram from the bishop-elect for the United States, Archimandrite Vitaly, inviting Evlogy to participate in his consecration in Belgrade, accompanied by a similar *official* telegram from Antony. "A strange contradiction," as Evlogy remarked, "the Karlovcians have suspended me as a cleric, and now are inviting me to participate in their church celebration." He then describes some details of his subsequent visit. Antony appeared totally decrepit but warm and friendly. The two hierarchs read

[8]See Sergii's response of September 30, 1931 (no. 7464) and Sergii's and his Synod's resolution "O prosinode" of July 29, 1932 (no. 113) in *ZhMP*, no. 7-8 (1932) 20-2, and no. 11-12 (1932) 2-3, respectively.
[9]See above in chapter 4, pp. 114ff.

prayers of absolution in sequence over each other. In the evening they discussed how they would concelebrate the next liturgy, but officials of the Synod intervened: "No, this has to be decided upon by the Synod." Thus, real concelebration was prevented for the time, although an official statement in a monarchist journal, signed by Count Grabbe, the Synod's chancellor, stated that the ban on Evlogy would soon be removed.

The metropolitan was invited to the August 1934 session of the Karlovci Synod, but responded that he could not come as a petitioner for the revocation of the ban since it was illegitimate and therefore should be revoked on the Synod's own initiative. Evlogy should have thought about this earlier, prior to the absolution prayers, for, canonically speaking, recourse to these prayers by both hierarchs meant that both considered themselves guilty of ecclesiastic apostasy. It also meant that all the rites performed by the churches under the jurisdictions of both Antony and Evlogy during the years of apostasy were invalid. If both saw themselves as guilty of apostasy, they had no right to absolve each other, but should have sought absolution from their supreme ecclesiastic authority—i.e., from Metropolitan Sergii or from a Russian council of bishops.[10] Stretching out the canons somewhat, the two metropolitans could have resorted to the Patriarch of Serbia and his council of bishops for the absolution, on the grounds of their physical presence on Serbian church territory. But nothing of the sort was done. Moreover, the Synodal revocation of the ban that followed was dressed as an act of magnanimous forgiveness toward Evlogy, a concession to the personal petition of Antony for the good of the Church, based on Evlogy's alleged personal appeal to Antony, which in fact never took place. Evlogy immediately and vehemently denied, in the press and in his sermons, the accuracy of this formulation, emphasizing the illegitimacy of the ban to begin with.[11]

In response, the Karlovcian bishops renewed their attacks on Evlogy's "sell-out" to Constantinople, and Karlovcian bishops visiting their clergy within Evlogy's diocesan territory deliberately

---

[10]Stratonov makes these points in two articles he wrote in 1934, apparently offprints from an unnamed publication. See in the Lieb Archive, Hd 50, Nr. 37, Beil 2 and 3.

[11]Evlogy, Put', 621-32; Deyaniya vtorogo sobora, 568-75.

ignored the Evlogian bishops and clergy.[12] Evlogy's complaints to this effect in his correspondence with Antony were followed by an invitation extended by the latter to Metropolitans Evlogy and Theophilus of North America to a reconciliation council of émigré bishops, to take place in November 1935 under the chairmanship of Patriarch Varnava of Serbia. Evlogy agreed on the condition that he would remain under the Patriarch of Constantinople and that the émigré church structure would consist of four fully self-governing autonomous metropolitan districts: the Balkans, under Archbishop Anastasy; Western Europe, under Evlogy; China and the Far East, under Archbishop Dimitry of Hailar; and America under Metropolitan Theophilus.

At the council Evlogy was presented with a fully prepared draft of a "Temporary Statute," which substantially increased the central powers of the Synod of Bishops (i.e., the Karlovci center), granting it the right to appoint diocesan bishops to the "autonomous" districts over the heads of their official administrators. At the same time, it substantially increased the powers of the diocesan bishops within the districts. The whole exercise was obviously geared at curbing the prerogatives of such "unreliable" metropolitans as Evlogy and Theophilus. Remaining in a minority of one against all the others (Theophilus stated that he would go along with the majority and Anastasy said that he would act in accordance with the decisions of the Synod), Evlogy reluctantly signed all the papers, with the proviso that he and his metropolitan district would remain under Constantinople while fully cooperating with the Karlovci Synod and that the agreement would be valid for him only if approved by the Ecumenical Patriarch and his own diocesan assembly. The other amendments accepted on Evlogy's insistence were: (1) concelebration of clergy of all émigré districts; (2) condemnation of all hostile activity of the clergy of one district against those of another, whether in print, speeches or sermons; (3) ban on the opening of parallel parishes of Karlovci orientation on the territories of Evlogy or Theophilus, and vice-versa; and (4) ban on the acceptance of clergy from one diocese by another without canonical release.

Evlogy's diocesan assembly of June 1936, after a careful study of the statute, came to the conclusion that it had deprived

[12]Evlogy, *Put'*, 633-4; *Deyaniya vtorogo sobora*, 568-85.

the diocese (or the West European district, to be exact) of all autonomy, and therefore refused to endorse it. This brought Karlovcian accusations of fomenting schism levelled at Evlogy. Simultaneously, they reactivated their efforts to wrest all the remaining Evlogian parishes in Germany away from him, but under the pressure of events were forced to replace Bishop Tikhon with a German national, Archbishop Serafim (Lade), whom Evlogy characterized as decent but weak. These efforts were crowned by Hitler's decree of February 25, 1938, according to which all Orthodox church property became subject to the total control and administration of the German Ministry of Religious Cults. The latter, in turn, handed them over to the Karlovcians. This was often done by Gestapo intimidation of parish councils and priests. Thus, by 1938, only three parishes in Germany remained under Evlogy: in Berlin, in Dresden and in East Prussia.[13] Meanwhile, the 1936 Council of Karlovcian Bishops declared the temporary statute null and void because of Evlogy's withdrawal, and likewise annulled the stipulation banning the opening of parallel parishes, establishing a Karlovcian parallel diocese even on the territory of the Evlogian diocese of Nice, with the episcopal seat in the nearby city of Cannes.

At this point, Metropolitan Sergii's and Moscow's efforts in relation to the Orthodox diaspora should be mentioned. In 1931, in a letter to the Ecumenical Patriarch, Sergii protested the un-canonicity of the acceptance of the banned bishops and clergy (Evlogy and the Evlogians) into Constantinople's jurisdiction. Patriarch Photios' reply was couched in terms of the traditional claims of the Ecumenical Patriarchate to all territories outside the national frontiers of local autocephalous Orthodox churches.[14] In conciliatory terms, however, it assured Sergii of the temporary character of this arrangement, "until unity has been restored in the Russian Orthodox Church and a pan-Orthodox council has met," and it requested that Metropolitan Elevfery of Lithuania abstain "from interference into other bishops' canonical districts."

[13]Evlogy, Put', 646-8.
[14]See the already cited canon 28 of the Fourth Ecumenical Council (Chalcedon). Its validity is likewise rejected for the contemporary situation in the West by the Very Rev. Prof. John Meyendorff in his Living Tradition (Crestwood, N.Y.: SVS Press, 1978) 114. See also G. Troitsky, "Patriarkh Sergii i russkii zarubezhnyi tserkovnyi raskol," ZhMP, no. 6 (1968) 19-20.

Sergii expressed disagreement with this position. In October 1931 he addressed Patriarch Photios once again, explaining that anti-Soviet political activities of the émigré clergy were hurting the situation of the Church inside the USSR and that therefore he had asked the émigré clergy to pledge to abstain only from public attacks against the Soviet government. As Evlogy had not responded, this was followed by Sergii's synodal announcement that Evlogy and his clergy were suspended, pending a decision by an episcopal court to be convoked in due course.

In the meantime, Sergii corresponded with Patriarch Varnava of Serbia, who was rather critical of Evlogy's subordination to Constantinople, considering it canonically irregular. But it was the fate of the Karlovci Synod that was the main subject of the correspondence between the two hierarchs. Sergii stressed its complete uncanonicity, particularly its claims to head and represent the whole Russian church diaspora, and asked Varnava to act as an intermediary. He reiterated the limited context of his request of a pledge of loyalty and saw only two possibilities of solving the émigré problem: either their return to the jurisdiction of the Moscow Patriarchate or their absorption by the Serbian Patriarchate. Varnava chose the latter and disclosed his plans to turn the Karlovci Synod into an autonomous church administration for Russian émigrés within the jurisdiction of the Serbian Patriarchate, arguing that Sergii's own act of July 1927, releasing from his jurisdiction those clergy who would refuse to sign the pledge of loyalty, authorized such an act by the Serbian Patriarchate. Sergii, however, maintained that the Karlovci clergy could be absorbed by the Serbian Church only as individuals, to be appointed to dioceses and parishes within the Serbian church structure, and not as a self-governing body with extraterritorial rights. Upon joining the local Orthodox churches, the émigré bishops should return all original Russian church property to the Moscow Patriarchate, or to its official representative for Western Europe, Metropolitan Elevfery. In response, Varnava criticized Sergii for reneging on his own advice to the Karlovcians in his already cited private letter to them of 1926.[15] This accusation,

---

[15]The original texts are in *ZhMP*, no. 14-15 (1933) 1-8; and no. 22 (1934) 1-2. The pro-émigré view is in S. Troitsky, "Mitropolit Sergii i primirenie russkoi diaspory," *RAPV*, no. 9 (November 1936) 133-5; the pro-Moscow view is in G. Troitsky, "Patriarkh Sergii," 20-3.

however, is only partly valid, for although Sergii had suggested in that letter that the émigrés could form local territorial church administrations in non-Orthodox countries, for Orthodox countries (and he singled out Serbia in particular) the best solution would be simply to join the local Orthodox churches. Thus, strictly speaking, he was not reneging on anything.

Given the obvious pressure by the Soviets, Sergii's conciliatory tone is remarkable. He stresses that, although the Karlovci schism has been condemned by the Moscow Patriarchate ever since 1922, no definite datelines have been set for resolving the problem. Eleven years have gone by; this is about the limit, he writes. He hints quite clearly that the Karlovci Synod's politicization has caused the Church in Russia a great deal of harm, and he insists that his pledge of loyalty requires of the émigré clergy only one thing: abstention from participation in any politics. Thus, it gives the clergy greater freedom to concentrate on pastoral and spiritual work, while leaving the politics to the laity, to whom the pledge did not extend at all. The Soviet pressure is also noticeable when Sergii suggests that the main pragmatic reason why the Karlovcians should cease to exist as an extraterritorial independent or autonomous unit is because of their overt, declared and active hostility toward the Soviet government and toward the Church in Russia. He cites the example of a Chinese Orthodox priest, Fr. S. Chang, who, after he had dared to say a public prayer for Sergii and the Church in Russia at the 1934 Easter Liturgy in Tientsing, was banned by the local Karlovcian Bishop of Peking.[16]

Receiving no satisfaction from Patriarch Varnava, Metropolitan Sergii and his Synod resolved, on June 22, 1934, that all bishops of the Karlovcian church group be banned from performing any pastoral duties and rites subject to an ecclesiastical trial. This occurred a full six years after Sergii's own order of May 9, 1928 (no. 104) to immediately disband the Karlovci organization. Such a long interval between the order and the enactment of punishment for its nonfulfilment demonstrates Sergii's unwillingness to bring the matter to a head and his resistance to Soviet

[16]Ibid., 23. This was the same Archbishop Viktor of Peking who in 1945 would join the Moscow Patriarchate and later return to the USSR to head one of its dioceses. See the ukaz of Patr. Aleksii of June 13, 1946, in Ioann (Shakhovskoi), *Utverzhdenie*, 12-3; see also Sergii's address to Varnava, *ZhMP*, no. 14-15 (1933) 1-8.

pressure. Characteristically, none of the threatened trials has ever taken place to the present day, once again indicating the remarkable restraint and caution of Sergii and his successors.[17]

In August 1938 the Karlovci Synod engaged in another questionable operation: it convoked a clergy-laity conference, calling it the Second All-Émigré Sobor. But although it was styled all-émigré, Evlogy's West European exarchate was not represented, and France was the main center of Russian emigration and of the intellectual and scholarly life of Russian Orthodoxy outside Russia. The dubious nature of this assembly is also evident from several other factors. As Metropolitan Antony had died, it was convoked by Anastasy, who called himself a metropolitan, although the white metropolitan's cowl had been placed on his head by Patriarch Varnava of Serbia over tea in 1935, while the Karlovci Synod claimed to have been independent from the Church of Serbia; moreover, such acts are to be made by the decision of synods, not by an informal arbitrary decision of a patriarch. Also, the bishops from the Far East did not arrive and were "represented" by European bishops, who thus had extra votes.[18]

The "sobor" accused Evlogy of fomenting divisions, of "selling out" to Constantinople and even of acting uncanonically.

[17]Antony reacted by a long letter to Metropolitan Elevfery of Lithuania (August 20, 1934) disputing the legality of Sergii's actions on the grounds that bishops may not be banned without an ecclesiastic trial by a council of bishops, and this is to take place after three warnings given in personal visits by a delegate-bishop of such a council. A trial, he says, is impossible because it would mean certain death to the émigré bishops, and they would not go to Moscow even if called there by Sergii. To this Elevfery replied: (1) that precisely because their journey to a Moscow ecclesiastical trial would have been too risky, Sergii, making use of the fulness of power granted to him as locum tenens, banned them by administrative decree; (2) how dare he, Antony, call Sergii an apostate when he states a priori that he would not take the risk of a trip to Moscow while Sergii had been imprisoned four times for the faith; and (3) obviously, given the Soviet conditions, Sergii could not send personal messengers to the émigré bishops, but he gave them plenty of warning and waited for nearly six years before taking the decision, while Antony banned Evlogy of Paris and Platon of the US without sending any messengers or calling them to any ecclesiastic trials, although he had the full opportunity in the free world to do both, and without possessing even the canonical powers of a diocesan bishop, without which his bans were illegal anyway. Elevfery, *Moi otvet mitr. Antoniyu* (Paris, 1935) 10-58.

[18]Evlogy, *Put'*, 646-7. The informality of the ceremony with the cowl seems to be another indicator of Patriarch Varnava's real intentions of regularizing the Synod's situation by turning it into a Russian branch of the Serbian Church.

The only formally strong point in the accusations is a detailed account of the waverings and inconsistency in Evlogy's behavior on the whole issue of relations with Karlovci: his active participation in amending the draft statute and hence its acceptance, and then its subsequent rejection under the influence of the laity-clergy conference of his diocese.[19]

Among other business of the "sobor" there was an interesting and very detailed account on Orthodox Church-Polish state relations and on the mounting persecution of Orthodoxy in Poland. The report, however, showed the characteristically arch-conservative Russian nationalism of the Karlovcians: the use of the Polish language and the "Ukrainization" of Orthodoxy in Poland were condemned as a betrayal of the only "legitimate" Russian culture and basis of Orthodoxy there.[20]

The "sobor" criticized Evlogy for resisting the liquidation of his parishes in Germany, arguing that there should be only one ecclesiastical power there and it should "be the one, of course, which is recognized by the law of the state," i.e., by the Nazi state.[21]

The other curious documents of the "sobor" include a rabidly anti-Semitic report, alleging that world Jewry was engaged in demoralizing the Christian world by the dissemination of narcotics. Moreover, at the height of Hitler's attack on the Jews (and on Christianity) the report accuses the Roman Catholic Church of rapprochement with Judaism and attacks the Catholic Church of Germany for defending the Jews from Hitler and for protesting against anti-Semitism.[22]

The sessions concluded with an address to the Russian people in the USSR, containing a rather sober and intelligent assessment

[19]Ibid., 621-32; Deyaniya vtorogo sobora, 568-75.
[20]Ibid., 641-77.
[21]Ibid., 581-3.
[22]Ibid., 492-556. A characteristic representative of this extreme wing—which, with time and the increasing self-isolation of the Synod, took the upper hand in it—is N. Talberg, a member of the Higher Monarchist Council who after World War II became a professor at the Synod's only seminary in Jordanville, N.Y. and one of its foremost ideologists. In his publications, from 1927 to the 1960s, he consistently criticizes Tikhon for the attempts to make peace with the Bolshevik regime from 1919 on and attacks the leading "Evlogians" as agents of the Masons. See his Tserkovnyi raskol (Paris, 1927); and K sorokaletiyu pagubnogo evlogianskogo raskola (Jordanville, N.Y.: Holy Trinity Monastery, 1966).

of communist ideology, of the emotions that had been stirred across the world by the *Communist Manifesto* and of how these were frustrated by the materialization of the idea. The analysis concludes with the statement that throughout history only Christianity has been realistic enough to preach that complete equality and social utopia cannot be realized in this world of imperfect beings and can only result in their caricature. Inevitably, the document overidealizes the tsarist past and lists Nicholas II and his family, among others, as martyrs. In contrast to the 1921 "Sobor," this one does not directly call for a restoration of the monarchy, only for a healthy, strong and unified national Russian state.[23]

The Postwar Emigré Synod: From Munich to New York

The wartime fate of the Karlovci Synod has already been discussed. Let us now turn to the most salient points of its postwar development.

On August 10, 1945, Patriarch Aleksii issued an appeal "To the Archpastors and Clergy of the So-called Karlovcian Orientation," calling on them to return to his fold. He repeated all of Sergii's earlier admonitions, but significantly did not request a pledge of loyalty to the Soviet state.[24] Metropolitan Anastasy of the newly reconstituted Synod responded in the equally traditional Karlovcian terms, of which the strongest and most appropriate statement was: "To please the government, even the highest . . . bishops are not ashamed to propagate the manifest untruth that there was never any religious persecution in Russia, and in so doing blasphemously mock the masses of Russian martyrs, whom they openly describe as political criminals."[25] Characteristically, the reply was not even addressed to the Moscow Patriarchate, but to the "Russian Orthodox people." At least in this document, Anastasy still recognized Patriarch Aleksii as "the new Primate of the Russian Church." Seventeen years later the émigré Synod would assure its flock that the Moscow Patriarchate had nothing

[23]*Deyaniya vtorogo sobora*, 681-95.
[24]*ZhMP*, no. 9 (September 1945) 9-12.
[25]*A Pastoral Letter to Russian Orthodox People, Being a Reply to an Address by Patriarch Alexis*, an undated English-language printed brochure of eight pages.

to do with the true Russian Church, since it was but "a small group of clergy which enjoys the rights of legal existence . . . and is a toy in the hands of the communists . . . we appeal to you to avoid contacts with the clerics enslaved by the communists . . . They belong to that world which is diametrically opposed to ours . . . and we do not want to see any infiltration . . . and any influence of it. . . . You should not frequent churches of the Moscow Patriarchate."[26]

This encyclical is characteristic of that sorry degeneration of the Church that so closely associated herself with émigré politics. Every emigration is destined to wither away through death of the first generation and the assimilation of the generations that follow. With the physical reduction of the emigration and its increasing loss of touch with the reality of its nation of origin, a growing sense of insecurity becomes inevitable. A Church that marries herself to the emigration and its political aims and ideals suffers from the same ailment, gradually develops fear of the outside world and tries to hide from it by condemning it and by isolating herself from it. Hence, the Church that had shown all signs of rejuvenation in postwar occupied Germany, where, with over two hundred priests and close to twenty bishops, she was tending to the spiritual and cultural needs of some 200,000 displaced persons—establishing and running churches, schools, libraries, study groups and seminars of all kinds and helping to save many Soviet citizens from forced repatriation to the USSR—would by the 1960s degenerate into a paranoid body, fearful of and hostile to all who disagreed with her. She condemned the World Council of Churches for its secularism, but instead of participating in it in order to try to somehow influence it, like all the other local Orthodox churches have done, she isolated herself from it and condemned the other Orthodox churches for their participation.[27]

The Synod again condemned the Moscow Patriarchate. Her

[26]From an official Synodal publication, *Russkaya pravoslavnaya tserkov' zagranitsei, 1918-1968* (New York, 1968) 1:306-15.

[27]On the numbers of clergy and laity see *Tserkovnaya letopis'*, 15-20. On the World Council of Churches see the encyclical of the 1962 Council of "post-Karlovci" bishops in *Russkaya pravoslavnaya tserkov'*, 1:306-15; and the Synod's "Skorbnye poslaniya . . ." *Pravoslavnaya Rus'*, no. 15 (August 1969) 1-5; and no. 4 (February 1972) 3-8.

arguments regarding the questionable canonicity of its structure, however, may be quite valid. They begin with Sergii's own earlier assurance that his prerogatives as deputy locum tenens would disappear upon the death of the locum tenens, and with the fact that when Metropolitan Peter died in 1936, however, Sergii did not abandon his position.[28] Then there were the sobors of 1943, 1945 and 1971, which the "Synodals" claimed were invalid because they contravened the canons of 1917-1918, which stipulated that any member of the sobor had the right to propose candidates for the patriarchal throne, and then the election is to be by secret ballot. At each of the above sobors, however, there had only been one candidate and the "elections" were open. According to the canons, only a greater or larger sobor can change the regulations of a smaller or lesser sobor. Since all three sobors and, in particular, the councils of bishops preceding them which had set the procedures, were smaller than the 1917-1918 Sobor, any procedural changes established by them were invalid and, hence, the sobors and the resultant offices were uncanonical.[29]

This is the official position of the "Synod," which, as will be seen, was not even clearly reiterated at their main postwar assembly: their Third Sobor in 1974. Apparently, the "post-Karlovcians" are having second thoughts about the validity of such a purist approach, particularly in view of their own more than questionable canonicity and in view of the fact that the whole Russian Orthodox Church from 1721 to 1917 could be judged uncanonical, as Peter the Great's abolition of the patriarchate and of all conciliarism in the administration of the Church made the whole administrative structure of the Church uncanonical, precisely in the above terms.

But, whatever the Synod's attitude to the Moscow Patriarchate, its admonition that the flock must avoid any contact with the Patriarchal clergy and laity implies the Synod's sense of its own weakness and inner insecurity—even an uncertainty as to the validity of its position. Moreover, by banning any liturgical contacts and concelebrations with any Orthodox churches who did

---

[28]See above in chapter 5, pp. 189f.

[29]Protopresbyter George Grabbe, *The Canonical and Legal Position of Moscow Patriarchate* (Jerusalem: The Russian Ecclesiastical Mission, 1971) passim.

concelebrate with the Moscow Patriarchate, the Synod isolated itself from the whole Orthodox *oikoumene.*

But let us return to a more chronological overview. In Paris, as already stated, the aged Metropolitan Evlogy, overcome by emotion, sent a letter to Aleksii requesting to be accepted into the Moscow Patriarchate. When visited by Metropolitan Nikolai (Yarushevich), at the head of an impressive church delegation from the USSR in September 1945, he unilaterally rejoined the Moscow Patriarchate. Metropolitan Nikolai concelebrated with Evlogy with no question of any bans or suspensions, which showed that the patriarchate itself viewed them as political rather than canonical acts. Both the Moscow Patriarchate and Metropolitan Evlogy petitioned the Ecumenical Patriarch to release him and his exarchate, but no answer followed. Thus, in a canonically irregular way, Evlogy became a dual exarch: simultaneously of the Moscow and of the Ecumenical Patriarchate. But in August 1946, Evlogy died. The next hierarch in seniority in France was Metropolitan Serafim (Lukyanov), formerly a Karlovcian of the most aggressive kind and of an actively pro-Hitler orientation during the war. He had been the first to join the Moscow Patriarchate in 1945 and now was appointed by Moscow as the exarch for Western Europe. Even earlier he had been appointed by Moscow as the chief vicar of the aging Evlogy, which had made the latter very unhappy. This situation was utilized by an Extraordinary Diocesan Conference in Paris, October 16-20, 1946, to vote in favor of remaining under Constantinople. Since the latter had never released the exarchate from under its jurisdiction, the operation was quite simple. Archbishop Vladimir of Nice was elected metropolitan-exarch and was soon confirmed by Constantinople.

On this occasion, the Moscow Patriarchate did not act as rashly as it did in 1930-1931. By its decree of May 16, 1947, Vladimir and his other two bishops, Ioann and Nikon, were simply removed from the lists of the Moscow Patriarchate's bishops and deprived of the right to call themselves clerics of the Russian Orthodox Church. No ban was proclaimed.[30]

[30]Evlogy, *Put'*, 671-6; "Po tserkovnomu zarubezh'yu," *Pravoslavnaya Rus'*, no. 9 (April 1947) 14; Fletcher, *Nikolai*, 72-6 and 81-2. Also, oral testimony to this author by the Rt. Rev. Alexander Schmemann, Dean of St. Vladimir's Seminary, who participated in the above-described events of 1946-1947.

The reconstituted postwar émigré Synod, in its turn, suffered a very heavy blow when the Russian Orthodox Church of America withdrew its associate membership from it. We shall treat the American issue separately. Suffice it to say here that subsequently to the reestablishment of the patriarchate in Russia, the Orthodox Church in America or, as she was better known then, the "Metropolia," began negotiations with the Moscow Patriarchate. In the meantime, Metropolitan Theophilus of North America suggested to Metropolitan Anastasy that the Synod in Europe likewise recognize the spiritual authority of the Moscow Patriarchate again (as, at least in theory, it had done in the 1930s). But, psychologically, this was impossible in the climate of the DP camps and the sycophantic pro-Stalinist pronouncements of the Moscow hierarchs while the DPs were being hunted down by Soviet repatriation agents.

In the meantime, masses of DPs began to emigrate overseas, mainly to the United States. Having been highly politicized by the Karlovcians against the Moscow Patriarchate while in the camps,[31] and often nationalistically Russian oriented, many could not adjust to the partly assimilated and mostly American-oriented parishes of the Metropolia, which often cherished sympathetic attitudes toward the Russian Patriarchal Church, sometimes with a certain admixture of enthusiasm for the "Russian victory" in World War II. Directly pro-Soviet attitudes were also quite common in America of the 1940s and even of the early 1950s. All this led to the establishment of Synodal churches in America and Canada by the new refugees from Germany. In 1950 the Synod itself moved from Munich to the US, thus creating a canonical absurdity: two separate church administrations, both originating from the same common Russian cradle, with their ruling metropolitans on the territory of one and the same country. The "hosts," i.e., the Metropolia, proved to be much friendlier to the newcomers than the latter would be to the "hosts."[32]

[31]This author's personal recollections from life in DP camps in 1945-1949. See also the brochure *Raz'yasnenie dlya priezzhayushchikh v Ameriku DiPi* (New York, 1950); and *Lzhe-pravoslavie na pod'eme*, a collection of articles from *Pravoslavnaya Rus'* (Jordanville, N.Y.: Holy Trinity Monastery, 1954) passim.

[32]A letter from Metropolitan Leonty (Turkevich, the head of the Metropolia after Theophilus' death in 1949) to Anastasy warns of the uncanonical character of the Synod's emigration to the US without joining the local Church, but wel-

The Synod, while retreating deeper and deeper into a self-imposed ghetto, in its posture of self-righteousness began to totally ignore the canons. Having elevated the obligatory observation of the Julian calendar to the status of a theological issue, it began to encroach upon the jurisdictional territories of other churches to the extent of the illegal consecration of "Old Calendarist" bishops for a parallel Greek Church on the Greek mainland. In 1965 it canonized John of Kronstadt (d. 1909), a famous Russian priest who has been widely recognized as a saint in Russia and is known for his miraculous healings and other wonderworkings.[33] According to the tradition of the Orthodox Church, only a local Church canonizes the saints who lived and died on its territory. Thus, by this act the Synod, whose headquarters are in New York, appropriated for itself the rights of a territorial local Church of Russia, in total contempt of the Patriarchal Church. Somewhat later a saintly woman, Xenia of Petersburg, who had lived and died in that city in the eighteenth century, was similarly canonized by the émigré Synod; and, most recently, the canonization of Nicholas II and his family has taken place.

The "ivory tower" mentality was further exemplified in the 1971 Karlovcian Council of Bishops. Its session of August-September ruled that the autocephaly granted by the Moscow Patriarchate in 1970 to the Metropolia, which henceforth became known as the Orthodox Church in America, be recognized as invalid because, allegedly, the Moscow Patriarchal Church is

comes fellow bishops nevertheless in the spirit of love and the hope that they would fulfil the need to spiritually feed the new wave of emigration from Europe (letter of February 8, 1950, in the Archives of the OCA). Even a hostile article in *Pravoslavnaya Rus'* ("Sobornaya zagranichnaya tserkov' i amerikanskaya mitropoliya," no. 6 [March 1951] 3-6) admits that the Metropolia's attitude to the Synod is fraternal and that the former invites its parishioners to visit the Synodal parishes. An example of the hostile attacks on the Metropolia is an editorial in *Pravoslavnaya Rus'*, no. 1 (January 1954), alleging that she has been losing her Orthodoxy and will soon become simply a Protestant sect "of the Eastern Rite." Even a 1947 statement criticizing the Karlovcian bishops for splitting tactics after the Cleveland Sobor by Archbishop Leonty concludes on a peaceful note: "In free America . . . there is room for people with different views. One thing remains desirable: let us not lose our Orthodox . . . consciousness." *RAPV*, no. 9 (1947) 138.

[33]See the theological explanation to this effect in "Obrashchenie arkhiereiskogo sobora russkoi pravoslavnoi . . . tserkvi v Amerike," *VRSKhD*, no. 74 (1964) 67-8; and the Metropolia's statement of October 25, 1965, in *OC* 1:5 (1965) 3.

devoid of charisma, having grown out of Sergii's allegedly un-canonical Synod. Also, no intercommunion or any other churchly contacts with the Orthodox Church in America are to be permitted because of its intercommunion with the Moscow Patriarchate. Thus, by implication, the Synod was severing any ecclesiastical and liturgical connection with the rest of the Orthodox world. All Western Christians, the council further ruled, are to be con-sidered heretics and to be accepted into the émigré Church only via rebaptism. To this was added a theologically questionable proviso allowing individual clerics to make special exemptions to some individuals, entirely at the discretion of the former. Finally, the council called on all émigré meetings and conferences to conclude with the singing of "God Save the Tsar," as the Russian national anthem (ignoring the problem of there being no tsar), and stipulated that a special committee is to be set up to prepare the canonization of Nicholas II and his family along with other martyrs under communism.[34]

The culmination of the postwar events in the life of the post-Karlovci Synod was its Third Sobor of Bishops, Clergy and Laity, which met in September 1974 at its Holy Trinity Monastery in Jordanville, New York. Patriarch Pimen had sent an address to the Synodal clergy, but it was neither read at the sobor nor published in the Synod's organ, *Pravoslavnaya Rus' (Orthodox Russia).* The address is remarkable for its tolerance and modera-tion. It states emphatically that it *does not* call upon the Russian Orthodox émigrés to give up their loyalties to the countries in which they live or have become citizens of, or to pledge loyalty to the Soviet Union. All it asks is for them to reenter the Orthodox *oikoumene* by recognizing the Orthodox Church of Russia as a spiritually valid Church and by allowing their clerics and laity intercommunion with the clergy of the Moscow Patri-archate as well as with any other valid Orthodox clergy. It assures the Karlovcians that:

> The Russian Orthodox Church bears no grudge against her children who have broken with her. . . . Without any sense of pride, however, it is her duty to remind those of

---

[34]"Vazhneishiya opredeleniya arkhiereiskogo sobora russkoi pravoslavnoi tserkvi zagranitsei," *Pravoslavnaya Rus'*, no. 20 (October 1971) 9-13.

her children who have alienated themselves from her that thereby they have entered upon a road of spiritual dangers . . . of hostility and hate which dry up all the spiritual charisma of life. . . . Beloved brothers and sisters, children of the Church, we are praying to God, the Father of all generous gifts and mercy, that He instruct you not to ignore this appeal to love and peace . . .[35]

The Synodal organ did publish, however, its governing Metropolitan Philaret's angry response. Philaret admits that "The current address differs from the previous ones only in that it does not contain the absurd request of loyalty to the Soviet government." But is "only" the right word? Was this not, at least officially, the cause for the Karlovcian break with Sergii's administration in 1927? Hence, if this request has disappeared, there is no reason for the Synodal Church to persist in refusing concelebration with and recognition of the spiritual validity of the Moscow Patriarchate.[36] Moreover, Philaret seems to be nearly thirty years *behind* the time: in none of the postwar contacts of the Moscow Patriarchate with the émigrés was there any repetition of the 1927 demand of a pledge of loyalty to the Soviets. In fact, the late Metropolitan Nikolai stated this explicitly in 1956:

Metropolitan Sergii's . . . 1927 . . . request . . . of the Russian émigré clergy to give a written guarantee of loyalty to the Soviet power . . . was only of temporary character and was dictated by the circumstances of that time, when the Patriarchal Synod was extending itself to normalize

[35]"Poslanie patriarkha . . . Pimena," *Novoe russkoe slovo* (October 18, 1974) 3. The moderation was probably the result of warnings against rash actions in relation to the Karlovcians made in a moving speech by Metropolitan Anthony (Bloom) of England at the Moscow Sobor in 1971.

[36]They argue, of course, that the patriarchate is canonically invalid because it originates from the proclamation of Metropolitan Sergii as the locum tenens on the death of Metropolitan Peter, while Metropolitan Kirill, the real patriarch's second choice for locum tenens, was still alive. Yet the very practice of appointing locum tenentes in patriarchal wills is uncanonical (see chapter 4). The same *oikonomia* considerations applied to accepting Sergii rather than the imprisoned Kirill, particularly at the height of Stalin's 1930s terror. Their 1962 argument that the patriarchate represented but a minority of the Orthodox clergy and laity in the USSR had to be discarded and reversed by the 1970s—in their response to

relations between the Russian Orthodox Church and the state in the new conditions. . . . this request has lost all its power long ago.[37]

Metropolitan Philaret denies that the Synod cherishes any hostility toward its Orthodox brothers and sisters in the USSR, and maintains that the only thing is that this "free part of the Russian Orthodox Church . . . never did and does not recognize . . . the hierarchy, controlled by the enemies of the Church . . . as a lawful Russian ecclesiastic authority." As his only justification for this nonrecognition he cites Patriarch Pimen's fraudulent statement in Geneva during his visit there to the World Council of Churches headquarters on September 17, 1973 that there was no social injustice or oppression in the USSR. Philaret then pledges to continue to unmask the tyrannical character of the Soviet political system, "so brilliantly reflected in Solzhenitsyn's books," and never to "bend under one yoke with the infidels . . ."[38]

In this Philaret seems to be off target: the Patriarchal appeal clearly states that it does not expect the émigrés "to share the views of the Orthodox Christians living in their fatherland" on social and political matters. Moreover, it does not even ask them to join the Moscow Patriarchate administratively (and in this Pimen's address differs radically from Patriarch Aleksii's of 1945, for instance), only to recognize its ecclesiastical validity— to recognize it as a Church and to reestablish intercommunion with it.[39]

Solzhenitsyn, Fr. G. Grabbe stated that there are still "small numbers" of "catacomb" priests and laity. See his comments following Solzhenitsyn's address in *Pravoslavnaya Rus'*, no. 18 (September 1974) 11-4. One of their ideologists and professors at the Jordanville seminary even argues that the Moscow Patriarchate's churches are devoid of charisma because they are loyal to the Soviet regime— which is the mystical body of the antichrist, just as the Church is the mystical body of Christ. Ivan Andreev, *Blagodatna li sovetskaya tserkov'?* (Jordanville, N.Y.: Holy Trinity Monastery, 1948) 4-22.

[37]"Raz'yasnenie nedoumeniya," *ZhMP*, no. 9 (1956) 22-3.

[38]"Zayavlenie pervoierarkha russkoi zarubezhnoi tserkvi po povodu poslaniya patriarkha Pimena," *Pravoslavnaya Rus'*, no. 17 (September 1974) 1.

[39]Some of the leading members of the Russian Patriarchal clergy have likewise pointed out to this author that the Karlovcians' claim to be "the free branch of the Russian Orthodox Church" would have validity had they recognized the spiritual supremacy and authority of the Patriarch of Moscow even while they

The "sobor" proved that Philaret's reference to Alexander Solzhenitsyn as a rationale for a boycott of the Moscow Patriarchate was likewise misdirected. In his letter to the sobor, sent in response to an invitation to attend the gathering, Solzhenitsyn emphasized that despite all his disagreement with the political declarations of some bishops of the Moscow Patriarchate, he was still its spiritual child and was happier there as such than in emigration, where he sees the Church torn asunder by mutual conflicts. He maintained that there was no longer any such thing as a "catacomb Church" in the USSR—the Russian Church meant the Patriarchal Church. He criticized the "Karlovcians" for underestimating this Church and her spiritual dynamics: "The contemporary Church in Russia is imprisoned, persecuted . . . but she is by no means fallen." However, as far as the émigrés were concerned, he agreed that there was no reason to submit oneself voluntarily to an *administrative* subordination to the Moscow Patriarchate: why voluntarily put oneself into the chains in which the Moscow Patriarchate is forced to exist not by its own choice? Furthermore, Solzhenitsyn stressed that he idolized the memory of Patriarch Tikhon and could not condone any insubordination to his orders, thereby hinting that he could not approve of the very basis on which the Karlovci Synod and its successors were founded. In the end, Solzhenitsyn appealed to all émigré churches to resolve their differences and reestablish unity.[40]

The official speakers at the sobor, including Philaret in his reply to Solzhenitsyn, disagreed with him on the catacomb church issue and maintained that no one but themselves have been struggling for unity all these years. The sobor then proceeded to draft appeals to the "Evlogian" Church in Paris and to the Orthodox Church in America to begin negotiations on unity. Solzhenitsyn's main criticism was that the split has resulted in the banning of intercommunion (by the Karlovcians, as we have seen) with

refuse, however, to subject themselves to him administratively on the perfectly valid grounds that he was politically controlled by the Communist Party. Had the Synod taken this position, its criticism of Soviet policies toward the Church in Russia would have had much more effect and would help the position of the Church in the USSR, because it would be appreciated as a free voice of the uncensored part of the same Russian Church—i.e., representing the genuine voice of the Church in Russia.

[40]*Pravoslavnaya Rus'*, no. 18 (1974) 6-11.

the other Russian Orthodox churches. He argued that all church organizations followed some canons in their positions and broke others, which was inevitable in the unprecedented twentieth-century conditions, and that therefore it was absurd to ban intercommunion on the grounds of incomplete observance of the canons. The correspondence that followed between Philaret and Metropolitan Ireney of the Orthodox Church in America (henceforth, OCA) showed, however, that the Synod was not prepared to give up its ban on intercommunion. The Synod offered the Orthodox churches its readiness to show their mutual rapprochement by joint participation in social or political manifestations— e.g., protests against Soviet policies regarding the Church, the dissidents, etc. The OCA responded that her parishioners were free to participate in any such actions without any special decisions by the Church, while the only significant manifestation of cooperation between churches of the same religion is intercommunion, and that this should be permitted by the Synod and concelebrations between the hierarchs of both churches should begin. Thereafter, pledged the OCA, she would take upon herself the role of intermediary in reestablishing liturgical relations between the Karlovcians and the other Orthodox churches (non-Russian). But Philaret replied that no intercommunion was possible as long as the OCA had intercommunion with the clergy of the Moscow Patriarchate. This ended the correspondence without any positive results.[41]

The sobor's traditional "Address to the Orthodox Russian People in the Motherland" amply quoted the "convenient" parts of Solzhenitsyn's letter, reproaching the Moscow Patriarchate for its subservience and "assuring" it that it would gain much more for the Church by a steadfast policy of resistance to the regime's pressures. It thus ignored that part of Solzhenitsyn's letter where he said that, after his departure from the USSR, he had lost the moral right to attack the patriarchate and its policies.[42]

[41]Philaret's reply in *Pravoslavnaya Rus'*, no. 19 (October 1974) 5-6. The whole correspondence between Philaret and the OCA is to be found in *VRKhD*, no. 114 (1974) 89-104, and no. 115 (1975) 108-11.

[42]Similarly, on the occasion of the fiftieth anniversary of Tikhon's death, *Pravoslavnaya Rus'* (no. 6 [1975] 11-3) published only his encyclical calling for civic loyalty to the Soviet regime, failing to mention either his statements regarding the Church's political neutrality or his 1922 and 1925 anti-Karlovci documents.

The sobor's address cites the examples of Fr. Dimitry Dudko and a few other members of the Patriarchal clergy and laity as examples to be emulated, thereby entering into an intrinsic contradiction between condemning the Moscow Patriarchate and refusal of liturgical contacts with it, on the one hand, and approving clergy and laity who are members of that patriarchate, on the other.[43] This inconsistency led, for instance, to a case where the dean of the Synodal cathedral in London, England refused to give communion to children baptized in Moscow by none other than Fr. Dudko, on the grounds that no rites administered by any cleric of the Moscow Patriarchate were valid—an argument consistent with the official Synodal position. Fr. Dudko responded by requesting some form of disciplinary action against the priest concerned. But Metropolitan Philaret, who had exchanged several letters with Dudko and to whom the Dudko letter had been addressed, took no such action. Dudko continued to elicit much praise in the Synodal press for his steadfast posture in Moscow and for having made rather risky political statements, including remarks about the saintly martyrdom of Nicholas II. But the same Dudko, in his letters to Philaret, deplored the émigré church disunity and assured him that the "catacomb Church" was practically nonexistent and that the only real Church in Russia was the Patriarchal one, which deserves a more charitable attitude. Alas, Dudko's statements to the effect that the behavior of the clergy and hierarchy of the Moscow Patriarchate was too cowardly and that the Church should follow more independent and actively missionary activities misfired in early 1980, when he was released from a three-month imprisonment after making a public confession over the Soviet TV network, promising "good behavior" for the future.[44] This act, as it were, implied that the road taken by the Moscow Patriarchate and followed by the vast majority of the clergy and hierarchy was the only realistic one in the current circumstances. Whether this is so or not is another matter, but this is the logical conclusion from Fr. Dudko's statement, if

[43]*Pravoslavnaya Rus'*, no. 20 (October 1974) 3-4.

[44]See some of his letters to Philaret on this subject in Dudko's collection *Vrag vnutri*, reprinted in *VS*, no. 33 (1979) 12-30. The letter on the London church issue is in Dudko's parish bulletin, *V svete preobrazheniya*, reprinted in *VRKhD*, no. 129 (1979) 271-2. See also Dudko's "Zapad ishchet sensatsii," *Izvestiya* (June 21, 1980) 6.

calendar and the English language be introduced, and that the Church be called the "Orthodox Church in America."

But ethnic troubles were gnawing at the Church already in those years. While in the western states Greeks generally accepted the jurisdiction of the Russian Church, on the east coast problems developed. When Tikhon claimed jurisdiction over the Greek parish in New York City, the Greeks evaded this by incorporating the parish with the American authorities as a private church under the name "Hellenic Eastern Christian Church." Platon (Rozhdestvensky), the new archbishop who replaced Tikhon (Platon's first period of tenure was from 1908 to 1914; his second, from 1922 to 1934) continued the work of his predecessor. He ordained Fr. Theofan (Noli, 1908) to head the American Albanians (in fact, he was the first clergyman to use Albanian as a liturgical language, and to introduce it from Boston to Albania). But ethnic problems continued. In 1913 a Serbian clergy convention in Chicago considered withdrawing from the archdiocese and going under the Metropolitan of Belgrade; of the Greeks, Platon complained that "they do not contact the Russian bishops. . . . I haven't seen a Greek at my place in the four months of my stay here."[47]

The next ruling Archbishop of North America was Evdokim (Meshchersky), who was to leave for Moscow in 1917 at the head of the archdiocesan delegation to the Russian sobor. As already recorded, Evdokim did not return from the sobor, joining the Renovationist schism. But in the less than three years of his activities in America, Archbishop Evdokim left a very deep and positive impression by his missionary zeal, great administrative and pastoral qualities and democratism, which fitted the American scene so well. This might be one of the reasons for the relatively extensive inroads of the Renovationists in America and for the prolonged and very costly struggle of the Orthodox Church in America against them, involving many complicated litigations, but with an eventual overall victory for the regular Orthodox

---

[47]Platon is cited in Michael Johnson, "Archbishop Evdokim and the Orthodox Church in America, 1914-1917," Master of Divinity thesis, St. Vladimir's Seminary, 1976, 5-6 et passim. Other data from *Orthodox America*, 15-51, 69-71, 83-101, 191-5; and Archbishop Tikhon's report (no. 25), in *Otzyvy eparkhial'nykh arkhiereev* (St. Petersburg, 1906) 1:530-7.

---

one is to take Dudko as an authority, as a man who has tested the possibilities of extending church activities beyond the liturgical cycle alone. It was the Karlovcians who had elevated Dudko to such a status of unquestionable authority. Hence, logically (since it has become common knowledge that he had not been subjected to any tortures), the Karlovcians should now make their peace with the Moscow Patriarchate, or at least scale down their intolerance toward it.

From the "Russian Metropolia" to the OCA

The Church that since 1970 has been known under the official name of the Orthodox Church in America (OCA) goes back to 1794, when the first group of missionaries arrived in Alaska from the ancient Russo-Karelian Monastery of Valaamo on Lake Ladoga, bordering on Finland. With the rapid conversion of Aleuts, Eskimos and Indians, the need arose for a regular ecclesiastical administrative and educational system for Alaska. Much was accomplished toward this end by a brilliant young priest, Ivan Venyaminov-Popov, from Irkutsk in Siberia. Active in Alaska since 1824, he had mastered the Aleutian and the Tlingit Indian languages, founded schools for these natives[45] and translated the principal service books and the catechism into their languages, having devised a phonetic alphabet for them based on the Cyrillic script. After the loss of his wife he was consecrated Bishop of Kamchatka, the Kuriles and the Aleutians in 1840, with his diocesan seat in Sitka (New Archangel, as it was known at the time) in Alaska.

In 1852 his diocesan seat was moved to Yakutsk in the Russian Arctic Far East, and an episcopal vicariate was formed six years later in Sitka. In 1868 Archbishop Innocent (Fr. Ivan's

---

[45]Alaska had both Russian-language and native-language schools, both open to any Alaskan resident. The Russian-language schools were founded for the children of employees of the Russian-American Company, irrespective of their ethnic background. Mixed native-Russian marriages were actively encouraged, and a number of offspring of the mixed marriages received higher education in Russia—at least one of them, Alexander Kashevarov, reaching the rank of major general in Russian service. In contrast, not a single school for the natives was ever founded by the Hudson Bay Company. See S.G. Fedorova, *Russkoe naselenie na Alyaske i v Kalifornii* (Moscow, 1971) 190-4 and 218-22.

monastic name) was elevated to the position of Metropolitan of Moscow. He soon established the Siberian Missionary Committee, with special care for the conversion and religious and general education of the natives of Siberia, the Far East and Alaska. This began the regular development of Orthodoxy in North America, with the faith spreading beyond the borders of Alaska after its incorporation into the US. Clergy and lay servants of the Church and her educational establishments hired by the committee were to serve in America for ten years with a relatively generous remuneration, after which time they were free to return to Russia and were entitled to a pension. This system attracted a high caliber of clergy and other churchmen, as the prospect of a pension and financial security was equally a promise of freedom from want, independence and the possibility for research and work according to one's vocation, free from administrative interference.[46]

During the tenure of Bishop Paul (Popov, 1867-1870) the first regular Orthodox parishes were established in the "lower forty-eight": an immigrant parish in San Francisco (1868) and an English-language parish in New York City (1870), founded by an American convert to Orthodoxy, Fr. Nicholas Bjerring. In 1870, the Alaskan vicariate was elevated to the rank of a full-fledged diocese of the Aleutian Islands and Alaska, and Bishop John (Mitropolsky, 1870-1876) was consecrated its first bishop. In 1872 the episcopal seat was moved to San Francisco. These developments indicated the direction of prospects and problems for the Church in the future: the San Francisco parish would become the cradle of the multinational ethnic Orthodoxy of the waves upon waves of immigration from Eastern Europe and the Middle East that began in the last decades of the nineteenth century; the short-lived English missionary parish would show the American missionary future of the Church in the English language; while Alaska would continue to remind the over-zealously ethnicist trends, which were to rock the Church in the twentieth century, of the original purpose and meaning of Orthodoxy on the American continent.

But the first mass influx into Orthodoxy in America came in the form of the conversion of some ninety thousand Galician

[46]Oral testimony of Prince S. Trubetskoy, the Syosset archivist (April 19, 1980).

and Carpatho-Russian Catholics of the Eastern rite (Uniates) to Orthodoxy, roughly during the two decades from 1891 to World War I. The work of returning to Orthodoxy was begun by a Uniate missionary priest from Carpatho-Russia (now known as the Carpathian Ukraine), Fr. Alexis Toth, with the conversion of the Minneapolis Church of the Protection of the Virgin Mary. Another substantial group of Carpatho-Russians returned to Orthodoxy in the 1930s. In the meantime, waves of Orthodox immigrants began to arrive from the Balkans, the Middle East (Syria, Lebanon, Palestine) and, to a lesser extent, from the Russian empire. The missionary diocese was thus becoming nationally more diversified.

It was during the tenure of Archbishop Tikhon (1898-1907), the future Patriarch of Russia, that the diocese came of age, thanks to Tikhon's deep understanding of the needs and the future of Orthodoxy in America. First, its name was changed to the Greek Orthodox Church of the Aleutian Islands and America (1900). Elevated to an archdiocese in 1905, a number of vicariates were created, the first ones being the Alaskan one and the Arab-Syrian one of Brooklyn, and along with them came the consecration of the first Orthodox bishops on American soil. The first theological seminary in the "lower forty-eight," in Minneapolis, and the first Orthodox monastery, in South Canaan, Pennsylvania, were established in 1905. A complete translation of the principal Orthodox church services was begun, and English began to be used in a number of parishes. The archdiocesan seat was moved to New York in 1905, and in 1907 the first sobor of the clergy and laity took place in America, establishing a canonically correct system of conciliar church administration ten years prior to its reestablishment in Russia. A Serbian mission was established within the archdiocese in 1905, under the administration of a Serbian Archimandrite Sebastian (Dabovich), with a view toward his eventual consecration as bishop for the Serbs in America.

In his report to the Preconciliar Commission and to the St. Petersburg Synod, Archbishop Tikhon prophetically requested that the archdiocese be granted autocephaly, or at least wide autonomy from the Russian Church, as it was becoming a truly local American Church. Moreover, he suggested that the western

Church, despite the loss of the cathedral in New York in 1925.[48]

With the revolution and the Bolshevik victory, the Church in America lost her very substantial annual subsidy from the Church of Russia (a prewar total of 185,000 rubles, which in 1916, on Evdokim's appeal, was raised to 550,000 per annum). Inexperienced in financial matters, the caretaker Archbishop Alexander (Nemolovsky) began to sell and mortgage church property and to advise the non-Russians to find their own ways of ecclesiastical survival. In the meantime, the Russian politically and nationally oriented emigration began to arrive in America. Though relatively small in numbers, because of their education and social status they began to play a disproportionately important role in the Church, diverting her from her prewar American orientation back to a Russian national one. The nascent East European nationalism began to take further toll in the Church: Ukrainians, particularly in Canada, began to break off after being told by the Ukrainian-speaking and ethnically Ukrainian Archbishop Alexander that the Ukrainians were not a nation but a political party, and hence no church services should be conducted in Ukrainian.[49]

In short, by the time the newly arrived Platon (who since his return to Russia had been first exarch of Georgia and later Metropolitan of Odessa) was elected the first Metropolitan of America and Canada by the Third All-American Church Sobor in Pittsburgh in September 1922, the process of the breaking up of the Church into a totally uncanonical maze of ethnic dioceses was well underway. This process was headed by the Greeks, who established a Greek archdiocese in 1921, at first under the Archbishop of Athens but later transferring to the jurisdiction of the Ecumenical Patriarch.

Metropolitan Platon's election had Patriarch Tikhon's backing, originally transmitted verbally through several reliable per-

[48]A major victory was gained in the courts in December 1924 (see "The Conclusion of the Court" [official document], *APV*, no. 1 [1925] 4-10), but the struggle for individual churches continued until 1932. The Renovationists were trying to wrest all church property from the American Church that was established before the revolution with any participation of finances from Russia—a total of 115 parishes being involved. The American Church retaliated by creating boards of trustees with the ruling metropolitan as the head of each, in whose name each church building was registered. See the voluminous legal correspondence in the Syosset Archives; also *Orthodox America*, 187-8.

[49]Ibid., 175 and 193.

sons traveling from Moscow to America. The Karlovcian Higher Church Administration was not convinced by the oral testimony, but, as the American conciliar act confirming Platon correctly states, "the Higher Church Administration had been abolished by the patriarchal ukaz issued several months earlier, which also established Metropolitan Evlogy as the sole [legitimate] administrator of Orthodox parishes abroad." As Evlogy received additional proof of the validity of the patriarchal appointment of Platon, and the newly formed Karlovci Synod confirmed it, Platon's election was validated.[50]

The "triangle" of Platon's position, however, is evaded in the above citation. It seems that the conciliar character of the "Metropolia," confirmed by the statutes enacted by the 1917-1918 Moscow Sobor setting up self-governing metropolitan districts coinciding with provinces and made up of local dioceses coinciding with districts or counties, required simply the legitimacy of the election of Platon at an all-American sobor.[51] However, Platon had been Metropolitan of Odessa, and hence he could not take any new episcopal post without a canonical release by the mother Church. That he now received in the patriarchal decree, but the emotional climate of the new *political* emigration required also an "émigré legitimization context," and this Platon received in the confirmation of his appointment by the Karlovci Synod. But let us remember the wise point of the act, which made it clear that the Synod's approval was legitimate only insofar as Evlogy, the patriarchal appointee, participated in it—i.e., its legitimacy was only by the authority of the Patriarch of Moscow. By logical implication, this legitimacy would cease to exist as soon as the Synod broke with the patriarchate or as soon as Evlogy withdrew from it. This is the fine point that the Synodals constantly ignore in their attacks on the maneuvers of both the Metropolia and Evlogy.[52]

[50]"Akt," *APV*, no. 25 (October 31, 1922) 174-6. In 1923 it was confirmed in an official patriarchal ukaz. See "Poslanie . . . Platona mitropolita . . . Ameriki i Kanady . . . russkim pravoslavnym lyudyam v Amerike," *RAPV*, no. 1 (1930) 2.

[51]See Fr. Prof. Alexander Schmemann's view in "Kanonicheskoe polozhenie russkoi pravoslavnoi tserkvi v Sev. Amerike," *RAPV*, nos. 6-8 (1953) 90-2, 106-7 and 116-8 respectively.

[52]See, for example, Polsky, 132-84. The most competent analysis of the émigré church problem from the canonical point of view is Troitsky, *Razmezhevanie ili*

Unfortunately, the subsequent events and the pressures to which the Moscow Patriarchate was to be subjected would practically close this canonical path to both churches. But the intention to return to it always remained, and this return would be attempted several times—hence, the maneuvers and the apparent waverings.

A situation illustrating the case in point arose in 1924. Platon's appointment to America obviously displeased the Soviet government. First of all, he had an extremely activist anti-Bolshevik record on the eve of the Bolshevik occupation of Odessa, where he had personally formed an armed anti-Bolshevik "Holy Squad." While the Bolsheviks, upon entering the city, executed over a thousand young men who had enlisted, the metropolitan had managed to escape to a foreign ship, which sailed with him on board. It was, probably, because of this record that the Soviet regime put pressure to bear on Patriarch Tikhon, who, allegedly, deposed Metropolitan Platon from the North American church administration by a decree of January 16, 1924 and ordered him to return to Russia to face an ecclesiastical trial. Secondly, Platon staged an extremely energetic and eventually successful struggle against the Renovationists in North America, where their impostor "Metropolitan" Kedrovsky, a married priest who had gone to Moscow for Renovationist consecration, had full Soviet backing and was trying to wrest away from the Metropolia all the church property in America. But on December 23, 1924, Kedrovsky suffered a major defeat in the courts.[53]

Had Platon been ecclesiastically deposed by the alleged patriarchal ukaz of January 16 of that year ("alleged" because, as Platon would later state, he never received such an ukaz and

raskol? He entirely rejects any canonical validity of the Ecumenical Patriarchate's claims over Western Europe, while also condemning Karlovcian meddling in Evlogy's affairs and in the American Metropolia as uncanonical and also harmful from the point of view of *oikonomia*. For the Metropolia's official position, see the minutes of the session of the Diocesan Council of September 1922, in *APV,* no. 21 (1922) 146-7. Characteristically, a resolution of a conference of the bishops, clergy and laity of the Metropolia in New York City (May 27, 1922), which approved Platon's appointment as the administrator of the Metropolia, stresses that the legitimacy of his new position comes "from the highest source of this power—from His Holiness Patriarch Tikhon." "Akty sobraniya episkopov," etc. (document found in the Kartashev Collection of the Bakhmeteff Archives, box 3232).

[53]Polsky, 156-7; see also n. 48 above.

never physically saw it), Kedrovsky would have had a much greater chance of winning. The already cited pro-Karlovcian priest, Fr. Mikhail Polsky, in his first book since his escape from the USSR, written when he was still relatively independent from émigré church politics, says that the order to remove Platon was composed by the GPU in the name of Patriarch Tikhon. When the patriarch learned of this, he reinstated the metropolitan in all his rights at a session of his Synod. A member of the Synod, Metropolitan Serafim, secretly took the new patriarchal-synodal ukaz to the GPU, which prevented its publication. (Naturally Serafim's behavior caused a scandal in the Patriarchal Synod.)[54] Hence, the revocation of the alleged patriarchal order never became officially known, while the order itself was never formally sent to Platon—although even in its published form it had a proviso that practically invalidated it: "Metropolitan Platon would be informed of this decision of his retirement, should . . . a candidate to replace him be found."

What is very strange is that, while Platon never received any of the above orders, two institutions were simultaneously disseminating statements that Platon had been deposed. According to Platon's information, the US State Department simultaneously received two messages: "from the Karlovci Synod, signed by Archbishop Feofan, . . . calling Metropolitan Platon a usurper . . . and the other from the Bolsheviks [the Renovationists?], declaring Metropolitan Platon's prerogatives illegitimate." Thus, at the height of his struggle against the Renovationists he was being stabbed in the back simultaneously by the Soviets and by the Karlovcians.[55] Was this a mere coincidence or was there a GPU agent in the center of the Karlovci Synod? At the time,

[54]Mikhail Svyashchennik (Polsky's early pseudonym), *Polozhenie tserkvi v sovetskoi Rossii* (Jerusalem, 1931) 61. Even the militantly Karlovcian author Count Olsufiev states that there is a GPU indictment against the greatest enemies of the Bolsheviks among the 1917-1918 Sobor participants, and Platon is listed among them. *Mysli soboryanina o nashei tserkovnoi smute* (Paris, 1928) 37-8. Fr. Shavelsky claims that the animosity between Antony and Platon was also personal and of a prerevolutionary vintage. Of the two he is very favorably disposed toward Platon. *Vospominaniya* (New York: Chekhov, 1954) 1:203-96 et passim.

[55]I. Nikanorov (September 1, 1926); also Platon's encyclical, n. 50 above. The editor of *ZhMP* cites this formulation of the ukaz and confirms that it was never officially sent to Platon. See A. Vedernikov, "Grekh protiv materi-tserkvi," *ZhMP* no. 7 (1950).

however, émigré church passions were running very high. The Karlovcians could not forgive Platon for the above-mentioned act of 1922. In addition, there was the April 1924 Fourth Sobor of the Metropolia in Detroit, which declared the full autonomy of the Church until a normalization of Church-state relations in the USSR had occurred. Hence, in the climate of the time, Platon's deposition probably did not cause too many eyebrows to rise. With historical hindsight, however, and given the cited 1931 information by Fr. Polsky, it is difficult to believe in mere coincidence. It is more likely that Karlovci was not immune to GPU agents at the time.

Attempts to break up the North American archdiocese continued. The Carpatho-Russian Bishop of Pittsburgh, Stefan (Dzubai), a former Uniate-Catholic, had gathered a parallel sobor in Philadelphia in 1922, claiming primacy over Platon. Although, by the time of the Detroit Sobor, Dzubai and his schismatic clergy had reunited with Platon, the incident shows the fragility and insecurity of the Church's canonical foundations once direct links with the mother Church could not be maintained. In fact, there was another attempt at a schism, by a questionable Bishop Adam (Filippovsky), who had been consecrated by Stefan while the latter was in schism.[56]

In short, to strengthen his position, Platon needed some form of émigré church acceptance, in order to protect his archdiocese from attack by the Karlovcians. Metropolitan Platon went to the sobor of bishops of the Orthodox Church in Exile, gathered in Karlovci in October 1924. There he satisfied the participants that the declaration of a temporary autonomy of his archdiocese did not constitute a self-proclaimed autocephaly or a break with "the lawful canonical head, His Holiness Patriarch Tikhon"—and thus, he again named the Moscow Patriarchate as the source of his legitimacy, not the Karlovci Synod. However, since the Synod itself still claimed subordination to the patriarch, this explanation was deemed sufficient, and an address was even issued by its sobor or council of bishops to the American flock, appealing to them

[56]*Orthodox America*, 183-8; *APV*, no. 4 (1924) 28-9. The dating of *APV* is occasionally incongruous: owing to lack of funds it developed quite a backlog, so, while coming out in 1925 and reporting events of that year, it appeared under 1924 datelines. See also Platon's resolution regarding Bishop Stefan in *APV*, no. 23 (October 11, 1922) 154-6.

to remain faithful to Metropolitan Platon.[57] The legitimacy of the independence of the Metropolia from the Karlovci gathering was, moreover, stressed in its official organ by one of its strongest theologians and architects of the future autocephaly, Fr. Leonid Turkevich (the future Metropolitan Leonty). At the time of Platon's announcement that he was departing for the Karlovci bishop's council, Turkevich analyzed the status of that body, stressing the legitimacy of Metropolitan Evlogy alone among the European bishops, and pointing out that the Karlovci council had no canonical authority of its own whatsoever. However, there would be no harm in participating in its meeting and working out some common policies.

> As long as the questions discussed by it relate to the protection of the Church from Bolshevism . . . our . . . metropolitan will fully cooperate with the bishops in exile. But if tendencies arise . . . to expand the powers and privileges of these bishops . . . to the role of an all-Russian central administration, the metropolitan, no doubt, will say his word.[58]

The conflict between this kind of canonical thinking and émigré emotionalism among the Metropolia's leading members is illustrated in an unsigned (editorial?) article appearing in the same journal soon after Platon's return from Yugoslavia. This one claims full canonical legitimacy for the Council of Bishops Abroad and the obligatory nature of its decisions for the whole Russian ecclesiastic diaspora. But even this article does not mention the Karlovci Synod.[59] Its argument concerns the whole body of *all* bishops in the diaspora gathered together, not the bureaucratic, permanent institution of *some* bishops in Sremski Karlovci. The Karlovci Synod, however, apparently interpreted the co-

[57]Platon's report (October 3, 1924) to his Diocesan Council on his departure for Karlovci, *APV*, no. 1 (January 1924); protocol no. 9 of the Synod of Russian Bishops Abroad (October 22, 1924), *APV*, no. 4 (1924) 28-9; *Poslanie arkhiereiskogo sobora russkoi pravoslavnoi tserkvi zagranitsei ko vsem chadam . . . v Amerike* (October 1924), Syosset Archives.

[58]"Arkhiereiskii sobor russkikh zagranichnykh arkhiereev . . .," *APV*, no. 1 (1924) 1-2.

[59]"Kompetentsiya arkhiereiskogo sobora . . . zagranitsei," *APV*, no. 6 (1924) 41-2.

operation of Platon in the same context as it did that of Evlogy
—namely, that it had the right to order them about and to treat
them and their sees as subordinate to the Synod. This resulted in
the already discussed conflict of January 1926, with the walkout
of both Evlogy and Platon. The Synod responded with the same
disciplinary actions toward Platon that it applied toward Evlogy:
it "deposed" Platon, on May 17, 1927, and appointed Archbishop
Apolinary in his stead to head the North American diocese. Thus,
a parallel Karlovcian jurisdiction was set up in America. But
except for Apolinary, all other bishops in America remained
faithful to Platon.[60]

In 1928, Platon asked Metropolitan Sergii to confirm that the
latter's church administration remained the canonical supreme
church authority for the Metropolia. According to Sergii, his
reply requested the loyalty pledge and reminded Platon about
Patriarch Tikhon's 1924 resolution deposing him as head of the
Church in America, which could be brought into effect. Sergii
received another letter from Platon in 1929, reproaching him for
the threat in his previous letter and saying nothing about any
difficulties in getting the pledges.[61] In reality, apparently, Platon
was playing for time while publicly stating in America that the
pledge would amount to subordination to the Soviet government
and to an act of disloyalty to America. Moreover, he accepted
the Karlovcian formula that the imprisoned Metropolitan Peter
was the head for whom prayers ought to be elevated in the
churches, not the deputy locum tenens Sergii.[62] In 1933, Sergii
decided to send Archbishop Venyamin (Fedchenkov) from Paris
to America to inspect the church situation there. On his report
on Platon's behavior, Sergii relieved the metropolitan of his post
and suspended him, subject to a trial by bishops, while appointing
Venyamin as his exarch for America. A few parishes joined the
Moscow exarchate, and some went over to the Karlovci jurisdic-

[60]See *Vozrozhdenie* (June 17, 1927). The newspaper commented that this was
a stab in the back at the height of Platon's struggle against Kedrovsky. See the
American reaction in *APV*, nos. 9-10 and 11-12 (1927) 116-21 and 138, respectively.

[61]See Sergii's address and his ukaz naming Archbishop Venyamin Patriarchal
Exarch for North America in *ZhMP*, no. 16-17 (1933) 1-9.

[62]Ibid., 5-7.

tion, but the vast majority—over three hundred parishes—remained faithful to Platon, who ignored Sergii's order.

Platon's attitude was clearly that of a head of a self-ruling, temporarily autonomous metropolitan district in accordance with the decisions of the Moscow Sobor and Patriarch Tikhon's decree of November 20, 1920 granting individual dioceses or groups of dioceses the right to become temporarily autonomous when regular contact with the ecclesiastic center became impossible. Although this was also the Karlovcian rationalization for canonicity, Professor S. Troitsky, the Russian-Serbian canonist, saw a stronger case for legitimacy along these lines for America, because its Church was truly established as a local Church and was even recognized as such by Sergii in his ukaz of July 14, 1927, wherein he says that "the missions in Japan, China and America have developed . . . into churches."[63]

In 1934 Platon died, having done nothing since his "suspension" to reaffirm his legitimacy in a sobor of his Church, the last of which was assembled ten years previously. The sobor that met upon Platon's death in Cleveland in November 1934 reaffirmed the Metropolia bishops council's decision to establish the Church as a temporarily autonomous metropolitan district, and elected Theophilus of Chicago as the new ruling metropolitan. The main report on canonical matters affirmed that both the Moscow Patriarchal exarchate and the Russian Synodal Church were valid, but questioned their relevance to the American situation, where an autonomous local Church was necessary.[64]

We have already discussed the initiatives of Patriarch Varnava of Serbia to achieve a reconciliation between the various branches of the Russian Church abroad. A reconciliation council was called by Varnava in Karlovci in 1936.

> . . . a joint meeting of the Council of Bishops and Diocesan
> Council [of the Church in America] . . . authorized Metro-
> politan Theophilus to enter into temporary agreements
> with the other hierarchs invited, on condition that the
> self-government of the Church in America would be fully

[63]"O kanonicheskom ustroistve tsentral'nogo upravleniya russkoi tserkvi v Amerike," *RAPV*, no. 3 (1930) 65-9.
[64]*Orthodox America*, 199.

preserved. Upon the return of Theophilus the Council of Bishops (this time including the bishops of the Church Abroad residing in North America) met in May 1936 and ratified the agreements made in Serbia, again stressing that the autonomy of the Church in America remained *inviolate*.

To the majority of Orthodox Americans, mostly of West Ukrainian descent, a group of monarchist émigré bishops from the Russian empire sitting in Yugoslavia meant absolutely nothing. This dichotomy (between the church people and their bishops, with their stronger links to the European Russian émigrés and their political predicament) manifested itself at the Sixth All-American Sobor, which met in New York in October 1937 to deliberate on Metropolitan Theophilus' actions in Yugoslavia and on its acceptance by the 1936 Council of Bishops. The majority of the laity and the American parish clergy was clearly opposed to those actions, but in their reluctance to undermine the metropolitan's authority most of them abstained. In fact, 122 abstained, nine voted against the accommodation and only 105 voted in its favor.[65]

The sobor reconfirmed the principle of autonomy and was assured by the bishops that the act of union with Karlovci in no way impaired the autonomy. It adopted provisional statutes establishing the autonomous principle of the metropolitan district with a number of dioceses. But troubles with the Karlovcians were not over. Although theoretically reunified, local Karlovcian parishes did not merge with the American ones. Even the Karlovcian Archbishop Vitaly, now in the unified Church with the title of Archbishop of New Jersey, uncanonically continued to keep

[65]Ibid., 199; Archbishop Ioann (John) of San Francisco, *Utverzhdenie*, 8-9. Curiously enough, a memorandum addressing itself to the problems of the then forthcoming Cleveland Sobor of November 26-29, 1946, and being apparently one of the manuscript variants of the so-called "Professors' Letter" to the sobor (by Professors N. Timashev, G. Fedotov, P. Zubov, etc.), denies the validity of the "current tendency to speak only of our association with the Synod." The memorandum claims that "the acts of 1936-1937 definitely subordinated our Church to the Synod Abroad." (Bakhmeteff Archives, Novitsky Papers, box 4, folder: "Russian Orthodox Church in America"; with the above memorandum and a very similar letter to Theophilus.) The confusion may have arisen because of a discrepancy between the agreement Theophilus signed in Karlovci and the resolutions of the 1937 New York Sobor, which reaffirmed the full autonomy of the Metropolia. See *RAPV*, no. 11 (1937), particularly 156-9; and appendix 4 below, pp. 489f.

his seat in a cathedral in the Bronx—i.e., in Metropolitan Theophilus' own diocese. Vitaly justified this on the grounds that he had no appropriate quarters in New Jersey.[66] Moreover, the statutes were never ratified by Karlovci.

In short, the Karlovcians remained in America in a "state of mobilization," ready to set themselves up again as a parallel jurisdiction at the first signs of disagreement with the "Americans." Such a moment came at the end of World War II, with the rise of pro-Russian and often pro-Soviet sentiment in America. In an attempt to restrain the passions on both sides and to prevent a possible split on political grounds, Theophilus warned his clergy in September 1942 to abstain from all political declarations.[67] The election of Metropolitan Sergii to the patriarchal throne in Moscow evoked from Theophilus a very friendly comment, with an expression of hope that Sergii would treat the American church issue with understanding. As if to stress once again the precarious position of the Church in Russia, Theophilus remarked that the last time he saw Sergii was when the latter had just been released from prison in 1922.[68] In October 1943, the clergy-laity Metropolitan Council decreed that, in the prayers "for the Eastern Patriarchs," the name of Patriarch Sergii should be likewise elevated. In 1944, on the occasion of Sergii's death, the same council sent condolences and decrees to similarly elevate prayers for Metropolitan Aleksii, the locum tenens. The Karlovcian bishops in America, Vitaly and Tikhon, participated in both sessions and signed both documents. Alongside these decisions there was printed a strongly anticommunist and anti-Soviet article by Fr. Mikhail Polsky, a Karlovcian priest in London, warning against being deceived by the current Soviet church policies.[69]

By the end of 1944 a number of parishes had joined the Moscow exarchate. Under all these pressures, the Metropolia began negotiations with the Moscow Patriarchate and was in turn invited to send a delegation to the 1945 Sobor in Moscow, which was to elect the new patriarch. On January 15 the delegates left New York for Moscow via Alaska, changing several military

[66]*RAPV*, no. 3 (1938) 34; and an earlier complaint to the same effect by Alexander Kukulevsky in *RAPV*, no. 1 (1936) 5-6.

[67]*RAPV*, no. 10 (1942) 145.

[68]*RAPV*, no. 10 (1943) 154-5.

[69]*RAPV*, no. 6 (1944) 82 and 89-92.

transport planes on the way. They were continuously delayed on the way through Siberia, under the pretext of fog. But the Moscow exarch, Venyamin, who had left New York at the same time as the American delegation, arrived in Moscow on time for the sobor while the American delegates arrived only after it had finished. They were very warmly received by Patriarch Aleksii, but were prevented from concelebrating on the grounds of the 1933 suspension. They presented the American petition, which amounted to two requests: for their acceptance into the fold of the Moscow Patriarchate; and for the retention of complete autonomy and administrative independence from the Moscow Patriarchate, with ruling metropolitans to be elected by American sobors and only then presented for confirmation by the patriarch.[70]

On their return from Moscow the name of Patriarch Aleksii, as "our master," began to be officially elevated at Metropolia churches. The delegates also brought back with them the patriarchal ukaz number 94 (February 1945), stipulating (1) that a sobor would meet the same spring in America under the chairmanship of Archbishop Aleksii of Yaroslavl, who would be specially sent there;[71] (2) that the sobor would elect a metropolitan for America, subject to patriarchal confirmation (the candidature of either Venyamin [Fedchenkov] or Aleksii was proposed, but the sobor would have the right to elect any other worthy candidate); (3) that all the clergy and laity of the Metropolia pledge to abstain from all anti-Soviet activities; and (4) that all contacts with the former Karlovci Synod be broken forever. Only after all these conditions have been met would the interdict be removed from the Church. Needless to say, Metropolitan Theophilus and

---

[70]See the first report on the journey by Bishop Aleksii of Alaska and Very Rev. Iosif Dzvonchyk in *RAPV*, no. 1 (1945) 34-6; and Dzvonchyk's report at the Seventh All-American Council (Sobor) in Cleveland, *Protokoly Sobora* (November 1946) 12-3.

[71]This Aleksii is described by Bishop Leonty (of Chile) as the man who betrayed to the GPU Archbishop Varfolomei (Remov) and his whole secret monastic theological academy, which he had run clandestinely in Moscow in the 1930s. Like Christ's Judas, Aleksii was Varfolomei's disciple and trusted spiritual son. Varfolomei was subsequently executed in 1936, and his whole learned fraternity received terms of incarceration and exile. Aleksii was consecrated bishop under Soviet pressure and in 1940 was sent to the newly annexed Moldavia as its ruling bishop. Later he was appointed Archbishop of Yaroslavl. Leonty, 42. It may thus be providential that Theophilus did not concelebrate with Aleksii on his visit to the US even though the American hierarchs were not aware of Aleksii's past.

the whole existing structure of the Metropolia were totally ignored by this document. In response, the Council of Bishops of the Metropolia, in its May 1945 session, declared reunification with the patriarchate on these conditions to be impossible and recommended that the status quo of the Metropolia—i.e., its continuing links with the "post-Karlovci" Munich Synod—should be retained.[72]

During this period—i.e., in the course of 1945 and 1946—many very strongly anti-Soviet and anticommunist articles were published in the chief organ of the Metropolia, expressing abhorrence of and sorrow over the subservience of the Moscow Patriarchate to the atheistic regime. Particularly noteworthy were the series of articles by Archbishop Leonty, the very person who had originally protested links with the Karlovci Synod on canonical grounds. Now he was indignant at the Moscow request to break with the Karlovcians:

> Would it be ethical to dispose of these bishops, with Metropolitan Anastasy at their head now, when they need our moral and material support more than ever before? At a certain time they helped us to make peace with a section of the American Orthodox flock; neither are they doing any harm to us now. . . . Now they are suffering a lot, like all other Europeans. . . . Of course, an all-American sobor may take another view on this matter; but up to now we have been moving along the line of cooperation.[73]

It seems that by these articles the Metropolia leadership was hoping to give a certain direction to the flock in anticipation of the coming sobor. The *Russian-American Orthodox Messenger* tried to steer a course of friendship and sympathy toward Anastasy's Synod, praising the hierarch for having achieved a reuni-

[72]Incomplete text of the ukaz in *RAPV*, no. 2 (1945) 34. The Chicago Session of the Council of Bishops' rejection of the ukaz is discussed in Dmitry F. Grigorieff, "The Russian Orthodox Church in America," diploma thesis, St. Vladimir's Seminary, n.d., 61-5. See a negative treatment of this in Archbishop Vitaly's "Sovremennoe polozhenie russkoi pravoslavnoi tserkvi v Amerike," *Pravoslavnaya Rus'*, no. 7 (May 1947) 1-3. Vitaly was the administrator of the Synodal parishes in North America following the split after the Cleveland Sobor.

[73]"Za kem poidete?" *RAPV*, no. 1 (1946) 9-12.

fication of bishops and clergy in Germany within his Synod while also emphasizing the independence of the American Church from it, using such terms as "Metropolitan Anastasy and his Synod."[74] "However," as one student of the subject writes, "the 'unanimous' opinion of the bishops was not shared by the majority of clergy and faithful in America," who continued to lean toward the Russian mother Church. Two bishops and a number of priests had left the Metropolia for the Moscow exarchate at the time, and its total number of parishes by 1947 surpassed fifty—the greatest number the exarchate has ever had in the US.[75]

At the Cleveland Sobor in November 1946, one could quite clearly perceive divisions among the laity and clergy along immigration backgrounds. While those of a "White émigré" background opted either for continuing links with the Munich Synod, or at best agreed to a spiritual link with the Moscow Patriarchate while strongly warning against any administrative links with it, owing to its captive status in a militantly atheistic dictatorial state, the Carpatho-Russians and other delegates of prerevolutionary immigration vintage mostly opted for reunification with the Moscow Patriarchate. However, in both camps, voices for the preservation of full autonomy under any circumstances prevailed. After considerable deliberations, the sobor resolved:

> . . . that His Beatitude, Alexy, Patriarch of Moscow . . .
> be assured that we . . . consider him as our spiritual, but
> not our administrative head . . . the Church in America
> retaining and continuing its present completely autonomous
> status and the right to self-government. That the periodic
> All-American Sobors . . . shall remain . . . the supreme
> legislative and administrative body of our Church; at these
> Sobors the Church continues to elect its own Metropolitan

[74]*RAPV*, no. 8 (1946) 125. The same issue reports the murder of six hundred Orthodox priests by Tito in Yugoslavia, emphasizing the incompatibility of the Church and communism. See also Alexander Kukulevsky, "Pryamyya rechi," *RAPV*, no. 3 (1946) 40-4; articles and letters by laymen in *RAPV*, no. 4 (1945) 60-2; and Grigorieff, 62.

[75]Grigorieff, 75. At its first sobor in February 1947 the Patriarchal exarchate had about one hundred delegates, including four bishops. The process of clerical and lay desertions for the exarchate began at least around 1944. See Rev. Silkin in *RAPV*, no. 10 (1944) 150.

and makes and adopts its own laws. . . . that any administrative subordination to the Synod of the Russian Orthodox
Church Abroad is hereby terminated, but we retain our
spiritual and brotherly relations with all parts of the
Russian Orthodox Church Abroad. . . . the administrative
autonomy . . . declared at the . . . Sobor at Detroit . . .
in 1924 is hereby affirmed.

The resolution was accepted by a vote of 187 to 61. The
sobor also resolved that it did not recognize the validity of the
Moscow interdicts and suspensions of the Metropolia clergy. To
accommodate the émigrés, the sobor even proposed the creation
of a Higher or Superior Church Council, in which all Russian
church administrations outside Russia, including the American
one, would be represented. Its seat would be in the US, and
through it coordination of actions and common policies would
be worked out. Another resolution, likewise adopted by the sobor,
provided that if the Patriarch of Moscow refused the conditions
on which the Metropolia deemed it possible to accept Moscow's
authority, the Metropolia would retain her status quo ante "until
the time when the Moscow Patriarchate found them acceptable
and granted us that which we had requested." Thus, there was
no question of renegotiating a compromise solution between these
conditions and those of patriarchal ukaz number 94. Legally
speaking, the principal resolution of the sobor amounted to the
return to the Church's status quo before 1933: recognition of
the Moscow Patriarchate solely as a spiritual authority; proclamation of readiness to coexist and cooperate with Anastasy's Synod,
but without even the indirect and conditional subordination to it
that stemmed from Theophilus' highly unpopular action of 1936;
and the preservation of the unity of the nascent local Church.[76]

But neither the Synodals nor the Moscow Patriarchate wanted
to see it that way. The four Karlovcian bishops refused to abide
by the resolution when their proposal to explain their reasons
for opposing it, after the vote had already been taken, was turned
down. In the newly established Synodal press it was claimed that

[76]*Protokoly,* 12-7 and 21-63. Even the Karlovcian Archbishop Vitaly recognized
that the Americans' "need for autonomy is legitimate." See his *Motivy moei zhizni,*
2d ed. (Jordanville, N.Y.: Holy Trinity Monastery, 1955) 33.

the Cleveland resolutions were invalid because they had been adopted by the whole house, whereas, according to the canons, they had to be separately deliberated upon by a council of bishops, which alone has final and veto powers on all canonical, theological and dogmatic matters.[77] This argument, however, totally ignored the *oikonomia* principle. The opinions at the time were so polarized, and the bishops and the laity differed in their assessments of relations with Moscow and with the émigrés so much from each other, that had the Cleveland decisions gone to a council of bishops and had the latter's decisions markedly differed from those of the sobor, a vast majority of the laity and a large section of the clergy would have probably simply revolted and left for the Moscow jurisdiction. In 1947, the pro-Karlovcian bishops were suspended from the Metropolia for their contempt of the Cleveland Sobor and its decisions. Also in 1947, a Synodal council of bishops in Munich resolved to restore its separate jurisdiction in America, with some forty parishes at the time.[78]

Future developments showed the wisdom of Metropolitan Theophilus' decision to accept the sobor's resolutions without any further ado. The uncanonical domination by laity over the clergy and bishops, which was so prominent at the Cleveland Sobor and which particularly prompted attacks from the post-Karlovcians, would be gradually replaced by a proper canonical, episcopal-conciliar structure after the adoption of the Statutes of the Russian Orthodox Greek Catholic Church in America at the Ninth Sobor in 1955. In 1971, at the Second Council of the Orthodox Church in America, the Statutes would be amended to suit the new autocephalous status of the Church.[79] But following the Sobor of 1946, Patriarch Aleksii sent Metropolitan Grigory (Chukov) of Leningrad to negotiate, informing Theophilus by telegram that in principle he accepted the Cleveland decisions. He also asked Theophilus to concelebrate with Grigory, in a gesture

[77]Ibid., 29; "Soveshchanie arkhiereev yurisdiktsii . . . arkhiereiskogo sinoda," *Pravoslavnaya Rus'*, no. 8 (June 1947) 1; Polsky, 170-3.

[78]Grigorieff, 74-7. See also "Rezolyutsiya po povodu deistvii v Amerike gruppy episkopov . . . zarubezhnoi russkoi tserkvi," *RAPV*, no. 11 (1947) 163-4.

[79]See the private letter of Bishop Serafim from Jordanville to, apparently, Archbishop Leonty (January 22, 1947), with Leonty's papers in the Syosset Archives; Polsky, 168-73, etc.; *Orthodox America*, 335-6; *The Statute of the Orthodox Church in America: Official Text* (New York: Chancery of the OCA, 1974).

of reconciliation—thus evidently shelving the issue of bans and suspensions. Grigory brought with him a Patriarchal draft statute for the Metropolia, which this time did not ask for pledges of loyalty and recognized the metropolitan district of America as autonomous and subject to decisions by its own sobors. There were, however, four provisos: (1) that metropolitans elected by the sobors be subject to approval by the Moscow patriarch; (2) that the Metropolia send delegates to the all-Russian national sobors and be subject to their authority; (3) that the patriarchate remain the ecclesiastical court of last appeal for the American clergy; and (4) that the Metropolia's relations with other local churches be conducted via the office of the patriarch. A bishops' council of the Metropolia rejected all this out of hand. Grigory responded by stating that what the Americans were demanding in fact amounted to autocephaly, not autonomy, and this the Moscow Patriarchate was not prepared to grant at the present stage.[80]

In November 1947, after the departure of Grigory for Moscow, the Metropolia Council of Bishops resolved that, owing to the political conditions in which the patriarchate had to exist in Moscow, only a spiritual, and not an administrative, link with the patriarchate was acceptable. Since the patriarchate was not able to accept this, further negotiations with it would be postponed "for an indefinite time," while the clergy would be free to elevate prayers for the Patriarch of Moscow and for the Russian land, "in spiritual recognition of the contemporary Russian Church."

To this the patriarchate responded by a December 1947 ukaz once again suspending Theophilus and his bishops and declaring them committed to a trial by bishops.[81] Evidently, after this, liturgical prayers for the Patriarch of Moscow were suspended in the churches of the Metropolia.

---

[80]See the full documentation, including the patriarchal ukaz, Grigory's letters to Theophilus, the draft of the autonomy principles presented to Grigory by the bishops of the Metropolia and Grigory's response and farewell message to the Orthodox of America, in ZhMP, no. 1 (1948) 13-24. The earlier texts of Theophilus' telegram to Patriarch Aleksii and the latter's response are in ZhMP, no. 4 (1947) 7.

[81]"Rezolyutsiya," RAPV, no. 11 (1947) 163; "Poslanie Patriarkha . . . Aleksiya . . .," ZhMP, no. 3 (1947) 9-11; V. Rev. P. Kohanik, "Dokumental'noe osveshchenie poslednyago patriarshago poslaniya i ukaza," RAPV, no. 3 (1948) 36-42.

The Metropolia thereafter continued to live as a de facto autocephalous Church, gradually evolving into a national American Orthodox Church. More and more English was used in its services, its St. Vladimir's Orthodox Theological Seminary graduated ever increasing numbers of American-born clergy, and a growing proportion of converts began to be found in its churches. Finally, a new series of negotiations began with Moscow in 1968, after the failure to regularize the American church situation with the help of the Ecumenical Patriarchate in 1967. At first, the leading clergy of the Metropolia were hoping to achieve a unified all-American autocephalous local Orthodox Church, irrespective of the ethnic origins of its members. With this purpose in mind, the Ecumenical Patriarch Athenagoras was approached in Constantinople. The hope was that he would grant autocephaly to his Greek Church in America, which then would be joined by the Metropolia and, it was hoped, by other Orthodox churches as well. But the patriarch flatly refused even to consider this.[82] Consequently, the Metropolia was forced to negotiate with her mother Church alone, and autocephaly was finally granted in 1970. The Russian Orthodox Greek Catholic Church of America, or the Metropolia, thus became the Orthodox Church in America (OCA), the fifteenth local autocephalous Orthodox Church—although still failing to gain recognition as such by several eastern patriarchates.

The same agreement also abolished the Moscow Patriarchate's exarchate in North America (leaving the ones for South America and Europe intact, however). The Patriarchal parishes (about thirty in the US and over twenty in Canada) became a temporary institution, with every individual parish possessing the right to join the OCA on a simple majority decision of the parishioners.[83]

This concludes the story of this Church as a part of the history

---

[82]"Autocephaly," *Orthodox America,* 262-3. Athenagoras replied verbatim to Fr. Alexander Schmemann, who was visiting him in 1965: "You are Russians, go to your Mother Church. . . . no one can solve your problem except the Russian Church."

[83]See all the documents on the autocephaly, including the text of the *Tomos* of the Moscow Patriarchate establishing the OCA as the local Church of America, in *Orthodox America,* 265-80; and, *Autocephaly* (Crestwood, N.Y.: SVS Press, 1971). Ironically, the most vocal of the eastern patriarchs in protesting the granting of autocephaly by the Moscow Patriarchate became the same Patriarch Athenagoras who had urged the American Church to turn to Moscow.

of the Russian Orthodox Church in the twentieth century. A new page in her history then begins—that of the building up of local North American Orthodoxy—but this is beyond the scope of this book.

CHAPTER 9

The Russian Orthodox Church during the First Postwar Decade

Church and State

With the end of the war, the Church had the task of proving her usefulness to Stalin even in peacetime, thus assuring the continuing toleration of overt, organized religion. The first premonition of forthcoming attacks against the Church came with the September 1944 CPSU Central Committee decree "calling for renewed antireligious efforts through 'scientific-educational propaganda.' Party members were reminded of the need to combat 'survivals of ignorance, superstition and prejudice among the people.' " Another Central Committee resolution calling for the intensification of atheistic propaganda by the mass media was issued in 1945, soon after the end of the war.[1]

But the renewed atheistic propaganda was at this stage still limited to words and was not accompanied by acts of vandalism against churches and believers, as before the war. The Church went out of her way to prove her usefulness to the Soviet state in its foreign and some aspects of its domestic policies. It has already been mentioned that, soon after his election, Patriarch Aleksii and other leading hierarchs were received by Stalin and Foreign Minister Molotov on April 10, 1945. Metropolitan Nikolai's report of the encounter, although couched in sycophantic

---

[1]David E. Powell, *Antireligious Propaganda in the Soviet Union: A Study in Mass Persuasion* (Cambridge, Mass: MIT Press, 1975) 38.

praise of Stalin, gives some solid information on the subject of the negotiations. In addition to the already functioning Moscow theology school, eight additional schools were to be founded in other cities, and a printing press was given to the Church on Stalin's orders, in connection with which the hierarchs asked Stalin for the right either to build or to obtain a block of buildings for a publishing establishment, a higher theological institute, pastoral courses, etc. "Stalin showed sympathy for everything we asked, and promised us support."[2] Thus, at the very outset, nine seminaries and at least two academies (graduate theological schools) were planned. According to other sources, ten seminaries and three academies were planned: four seminaries in the Ukraine, five in the RSFSR and one in Belorussia; and academies in Moscow, Leningrad and Kiev. This plan was only partly realized. A total of eight seminaries and two academies were in existence in 1947, but the mounting pressures against the Church soon forced her to postpone indefinitely any plans for further expansion. Subsequently, overt persecutions under Khrushchev were to reduce the number of seminaries to three. The plans concerning an independent church press were never to be realized, although the need to have a block of buildings for educational purposes was satisfied by the return to the Church of the huge Trinity-St. Sergius Monastery, where the Moscow theological schools were transferred in 1946.[3]

What Nikolai did not mention in his report was the apparent quid pro quo concordat concluded verbally in the two meetings with Stalin (1943 and 1945), according to which, in return for a relative liturgical freedom and tolerance for the Church, the latter would repay the state by serving its foreign policy interests and propaganda.[4] And Nikolai, as the head of the Church's De-

[2]"Na prieme u Stalina," ZbMP, no. 5 (1945) 25-6.
[3]The functioning seminaries, with dates of beginning of operation, were: Moscow/Zagorsk (1944), Odessa (1945), Leningrad (1946), Minsk/Zhirovitsy (1946), Lutsk/Volhynia (1946), Stavropol (1946) and Kiev (1947); the academies were in Moscow/Zagorsk (1944) and Leningrad (1946). William B. Stroyen, Communist Russia and the Russian Orthodox Church, 1943-1962 (Washington, D.C.: Catholic University Press, 1967) 71-9. The additionally planned seminaries were for Lvov and Novosibirsk, and the academy for Kiev. (Information provided to this author by the late Metropolitan Nikodim of Leningrad in a private conversation in London). See also Spinka, 118-20.
[4]See Archbishop Vasily (Krivoshein), "Poslednie vstrechi s M. Nikolaem,"

partment of External Ecclesiastical Relations, would be the main actor on this stage, although Patriarch Aleksii was also heavily involved.[5]

Aleksii's extensive pilgrimage to the Middle East soon after his visit with Stalin, a pilgrimage that was more political than spiritual in character, has already been discussed, as was Nikolai's diversion from the pilgrimage to Western Europe and his successes in returning considerable sections of Russian émigré churches to the Patriarchal fold. This was followed in 1946 by the incorporation of the Russian parishes in Hungary into the Patriarchal fold in the form of a Hungarian Orthodox deanery. But other tasks had to be done to extend Stalin's autarchy to church affairs as well. There was the matter of the Orthodox churches of Estonia and Latvia, nominally still under Constantinople, and the Autocephalous Orthodox Church of Poland, with ties to Constantinople, whence she had received her autocephaly; the Czech Orthodox Church and the Orthodox Church in the Carpathian Ukraine (Ruthenia), under the Serbian Patriarchate; and the Russian émigré churches in Czechoslovakia, formerly under Metropolitan Evlogy and now under Moscow. Finally, there were the large and quite nationalistic Uniate churches of the western and Carpathian Ukraine, with a combined nominal membership of well over three million, still under Rome; plus the whole question of closer relations with the Orthodox churches in the Balkan states. Along with the Soviet domination over Eastern Europe, Stalin obviously wanted the churches there to accept the leadership of the politically tamed Moscow Patriarchate.

The Church obliged as best she could. In the course of the year, Archbishop Grigory (Chukov, future Metropolitan of Lenin-

---

VRKhD, no. 117 (1976) 209-19, where Nikolai tells the author in 1960 that because the communist government has begun persecutions of the Church, he has responded by sermons attacking the persecutors, "not those sermons which are published in *ZhMP* but those which are preached in the churches" (210).

[5]See, for example, the patriarch's speech before a Te Deum in his cathedral on the occasion of Stalin's seventieth birthday (December 21, 1949), in which he says that Stalin "is the first among the fighters for peace among all the nations of the world . . . our leader whose charming personality disarms anyone who has met him by his kindness and attentiveness to everybody's needs . . . by the power and wisdom of his speech." Aleksii, *Slova, rechi, poslaniya, obrashcheniya, doklady, stat'i*, 2 (Moscow, 1954) 173. On Nikolai's role in the peace campaign, see Fletcher, *Nikolai*, passim.

grad) reintegrated the Baltic churches within the Moscow Patriarchate. Even before the end of the war he had gone to Bulgaria to assist at the enthronement of Exarch Stefan as the first *canonically* autocephalous head of the Bulgarian Orthodox Church (which became closely linked with the Church of Russia, at least in part because, after an eighty-year schism, Constantinople had at last recognized the originally unilaterally self-declared autocephaly of the Bulgarian Church, largely due to the pressure of the Russian Church). The Russian (formerly Karlovcian) parishes in Bulgaria, with their Metropolitan Serafim (Sobolev), returned to the jurisdiction of Moscow. A little later Grigory visited Finland, where the Orthodox Church enjoyed an autonomous status under the Patriarchate of Constantinople, which she had joined by unilaterally renouncing her allegiance to the Moscow Patriarchate in 1923. Metropolitan Grigory failed to return the Finnish Church to Moscow, but at least established personal contacts with the hierarchy of the Church and close relations with the two Russian émigré parishes and the New Valaamo Monastery, which continued to adhere to the Moscow Patriarchate. Grigory initiated talks with the ruling Archbishop German of the Finnish Church, and after some periods of tension, Moscow eventually recognized her status as an autonomous branch of the Ecumenical Patriarchate and returned the New Valaamo Monastery to Finnish jurisdiction in 1957.[6] Other bishops of the Russian Church carried out successful missions to Yugoslavia and Romania, resulting in the return of the Russian parishes in Belgrade (1945) and Bucharest (1948) to the jurisdiction of Moscow. In the autumn of 1945, Russian episcopal missions to Czechoslovakia, Austria, the recently annexed Carpathian Ukraine and Manchuria resulted in the return of the local Orthodox churches to the Patriarchate of Moscow.[7]

The church situation in Poland was rectified somewhat later, but in a much more regular fashion, with the initiative coming from the Polish Orthodox Church herself. We have already mentioned the unpopularity of Metropolitan Dionisy, who had changed his loyalties as befitted the political moment just too many times

---

[6]Rahr, 89-91; Struve, 107; Fletcher, *Religion and Soviet Foreign Policy, 1945-1970* (London: Oxford University Press, 1973) 19 and 25; and G. Troitsky, part 2, in *ZhMP*, no. 11 (1967).

[7]Ibid.; Fletcher, *Religion and Soviet Foreign Policy,* 16-21.

for his congregation to bear. Soon after the end of the war, Dionisy returned to Poland from West Germany and was permitted by the new rulers of Poland to head the Polish Orthodox Church, in accordance with the 1938 statutes, as an autocephalous body. Dionisy was enjoying the support of the Polish government in his proregime nationalistic Polish line, but not that of his coreligionists, who began to negotiate with the Moscow Patriarchate. In 1948 they petitioned the Moscow patriarch to grant the Polish Church canonical autocephaly, agreeing that the 1924 autocephaly granted by Constantinople was null and void. The Moscow Patriarchate complied, and on June 22, 1948, the Polish Orthodox Church received an Act of Autocephaly cosigned by the members of the Patriarchal Synod on the one hand, and on the other, by the two bishops (besides Dionisy, who did not participate in the action) and all the other members of the Consistory of the Polish Church. Forced into isolation, Dionisy petitioned the patriarch two months later to be forgiven and reaccepted into liturgical communion with the patriarchate. His request was granted, but henceforth he remained in retirement, while the Polish Church received "on loan" Metropolitan Makary (Oksiyuk) of Lvov, a Soviet Ukrainian and a highly learned man, as the first head of the new Church.[8] Since the death of Makary, the Polish Orthodox Church has been headed by Polish citizens.

The actions of the Moscow Patriarchate toward the Polish Church showed remarkable canonical regularity and ecclesiastical wisdom. Similar courses of action were followed vis-à-vis China and Czechoslovakia. In 1946, the Orthodox parishes of Czechoslovakia were consolidated under Moscow's jurisdiction with a metropolitan (Elevfery) sent from the USSR with the title of exarch. In 1951, after the abolition of the Uniate Church and her enforced merger with the Orthodox Church of Czechoslovakia, the latter was granted autocephaly, with Elevfery as her first administrator. In China, after the recall to Russia of the last Russian bishop there (Metropolitan-Exarch Viktor), a Chinese cleric, Bishop Simeon Du of Peking, who had been consecrated

[8]Svitich, *Pravoslavnaya tserkov' v Pol'she*, 203-13; Rahr, 86-8. In the early 1920s Oksiyuk, then a professor at the Kiev Theological Academy, switched to secular scholarship at the Soviet Ukrainian Academy of Sciences, yet Leonty of Chile (36) describes him as a very decent man.

the first Chinese Orthodox bishop five years earlier, was appointed head of the Orthodox Church in China.[9]

The Uniate issue was handled in a much less regular manner, to say the least. The tragedy of the "reunification" of the Uniate Church with Orthodoxy was that too many mutually incompatible interests coincided in bringing the legal existence of the Church to a quick end. Stalin wanted her quick death for three reasons. First, the predominantly Uniate Galicia was the cradle of Ukrainian nationalism and separatism, the Uniate Church having given her blessing and support to the Melnyk branch of the Ukrainian separatist movement in the 1930s and during the war.[10] Second, the Uniate Church, as a separate, openly tolerated, national-ecclesiastic organization confined to the areas of greatest national-istic and underground-partisan anti-Soviet agitation, could become a sort of "second government," a unifying and consolidating force, for anti-Soviet resistance in the western Ukraine. Finally, the Church's subordination to the Vatican, which was beyond Stalin's control, made her even more intolerable for him. In fact, the war was still on when, in April 1945, the ruling metropolitan of the Uniate Church in Galicia, Iosyf Slipy, and all four of his bishops were arrested "for treasonous . . . activities in support of the German occupiers." This was followed by large-scale, though selective, arrests of the most active Uniate priests.

At the same time, action groups for reunification with Ortho-doxy began to be formed in Galicia. By February 1946, of the 1,270 Uniate priests still at large, 997 submitted written applica-tions to be accepted into the Orthodox Church.[11] Many of them were probably quite sincere, for the Brest Union of 1596 had been forced upon the West Russian population of the Polish-Lithuanian state by the Jesuits. The whole of the seventeenth century was marked by resistance of the population to the union, which became one of the causes of the many rebellions, at first leading to the reunification of the eastern Ukraine with Muscovy

---

[9]Fr. Nikolai Getman, "Mitropolit Krasnodarskii i Kubanskii Viktor," ZhMP, no. 11 (1966) 16-9; Fletcher, Religion and Soviet Foreign Policy, 18; Rahr, 88-9.

[10]See, for instance, John A. Armstrong, Ukrainian Nationalism, 36-7. Had the Uniate Church remained intact it could have eventually played a nationally con-solidating oppositional role among the West Ukrainians, not unlike that of the Roman Catholic Church for the Poles or Lithuanians today.

[11]Rahr, 61.

and eventually contributing to the disintegration of Poland itself. Moreover, as already mentioned, masses of Uniates, once they had emigrated to the freedom of North America, rejoined the Orthodox Church there. In the early twentieth century, a movement for reunion with Orthodoxy began to spread quite spontaneously in Carpathian Ruthenia, among the Lemkos of what after World War I was to become part of Poland and among the Galician Ukrainians themselves. This process continued after World War I, although the Polish government discouraged it by increased persecution of the Orthodox Church in Poland.[12] Among the sincere enthusiasts for Orthodoxy was undoubtedly the Very Rev. Dr. Havrylo Kostelnyk, a highly learned and outstanding Lvov priest who became one of the organizers of the whole movement and was killed in retaliation by a Banderist partisan in 1948.

But in the conditions of the growing terror of the Soviet secret police against the Uniates and the unnaturally hurried pressure to liquidate the Church, many of the signatories were undoubtedly motivated by sheer fear. The elections of delegates to the sobor (*rada* in Ukrainian) which was to decide the fate of the Uniate Church showed further irregularities. In those deaneries where there was too much resistance against reunification, elections were not held and delegates were simply appointed by the deans; in the deaneries where the deans themselves continued to support "Uniatism," delegates were simply appointed by the local "action groups." No one bothered to check how representative these delegates were of the prevailing local opinion, and all of them received the right to vote at the sobor, which met at the end of February 1946 at the St. Iur (George) Cathedral of Lvov, with predictable results: the Uniate Church was liquidated in Galicia (former Polish western Ukraine) by uniting with the Orthodox Church. Through a similar combination of repression and genuine tendencies, the Uniate churches were liquidated in Romania in 1948, in the Carpathian Ukraine in 1949 and in Slovakia in 1951, after the condemnation of its ruling bishop to life imprisonment.[13]

[12]For example, in 1938 alone between 107 (Rahr, 86) and 150 (Svitich, 1-7, 75-95, 115-83) active Orthodox parishes in Poland were forcefully confiscated by the Polish government and were either transformed into Roman Catholic churches or demolished.

[13]Rahr, 62-4. Levitin is convinced the patriarch was not aware of the violence

It is still unclear whether Patriarch Aleksii and his Synod were aware of the violence and repression that went along with the process or if they saw it as the genuinely voluntary product of such enthusiasts as Kostelnyk. The direct and original contribution of the Moscow Patriarchate to the action was Patriarch Aleksii's "Message" to the Uniates of the western Ukraine, issued just after his election to the patriarchal throne. The message speaks of the finally achieved reunification of the historical Russian lands and of the sorrow that no joint prayers of thanksgiving to God for this reunification in the common Orthodox temples could take place because the western brothers belonged to a different faith, "torn away from their Mother-Russian Orthodox Church." Then follow two paragraphs on the inhuman face of Hitlerism and the victory over it as a sign that God blessed the struggle against Hitler, and a historically untrue allegation that the leaders of the Uniate Church, including the deceased Metropolitan Sheptytsky, "called on you to bow under Hitler's yoke. And where is the Vatican leading you, appealing in its Christmas and New Year's messages for mercy to the bearers of fascism, to Hitler, this greatest criminal ever known to history?" Aleksii refers to the recent national sobor which elected him and whose joint address, cosigned by two eastern patriarchs and representatives of all Orthodox churches, "quite contrary to the Vatican . . . gave witness . . . to their complete unanimity in condemning Hitler, the bloody madman . . . Pray you, brothers . . . break your ties with the Vatican, which leads you into darkness and spiritual destruction by its religious heresies . . . Make haste, return into the arms of your true Mother, the Russian Orthodox Church."[14]

The moment for such an appeal was certainly badly chosen: it coincided with, and gave support to, the NKVD terror against the Uniate clergy. Whether the patriarch was aware of it or not, he surely knew the nature and character of the Soviet regime too well to believe that no force would be applied by it, and therefore he could hardly disclaim any responsibility for such measures.

accompanying the "reunification." See volume 3 of his memoirs, *V poiskakh novogo grada* (Tel Aviv, 1980) 39.

[14]"Pastyryam i veruyushchim greko-katolicheskoi tserkvi, prozhivayushchim v zapadnykh oblastyakh Ukrainskoi SSR," *Slova, rechi,* 1 (Moscow, 1948) 121-3.

The Russian Orthodox Church leader could probably argue that once Stalin decided to do away with the Uniate Church he would do so as thoroughly as he had with the much more numerous Russian Orthodox Church in the 1930s, whatever the position of the Moscow Patriarchate. However, the blemish of slandering Metropolitan Sheptytsky[15] and of at least implicitly condoning the NKVD terror against the Uniate clergy cannot easily be erased from the record of the Moscow Patriarchate.

There is conclusive evidence that the Uniate Church has not been fully destroyed to the present day in the western Ukraine. She survives in the underground under various guises, and because her official liquidation was carried out in such a politically compromising manner she has gained for herself the aura of being the national Church in the eyes of Ukrainian nationalists, even those of Orthodox background.[16] But this was to become evident only much later. In 1945-1948 the Moscow Patriarchate needed success with the Uniates, as well as a leading role in the campaign against the Vatican, to once again prove to Stalin her usefulness. Now, moreover, she would be needed at least for the purpose of a lengthy, organic reintegration of the former Uniates within the *Orthodox* Church and of the formerly independent Orthodox West Ukrainians, Belorussians, Latvians, Estonians and Moldavians within the *Russian* Orthodox Church. To perform this function the Church had to be allowed a certain amount of inner freedom to win the necessary prestige and authority in the eyes of the new flocks.

In the same light should be seen Aleksii's maneuvers to gain for the Russian Church the status of primus inter pares in the Orthodox *oikoumene*. It has been argued by some western scholars (including Fletcher) that the Constantinople-Moscow rivalry was the reason why Aleksii's Middle East pilgrimage did not include a visit to Istanbul. A more likely reason, however, was

[15]Like many other Soviet citizens, Sheptytsky had at first welcomed the Germans as liberators, but then condemned their treatment of the Slavs and Jews in no uncertain terms, while supporting the Ukrainian nationalist resistance against communism, including the formation of the Ukrainian anti-Soviet military units under German command. Armstrong, 172-4.

[16]See, for instance: Bohdan R. Bociurkiw, "Religious Situation in Soviet Ukraine," in *Ukraine in a Changing World*, ed. Walter Dushnyck (New York: Ukrainian Congress Committee of America, 1977) 173-90; and Valentyn Moroz, "A Chronicle of Resistance," in *Boomerang* (Baltimore: Smoloskyp, 1974) 94-5.

the refusal of the strongly anti-Soviet Turks at the time to issue a visa to the Russian patriarch. He would visit Constantinople on another occasion anyhow. Meanwhile, the grand scale on which it was planned to celebrate the five hundredth anniversary of the autocephaly of the Russian Orthodox Church at the Moscow Trinity-St. Sergius Monastery (in Zagorsk) was a sign that Moscow might have hoped to be the initiator and convener of the next (eighth) ecumenical council. The celebration's agenda included consultations of pan-Orthodox importance that could be seen as preconciliar consultations (a prosynod). The very choice of the date, 1948, may have been intended as an implied slight to Constantinople: five hundred years before, Russia had unilaterally proclaimed her ecclesiastic autocephaly, but it took another 141 years before Constantinople and the other eastern patriarchates recognized it.[17] This time the ecumenical see reacted by pointing out that the convocation of pan-Orthodox councils or preconciliar commissions was its sole prerogative.

Consequently, the anniversary celebrations remained exactly that, although on a highly inflated scale, with a predictably politicized, anti-Vatican thrust. Patriarch Aleksii's opening address set the tone. It was followed by anti-Roman Catholic papers by Ermogen, the Archbishop of Kazan; by Fr. Havrylo Kostelnyk, the initiator of the liquidation of the Ukrainian Uniate Church; by the Bulgarian Metropolitan Kirill (the current patriarch), etc. The profile of most of these papers was predominantly political. By contrast, the papers on Anglicanism were much more theological in character and more sympathetic, although one of the conclusions was the invalidity of Anglican clerical orders, on the grounds that the Anglicans themselves could not even agree whether clerical ordination was a sacrament or not. One of the purposes of putting Anglicanism on the agenda may have been

---

[17]The immediate cause of the self-declared autocephaly was the 1439 Council of Florence, at which Greek bishops, including the ethnic Greek ruling Metropolitan of Russia Isidor, were forced to sign an act of union with the pope, in return for which the pope promised military help against the Turks. The help never came, Constantinople was sacked in 1453 and the Greeks discontinued their brief ecclesiastical dependence on the pope, but the union was cause enough for the Russians to break their ties with Constantinople. They deposed Isidor and elected their own metropolitan (Iona), and henceforth, in the eyes of many Russians the Orthodoxy of the Greeks has been suspect (which became particularly evident in the Great Schism of the seventeenth century).

a desire to pull the Anglicans away from the émigré and Greek churches by offering instead Moscow as the center for Anglican-Orthodox dialogue. (Another reason may have been purely theological: the Patriarchs of Constantinople and Alexandria had recognized the validity of Anglican orders in 1931 or earlier. At the time, Metropolitan Sergii declared that this question was a theological one of pan-Orthodox importance, and its resolution by a unilateral act of two patriarchates was invalid.) The magnitude of the celebrations in 1948 and of the questions discussed must have been aimed at proving to the Soviets the usefulness of the Russian Church as an international forum, in the hope of protecting the Church from any return of the Soviet state to its prewar anti-Church policies. But the conference failed to make the hoped-for imprint on the Orthodox world or to bring world Orthodoxy under Moscow's domination. Of the four eastern patriarchs, none were present, and only those of Constantinople and Antioch were even represented. Moreover, the Greeks participated only in the celebration, declining participation in the consultations that followed. The consultations therefore were limited to the churches dominated by communist regimes (plus Antioch, which at the time was receiving generous subsidies from the Moscow Patriarchate).[18] Having thus failed to become "an Orthodox Vatican," the Moscow Patriarchate lost its particular importance to Stalin.

The year 1948 marked a turning point in Stalin's foreign policy ambitions and their realization. The Cold War was beginning, and the Berlin Blockade proved to Stalin that the West was ready to retaliate and he had no chance for the time being to continue any expansion westward; the communist guerrilla warfare in Greece had failed and Stalin was folding it up; and there was trouble with Tito. Hence, in the realities becoming evident in 1948, Stalin's foreign policy was now aiming more toward entrenchment and internal consolidation of power both within the USSR and in the whole East European camp. Add to this the obvious failure of the Patriarchal Church to unquestionably dominate world Orthodoxy and it becomes clear that, in

[18]*Deyaniya soveshchaniya glav i predstavitelei avtokefal'nykh pravoslavnykh tserkvei v svyazi s prazdnovaniem 500-letiya avtokefalii russkoi pravoslavnoi tserkvi. 8-18 iyulya, 1948 g.* (Moscow, 1948) 88-382. Also, Fletcher, *Religion and Soviet Foreign Policy*, 25-8. See Sergii's reaction in *ZhMP*, no. 7-8 (1932) 20-1.

terms of Stalin's thinking, the Church was again becoming a nuisance—a nuisance, because she remained as incompatible as ever with Marxist ideology, even in the flexible Stalin's application of it, as well as with any notion of wholesome totalitarianism. Hence, her political usefulness was waning. In the words of William Fletcher,

> the establishment of Soviet control over Eastern Europe was proceeding well; the influence of the Moscow Patriarchate remained useful, but it was no longer quite so important. Unless some alternative sphere of service could be discovered, it appeared that the period of the Russian Orthodox Church's usefulness to Soviet foreign policy had drawn to a close.[19]

This usefulness was found in the peace campaigns. The world was tired of wars, and the Cold War was reminding the world that a new threat of war was rising. No matter that the cause of the threat was Soviet aggressiveness—large sections of apolitical humanity were ready to support any voice of peace, from whichever corner it came. Metropolitan Nikolai became the chief operator of these peace campaigns on the Soviet side. The Soviets must have calculated that the more vocal they became in the international peace forums at the time of the Cold War, the more the world public would become confused about the actual initiators of aggression and of the Cold War itself, particularly if such people as churchmen and men of arts (e.g., the former émigré Soviet writer Ilya Ehrenburg, with his intimate connections in the West European literary and artistic liberal establishment) were behind them. The Soviet government was concerned over the military imbalance of the late 1940s and early 1950s, when at first only the West possessed the atomic bomb, and feared that rearmament might result in a direct attack on the Soviet Union. In these conditions of growing tensions it needed a second front of self-defense against direct military conflict, and sought to find one by mobilizing world public opinion against the US—portraying the latter as a potential aggressor with no moral scruples whatsoever, using bacteriological weapons in Korea (which, of

[19]*Religion and Soviet Foreign Policy*, 29.

course, was untrue). The racist elements in the American tradition were blown out of all proportion and projected onto the Korean theater of war, to bring to people's minds analogies with the German Nazis while memories were fresh. And fraudulent pronouncements containing all these allegations would be made by Metropolitan Nikolai.

The World Peace Council was born in 1949 out of a 1948 meeting in Wroclaw (Poland). At the first USSR Conference for Peace in August 1949, Nikolai, inter alia, called the US "the rabid fornicatress of resurrected Babylon . . . [who] is trying to seduce the people of the world while pushing them toward war." During the Korean War he declared:

the spirit and the flesh of fascism have not disappeared . . .

No sooner had they begun their criminal aggression than the American neo-fascists began the planned, cannibalistic extermination of the "inferior" Korean race.

. . . Executions without trial . . . held in secret . . . they cut off ears, noses, and breasts, gouge out eyes, break arms and legs, crucify patriots, bury women and infants alive . . . they scalp Korean patriots for "souvenirs."

. . . the American criminals first of all slaughtered political prisoners (from 200,000 to 400,000 people), forcing them to dig their own graves beforehand. . . . The barbaric bombing of peaceful towns and villages has been carried out solely for the purpose of annihilating the civilian population . . .

In . . . death camps . . . people live on the bare earth. . . . They are not fed. . . . Under the pretext of affording them medical aid, American scientists and doctors experiment on the prisoners with the latest vaccines and chemical preparations. Every night executions take place. . . . First on the list are the intelligentsia of Korea: doctors, teachers, engineers, technicians, agronomists. . . .

They are manufacturing bacteriological weapons. . . . The
town of Chinhua . . . was subjected to bacteriological
bombardment which resulted in an epidemic of plague . . .[20]

These pronouncements were so crude in their fraudulent assertions, just like the whole Stalinist peace campaign, that they could
hardly have had a direct impact on western public opinion. One
could even almost excuse Nikolai's participation in it on the
grounds that as intelligent a person as he was must have thought
that his statements were so blatantly untrue that they could not
have any impact and were therefore harmless. This way of thinking is quite characteristic of Soviet citizens, who are used to reading between the lines and who to a certain degree are immune
to propaganda. Moreover, they tend to exaggerate the willingness
of the western public to make the utmost use of the available
channels of unbiased information and thus to render Soviet-style
propaganda harmless.[21] Indeed, Fletcher sees a difference of principle between the Moscow Patriarchate's role, on the one hand,
in the 1945-1948 campaign of establishing ties with churches,
carrying on propaganda against the Vatican and reintegrating
churches under the Moscow Patriarchate, and on the other, in
the post-1948 peace campaign. In the former, Metropolitan
Nikolai was the leader; in the latter, he was only a participant—
a useful one, but not indispensable.[22]

It seems, however, that Nikolai was trying to prove to the
state that even here there were important areas of propaganda
where he and the Church would be indispensable—namely, in

[20]Ibid., 32; Fletcher, *Nikolai*, 96-134. The congressional testimony of the
defector Deryabin, a former leading KGB official, that Nikolai was a KGB agent
is highly suspect. It is probably based on Deryabin's seeing some reports by the
metropolitan in KGB files, and in this sense every Soviet citizen who regularly
travels abroad can be dubbed a KGB agent. There is reliable evidence that Nikolai
never denounced anyone to the KGB (Levitin, *Likhie gody*, 85).

[21]Allegedly, Sergii privately expressed surprise that the émigré churchmen did
not appreciate the situation of the Church in the USSR. Recent arrivals from the
USSR are often shocked when they discover that the western public does not
make use of "the information explosion" and remains less informed than many
Soviet citizens, who go out of their way to listen to foreign broadcasts for information. Metropolitan Nikodim once said to this writer that fraudulent statements
by Soviet bishops shock only us in the West, while Soviet citizens have gotten
used to them and take them as a necessary part of life.

[22]*Nikolai*, 110.

involving the western churches by appealing to them in a Christian-theological context:

> It is necessary for all Christians . . . to understand . . .
> the childishly simple teaching of Christ . . . by virtue of
> which there cannot be Christian aggressive war . . . and
> force in the name of alleged preservation of Christian
> civilization is impossible.[23]

> As if to cheer thirsters after Truth, the prophet of the
> Old Testament said: "And the work of righteousness shall
> be peace; and the effect of righteousness, quietness and
> assurance for ever." (Isa. 32:17) . . . The spirit of all
> Holy Scripture testifies that war is not a primordial and
> natural phenomenon in the race of man . . . We are now
> against war because we ourselves created it.[24]

In the latter quotation there is even a sharing of responsibilities for the sin of the world, not just a crude blaming of the other side. Such statements must have rendered Nikolai's actions more effective by giving them a ring of sincerity—which most probably was there, for the Church, like any responsible Soviet citizen after the experience of the horrors of World War II, certainly wanted to preserve peace, almost at all cost and by any means.

But, apparently, the state was not convinced that this aspect of the peace campaign called for a privileged position for the Church within the USSR. The fact that despite the renewed attacks against the Church her leadership continued to serve the Soviet regime as faithfully as before—for example, celebrating special Te Deums on Stalin's seventieth birthday (December 1949) or shamefully returning, in 1950, Yugoslav decorations given by Tito to Patriarch Aleksii and other Russian bishops five years earlier[25]—must have convinced the Soviets that the Church was acting from a position of weakness and therefore would continue

---

[23]This was the same Nikolai who during the war had uncompromisingly condemned the Germans and, along with Patriarch Aleksii, criticized the Vatican for calling for clemency for war criminals.

[24]Fletcher, *Nikolai,* 106-7. Stalin's unsophisticated leaders of the *Agitprop* were probably not happy with the sharing of guilt implied in Nikolai's statement.

[25]See *ZhMP,* no. 1 (1950) 4-5 and 11-3; and no. 4 (1950) 5.

to perform whatever was required of her whether the state obliged by extending lenient treatment or not. As long as Stalin lived, the unwritten concordat mentioned above apparently retained some force. What probably happened was simply that, in the conditions of Stalin's iron centralization, no local administrators dared to frontally subvert a Church-state agreement reached personally with Stalin, which, never having been published, therefore could not have been officially revoked as long as Stalin lived. Therefore, the main targets of the renewed antireligious propaganda were mainly the Vatican and, to a lesser extent, the World Council of Churches, as Cold War mongers and anticommunist forces. On the local level, however, bishops, priests and believers had to fight for the survival of churches opened during and immediately after the war, and here and there the local officials of the Council for Russian Orthodox Church Affairs (CROCA) did occasionally close parishes and make life difficult, particularly for the bishops, by trying to prevent any disciplinary measures the bishops might take against immoral or otherwise unworthy clerics and church activists.[26]

The year 1947 was marked by a definite escalation of the antireligious campaign. For the first time since the end of the war the communist youth daily, *Komsomol'skaya pravda,* stated that Komsomol membership was incompatible with religious belief. The teachers' newspaper *Uchitel'skaya gazeta* said the same thing about the teaching profession, calling for a resolute fight against the "false" theory of nonreligious education—it had to be actively *anti*religious. The chief ideological organ of the CPSU, *Bolshevik,* proclaimed that the struggle against religion was a struggle against a reactionary, bourgeois ideology. The "USSR" volume of the *Great Soviet Encyclopaedia* came out with a reaffirmation of the CPSU's resolute and unwavering opposition to any religion. Just as before the war, the vanguard in the struggle was taken by the Komsomol and its chief organs, *Komsomol'skaya pravda* and *Molodoi bolshevik* (The Young Bolshevik). The same year saw the formation of the Znanie (Knowledge) society, in place of the defunct League of Militant Godless. Its official purpose was popular propaganda of "scientific and political knowledge." By 1972, of its 2,457,000 members,

[26]Popovsky, *Zhizn' i zhitie Voino-Yasenetskogo,* 414-22.

1,700 were from the top echelon of the Soviet scholarly official-
dom—members of the USSR and republican Academies of Sciences—and 107,000 were university professors and doctors of
sciences. The bulk of its publications and public lectures was
devoted to antireligious subjects. In many cities it established
"Houses of Scientific Atheism." Its atheistic activities reached
flood proportions again after 1958, coinciding with Khrushchev's
attack on religion. In 1964, for example, the total circulation of
atheistic publications exceeded six million copies.[27]

There must have been a near prohibition of new episcopal
consecrations (as claimed by Nikita Struve), for in the three
years between January 1950 and Stalin's death (officially, March
5, 1953) there had been only two episcopal consecrations, both
shortly before Stalin's death: the one of Ermogen (Golubev),
soon to become one of the staunchest fighters for the Church, and
that of Mikhail (Chub), on March 1, 1953, when Stalin was
already in a coma. There were also some disappearances of
bishops in those years, through arrests and state-imposed retire-
ments.[28]

A reflection of the fact that the peace campaign was largely
forced upon the Church is seen in the section "Defense of Peace,"
a very extensive feature in every issue of the *Journal of the Moscow Patriarchate* since 1949. Soon after Stalin's death, namely,
in early 1954, it was reduced in size to a total of three to six
pages per issue. This apparently was not to the Soviets' liking,
and by the end of the year the section again increased to some
ten pages per issue.

The Internal Life of the Church, 1945-1953

The propagandistic activities of the Church were the price her

[27]Ibid., 419; Curtiss, *Russian Church*, 320-1; readers' letters and editorials in
Nauka i religiya, nos. 3, 9 and 10 (1965); Simon, *Church, State*, 92-4.

[28]Struve, 139. A case in point was that of Metropolitan Manuil, who, after
spending many years in prisons, had received the diocese of Orenburg (Chkalov
at the time) only to be rearrested in 1948—apparently for opening too many
churches and raising religiosity among the population. Released only in 1955, he
then received the diocese of Kuibyshev. See Levitin, "Slovo ob umershem," a
samizdat ms. in this writer's possession dated September 19, 1968; and *OC*, no. 5
(May 1966) 2.

leaders were paying for being allowed to carry on real pastoral activities, for caring for the souls of the believers.

Almost every bishop (and to a lesser extent every priest) has acted as a two-faced Janus. If one reads the volumes of sermons, messages and encyclicals of Patriarch Aleksii and Metropolitan Nikolai, published by the Moscow Patriarchate, the contrast between the political and the pastoral utterances of both archpastors becomes tragically obvious, particularly in the writings of Nikolai. Nikolai's religious sermons have been excellently summarized and subdivided by topics in Fletcher's *Nikolai*. The inquisitive reader is advised to read the book and see for himself the religious sincerity, concern for Christian ethics and an eschatological vision of this world as gloomy and sinful in the late metropolitan's sermons—for which in fact he was dearly loved by Russian believers, who remember him in this light alone. And this is the tragedy: the people have not held his propaganda speeches against him, seeing them as a necessary evil to which they all are immune and for which they pity rather than condemn their pastors. The contrast with the late 1920s and early 1930s, when clerics were expelled by the parishioners for the mere utterance of prayers for Soviet leaders, is remarkable. The lie has become an accepted part of life![29]

On the occasion of the Japanese capitulation, Patriarch Aleksii wrote two contrasting messages. One, a congratulatory telegram to Stalin, sycophantically assured him of the Church's prayers for his health and long life and declared that his "military genius and . . . untiring toil for the good of our Motherland gave our peoples the great victory and victorious peace." The other, a message to the clergy and laity of the Russian Orthodox Church,

---

[29]See n. 21 above. When asked about the attitude to mendacious statements by bishops and priests on freedom of religion in the USSR or their participation in the peace campaigns, Tatyana Goricheva, a recent expellee from Leningrad (where she had been one of the founders of an unofficial religio-philosophic seminar as well as a Christian feminist movement and a number of *samizdat* publications), said that most laymen pity them for this and hold no grudge against them, understanding their position and knowing that it is the necessary price for keeping houses of prayer open. (Interview with this writer in Frankfurt am Main, September 1980). Fletcher (*Nikolai*, 86) confuses eschatological trends in Orthodoxy with pietism, which in fact is a characteristic of the German Protestant mysticism that influenced various Russian sects in the eighteenth century. See Dmitrij Tschizewskij, *Russian Intellectual History* (Ann Arbor: Ardis, 1978) 159 and 171.

contained some spiritually moving words about peace on earth: "Let us give thanks to God for granting us his heavenly help in the days of the war. Let us give thanks to God, who gave us . . . peace, which is the gift of God—the Creator of peace." Then he appeals to the nation not to forget God in these days of peace, to live in a way worthy of the gift of peace and the victory given by God. Only a short line praising "the Supreme Leader" mars this second message. But on many occasions the patriarch was forced to do much more than just make laudatory pronouncements about Stalin. On the anniversaries of the October Revolution and Stalin's birthdays special Te Deum services were celebrated by both the Moscow and the Georgian Patriarchates and sycophantic messages of congratulations were sent to Stalin and published in the *Journal of the Moscow Patriarchate*.[30]

In a number of addresses to newly ordained bishops Aleksii mentions the thorny road awaiting the archpastor, the great burdens and sufferings that the incumbents have gone through. He talks about the difficulties facing priests and bishops, because "many secular persons try to seize power for themselves in the Church which is not theirs, to criticize the pastors . . . and when faced with disciplinary measures on the part of the pastors, they respond by spreading slander about them and by threatening them." He appeals to bishops to stand firm in upholding church discipline and to keep up Christian morals.[31]

His encyclicals to bishops and priests implore them to concentrate on the spiritual education of believers, both by word of mouth through emphasizing the sermon, its quality and its teaching aspects, and by creating a prayerful atmosphere in church. The patriarch is against concert-like, secularized and overdramatized church singing and against too flashy decorations—electricity should be limited only to the central chandelier, and the rest of the church should be lit by candles. In his speeches at seminary commencement exercises Aleksii laid much hope in the spirituality of the new theological school. The prerevolutionary seminary "was gradually growing poorer and poorer in religious fervor"

[30]For example, *ZhMP*, no. 11 (1947) 4-5; no. 1 (1950) 11-3.

[31]*Slova, rechi*, 1:80-1; speech at the consecration of Bishop Roman of Tallin and Estonia, *Slova, rechi*, 2:50-1. It is hard to believe that this is the same Aleksii who in 1961 would force bishops to adopt new by-laws depriving the clergy of all power over their parishes.

because it was not only a pastoral school but also a general education school for the clerical estate. Consequently, there were even atheists among its teaching personnel. "Now only those come to our seminaries, both to teach and to be taught, who truly feel the beat of a religious heart within them." Therefore, it was the duty of the teachers to build up these resurrected theological schools in such a way that they could truly be called "*spiritual . . .* where the learning of the pupils would be predominantly that of the Spirit," with the emphasis on the teachings of the church fathers and of the Scriptures, not on the writings of secular authors, on which so many preachers rely.[32] These words reflected a sincere and deep hope for a spiritual renewal of the clergy, because, in the words of one observer, "the best priests had perished," while the ones who had survived and reentered church service in the immediate postwar years were mostly "the scum of the old clerical estate whom Ezhov and Beria had spared to breed." The same source continues: "I shiver at the thought of those impudent, fattened, slipshod priests of Stalin's vintage, who stored up money, bought summer cottages and cars at the cost of the poverty-stricken believers who donated their last kopeks to them." This same author confirms that the new generations of priests produced by the postwar seminaries are of an incomparably higher spiritual and moral caliber.[33] Thus, Patriarch Aleksii's hopes were not in vain.

The *Journal of the Moscow Patriarchate,* during the first postwar decade, occasionally printed some information on local ecclesiastical and archpastoral activities, illustrating some aspects of church life in those days. Despite the eight operating seminaries and two academies, each with a four-year course of study, the shortage of priests was apparently so acute in relation to the increased number of churches that bishops operated sporadic, brief pastoral courses to ordain priests outside the seminaries as well as to give some elements of theological education to poorly edu-

---

[32]*Slova, rechi,* 1:172 and 237-43. Another encyclical, addressed to the deans of Moscow parishes in 1953, emphasized the necessity of enhancing a prayerful mood in churchgoers by solemnity and severity of the services, singing, chanting, lighting, etc. S.N. Khudyakov, *O preodolenii religioznykh perezhitkov v SSSR* (Moscow, 1958) 41.

[33]Levitin, "Slovo ob umershem," 7; and *Bol'naya tserkov',* AS 886 (August 27, 1965) 23-4.

cated and hurriedly ordained priests. Most of these courses were only one month in duration. For instance, we read about courses aimed at raising the theological level of ordained priests in Grodno in western Belorussia in 1946, and again in 1947; in 1948 such courses are held in the summer at the Zhirovitsy Monastery, where the Belorussian Seminary is situated, again in the Grodno province.[34] This repetition of courses for practicing pastors in areas recently occupied by the Soviets raises suspicions that theology was not the only subject of study. But some of the reports on such courses deep inside Russian territory give details that show the clearly ecclesiastical aims of the diocesan bishops running them. For instance, Bishop Venedikt of Ivanovo and Kineshma (northeast of Moscow) not only ran a number of pastoral courses in 1952—he also built and consecrated a chapel attached to the diocesan residence and built a guesthouse "for visiting clergy, where courses' auditors also reside." From the text of the report it is clear that the bishop meant to make these courses a regular affair, perhaps eventually transforming them into a seminary. In fact, the length of his pastoral courses was not specified in the report.[35]

Venedikt apparently was not the only bishop who was hoping to form some type of a local religious-educational center at the diocesan headquarters. Another form of activity of this kind was the conference of diocesan clergy. Whereas in the 1960s and later such assemblies have been mostly political in nature, organized by the local plenipotentiaries of the state's Council for Religious Affairs (CRA), in the 1940s and 1950s their agendas dealt mostly with purely church and theological matters: "the sermonizing activities of the priesthood . . . and singing in the churches by the whole congregation . . . local reports on church attendance and parish life . . . on sectarians, impostor-priests and disorganizers of churchly discipline . . . organization of a diocesan fund to give support to the poorer parishes for repair and reconstruction of their churches[36] . . . financial support for seminarians . . . and elderly clergy." True, such conferences would contain one

[34]*ZhMP*, no. 12 (1946) 46-8; no. 8 (1947) 40; no. 9 (1948) 68-9.

[35]*ZhMP*, no. 9 (1952) 64.

[36]Such financial support of one parish by another was illegal in terms of the 1929 state legislation, which would again be strictly enforced after 1961.

political subject on the agenda as well—e.g., "On the participation of clergy in the forthcoming elections to the RSFSR Supreme Soviet."[37] But what is interesting is that one of the agenda subjects of a December 1946 conference of the Tula diocese was "On the organization of a diocesan library and a reading room."[38] Obviously, the aim of it was missionary: to make available to the interested reader the type of literature that was unavailable in a secular library. We are not sure to what extent these plans were realized (although the Ivanovo one was, by the late summer of 1952). But most probably the secular authorities confiscated and/or closed down all such facilities during Khrushchev's onslaught on religion, for nothing has been heard about the existence of such diocesan educational or library establishments since the 1950s.

Alas, by far not all bishops were as enterprising and dedicated to the Church and her mission as were the bishops of Ivanovo and Tula. This writer was informed by a respectable cleric of the Moscow Patriarchate that, for instance, in Belorussia the ruling bishop had originally been offered the prerevolutionary Minsk Seminary building for a theological seminary, but he refused, fearing that the Church would not have the funds to rebuild this war-damaged building. Next, he was offered the beautiful castle of Prince Lubomirski in western Belorussia, but again refused out of fear that the Church would not be able to keep up the palatial gardens and the vast buildings in proper order. When he decided to have the seminary at the rural Zhirovitsy Monastery, the Soviet authorities offered him the building of the former minor seminary there (*eparkhial'noe uchilishche*), but again he refused and chose instead a much more modest building on the monastery grounds. According to the same source, when pressures against the Church began to mount in Khrushchev's times, the Metropolitan of Kiev and the Ukraine, Ioann (Sokolov), and the Bishop of Stavropol rushed to close respectively the seminaries of Kiev and Stavropol without waiting for the secular authorities to put pressure to bear on them. Moreover, Ioann, a very learned

---

[37]In contrast, see the attacks on clergy for trying to participate in the elections before the war (chapter 5 above, pp. 182f).

[38]"S'ezd nastoyatelei tserkvei Tul'skoi eparkhii," *ZhMP*, no. 1 (1947) 45-7; "S'ezd dukhovenstva i miryan Chkalovskoi eparkhii," *ZhMP*, no. 3 (1947) 52-4.

man with two university degrees, hated educated clergy and often boasted of having personally prevented the reopening of the Kiev Theological Academy.[39]

There has never been complete data on the number of students at all the functioning ecclesiastical schools in the USSR in the 1940s or 1950s. The largest number of students cited for both Moscow schools (the seminary and the academy) was for 1949-1950—a total of 196 students. But in the early 1950s, apparently, there began a spectacular growth of applicants and students for the seminaries; Leningrad, for example, reports a combined student body of 320 in 1952, nearly double its 1950 figure of 172. But the student body in Moscow (actually at the Trinity-St. Sergius Monastery in Zagorsk, some forty-five miles from Moscow) has always been considerably larger than in Leningrad, and hence 350 to 400 students must have been in the two Moscow schools that same year. Another illustration of this growth is the report to the effect that in 1955, fifty-five students graduated from the fourth year of the Stavropol Seminary—thus, the student body there must have numbered close to 250, allowing for at least some attrition.[40] Henceforth, statistics on the numbers of students disappear until the late 1970s. Normally, in Soviet conditions, lack of statistics indicates the unprofitability of their revelation. In the peculiar conditions of the Church in the USSR, drawing attention to the growth of the student body in theological schools might arouse the antireligious zeal of the secular authorities. And, indeed, Khrushchev's persecutions and the closure of most of the seminaries were caused to a considerable extent by the growth of interest in religion among the younger generation. If the above figures concerning the three seminaries and two academies are any indicator, then the total number of students at the ten schools may have exceeded two thousand in the mid-1950s. In addition, there is the extramural sector, providing full theological education to ordained clergy over an extended period of years by correspondence. Since Russian hierarchs have stated on

[39]"A religiously believing enemy of the Church" is how our source described Ioann, shrugging his shoulders. But his distrust of the educated clergy may have come from a post-Renovationist syndrome, for the most active motivators of the schism were highly educated married priests.

[40]*ZhMP*, no. 1 (1950) 28; no. 11 (1952) 60; no. 8 (1955) 18; no. 11 (1950) 56.

several occasions that almost all graduates of the contemporary Soviet seminaries take ordination, the total number of ordained clergy per annum, at the above rate, should have reached at least five hundred. The vast majority of graduates, being under thirty years of age, would have a life expectancy after graduation of some thirty-five to forty years. At this rate, the seminaries would have provided some 18,000 priests, which could easily rise to 25,000 to 30,000 taking into consideration the extraseminary ordinations and the pastoral courses discussed above. Thus, we arrive at a figure not substantially less than the 1953 one, provided by the patriarchate—30,000 priests serving 20,000 to 25,000 parishes.[41]

Reports on the construction of new churches disappear from the *Journal of the Moscow Patriarchate* after 1948. Even prior to that we have found reports on the building of only five churches,[42] but numerous reports on reconstruction, repairs and reopening of already standing churches. In what state of repair had these been kept while in state custody was very well illustrated in a report on the transfer of the seventeenth-century church of the Novodevichy (New Maidens) Convent in Moscow to the Church in 1945. The elevated floor of the sanctuary, the altar table itself and the iconostas had to be built anew, along with the walls, ceilings and heating installation. In other words, after a decade of Soviet management of this outstanding historical and architectural monument, all that remained of it were the walls and the roof over them. Most other churches were received by believers in a similar state of disrepair and had to be reconstructed entirely at the believers' expense.[43]

[41]Spinka (118-20) doubts that there have ever been so many churches and priests functioning in the postwar Soviet Union, but given the above calculations of theology students in the 1950s, the numbers become quite realistic. Metropolitan Boris (Vik) cited the following figures to this writer at a press conference in Montreal in the mid-1950s: 35,000 clergy, 25,000 churches and four candidates for each place in the seminaries.

[42]In Magnitogorsk (1947), Samarkand (1946), Tambov (1948) and Bogdanovka in the Rovno province (1947). ZhMP, no. 6 (1956) 8; no. 3 (1947) 56-7; no. 3 (1948) 55-6; no. 6 (1948) 49-50.

[43]See the report in ZhMP, no. 1 (1946) 18-22. A good example is the Vladimir Cathedral of the Assumption, where there were "mountains of ice and garbage" at the time it was handed back to believers. I. Ratmirov, "Restavratsiya ili diskriminatsiya?" *Zemlya* (*samizdat*) no. 1 (August 1974); reprinted in *VS*, no. 20 (1975) 16-20.

In 1953 the reconstituted theological schools produced their first bishop, the first Russian Orthodox bishop entirely of the Soviet era. This was Bishop Mikhail Chub. Born in 1912, he held two university degrees prior to attending the seminary—one in meteorology and another in foreign languages—and had worked as a teacher of modern languages.[44]

Some idea on the numbers of believers can be obtained from the claim in one source that during Lent of 1947 the main cathedral of Leningrad had about 400,000 communicants; another source gives a similar figure for the patriarchal cathedral of Moscow for 1946.[45] The fact that there were individual cases of clerics refusing additional churches offered to them by the state does not necessarily prove their lack of desire to have more churches for the masses of believers. The point is that state taxes on churches and church employees, including clerics, have always been exorbitant, as both are treated as private entrepreneurs. In addition, local governments, completely arbitrarily, from time to time transfer large sums of money from the bank accounts of local parishes to the Peace Fund accounts. And, in accordance with the 1929 legislation, the Church may not impose regular membership dues on the parishioners. Hence, the income and its "reliability" in individual parishes are very precarious.[46]

[44]*ZhMP*, no. 1 (1954) 29.
[45]Robert Conquest, *Religion in the USSR* (New York: Praeger, 1968) 38; Rahr, 79. (Conquest erroneously cites Oleshchuk's book, which was published in 1939!)
[46]Information supplied by Fr. Konstantin Tivetsky, a Moscow priest until his emigration to the US in the spring of 1980, interviewed by this writer in San Francisco (June 20-26, 1980). The arbitrary Peace Fund transfers are characteristic of the 1960s and 1970s, as are high taxes on church buildings. In fact, high income taxes are true of any period since the 1930s. See the critical remarks regarding "cowardly" clerics who refused additional churches offered by the state, in Levitin, *Bol'naya tserkov'*.

CHAPTER 10

New Trials: Khrushchev's Attack on the Church

At first Stalin's death ushered in, as it seemed, an era of greater freedom for the churches as well. Between 1954 and 1958 the *Journal of the Moscow Patriarchate* periodically reported on the construction and reopening of new churches. A few were newly built,[1] but most were churches that were damaged or partly ruined during the war[2]—which seems to indicate that the immediate postwar reconstruction was cut short toward the end of the 1940s with the increased pressure against the Church, but then the work was resumed. However, reports on the construction or reconstruction of churches disappear by 1960, which coincides with the beginning of the mass closure of churches, monasteries and seminaries and the general persecution of 1959-1964.

With the consecration of Mikhail Chub in 1953 as the first bishop-graduate of the postwar Soviet theological schools, a new

[1] See reports in *ZhMP* on the building of a church in Ashkhabad in place of the one destroyed by the 1948 earthquake (no. 2 [1958]); another church built by Archbishop Ermogen in Kirgizia (no. 7 [1958] 19); a new church built in the Rovno province of the Ukraine (no. 11 [1955] 8).

[2] In almost every issue of *ZhMP* for 1954-1958 there are reports on one or more churches returned to the Church by the state, repaired by the faithful and reconsecrated for services. Archbishop Ermogen of Tashkent and Central Asia managed to completely rebuild the Dormition Cathedral in Tashkent in 1958 (*ZhMP*, no. 11 [1958] 13-5). According to information given to this author by a Moscow priest in 1964, this "reconstruction" amounted to the building of a new church more than double the size of the original one. This was one of the causes of the conflicts between the archbishop and the CROCA that resulted in his removal from the diocese.

generation of bishops wholly brought up and educated under the Soviets began to replace the old cadres. By the end of the 1960s, almost all ruling bishops of the Russian Orthodox Church were of this formation. The same process, of course, was taking place in the ranks of the parish clergy. In an internal report, a leading Moscow parish priest, Vsevolod Shpiller, a former émigré and a Bulgarian-educated repatriate who thus had the double experience of living and practicing as an Orthodox priest both in a noncommunist country and in the Soviet Union, made this penetrating observation on this *Soviet* generation of bishops:

> Our Church has perhaps more people . . . who have come to the Church through the personal experience of some form of "conversion crisis" [than any other church]. In their childhood . . . their environment was actively non-religious and often antireligious. . . . Suddenly they saw the Church with her truth and her beauty . . . and joined her.

Shpiller observes that their understanding of the Church is quite different from that of the traditional believers. Without using the word, he argues that they have mentally resigned themselves to secular totalitarianism to the extent that they cannot conceive of a society that tolerates simultaneously two types of law, one secular and one ecclesiastical. He refers to the experience of the Yugoslav-Russian canonist Troitsky who, as a visiting professor, delivered a series of elementary lectures on canon law at the Moscow Theological Academy only to discover that his students could not understand what he was trying to say. They simply could not conceive of autonomous legal bodies with separate systems of law governing their own existence within a society ruled by a different set of laws. In other words, the fact that the Church did not possess the status of a legal person in the Soviet Union appeared quite normal to these theology students of the 1940s, i.e., of the generation born and brought up under Stalin. Consequently, he continues, they are insensitive to the concept of the Church as an institution. They see her "only in a very narrow sense, as a 'praying assembly,' which totally excludes a juridical content."

Shpiller, further, cites concrete cases of bishops of the new generation sharing such a mentality, and maintains that its consequence is complete subservience to the civic authorities and their demands, laws and orders—not just out of fear but also out of a conviction that there can only be one authority and one law in a state. He sees a direct, logical connection between this mentality and the ease with which the changes imposed by the state on the Church in 1961 were accepted by the bishops and by the majority of the clergy[3] (but not by all, as we shall see). The addressee of the letter, Metropolitan Nikodim, must also be seen as an exception to this rule formulated by Fr. Shpiller (as will be shown later). Had this not been the case, Fr. Shpiller would hardly have addressed himself to him.

The changes imposed on the Church in 1961, however, will be discussed in the context of the general repression and persecution of the Church under Khrushchev. Within this context, Fr. Shpiller's observations will help us appreciate some of the aspects of the persecutions, as well as some oversimplifications in certain *samizdat* documents attacking the bishops as KGB agents and as conscious destroyers of the Church.[4]

Khrushchev's wholesale attack on religion in 1959 did not come out of the blue. Way back in 1950, articles began to appear in the Soviet press admitting that religion would not wither away on its own in a socialist society, and hence antireligious work and propaganda should be intensified. Soon, however, it was recognized that the propaganda itself was insufficient. A CPSU Central Committee resolution of July 7, 1954 stated that both the Orthodox Church and the sectarians were successfully attracting the younger generations to the Church by high-quality sermons, charity work, individual indoctrination and the religious press. This "activization of the Church has resulted in an increase in the number of people . . . participating in religious services." The

---

[3]"Ego vysokopreosvyashchenstvu Mitropolitu . . . Nikodimu," *samizdat*, reprinted in the Brussels Roman Catholic periodical *Rossiya i vselenskaya tserkov'*, no. 4 (1966)/no. 1 (1967) 59-72. The letter appears in a greatly abbreviated translation in *Patriarch and Prophets*, 321-9.

[4]See, for instance, Boris V. Talantov, "Sergievshchina ili prisposoblenie k ateizmu" (Kirov, August 1967-March 1968), AS 745; Talantov in Bourdeaux, *Patriarch and Prophets*, 140-52; anonymous, "Rossiya i tserkov' segodnya" and "Tserkov' i vlast' " (n.d., but probably 1970-1971), AS 892 and 893.

resolution called on the Ministries of Education, the Komsomol and the trade unions to intensify their antireligious propaganda.

Lack of unity in the Soviet leadership after Stalin's death was demonstrated by the fact that four months later (November 10, 1954) there appeared another CPSU Central Committee resolution criticizing arbitrariness, the use of slander and libel against the clergy and the believers and insulting epithets in the antireligious campaign.[5] This slowed down the attack. The period from 1955 to 1957 could be considered the most "liberal" for the Christians since 1947, despite the fact that atheistic "education" was enhanced in the armed forces at least since 1955, and since 1957 a relatively scholarly *Yearbook of the [Leningrad] Museum of the History of Religion and Atheism* of over four hundred pages began to be published. Although the November resolution resolved to build up a systematic Soviet antireligious scholarship, its emphasis on scholarship rather than propaganda delayed the appearance of a journal specially dedicated to the propagation of atheism among the masses. The journal, *Science and Religion,* first promised for 1954, in fact began to be published by the Znanie society only in 1959, reaching a circulation of over 400,000 copies by 1978.[6]

It may be of interest to note that the more hostile resolution of July 1954 mentioned the church press as a dangerous threat to atheism in the USSR, although at the time it consisted of one Russian Orthodox monthly with a circulation of some fifteen thousand copies,[7] one Baptist journal and a Ukrainian Orthodox journal—both published six times a year, each with a circulation of perhaps ten thousand copies or less. None of the church publications were ever openly on sale, and they were always very difficult to subscribe to, while atheistic pamphlets alone in 1950 numbered forty, with a total annual circulation of 800,000 copies (not to mention the atheistic monopoly in the educational and mass media). Moreover, the resolution ordered that "the teaching of school subjects (history, literature, natural sciences, physics,

[5]Powell, *Antireligious Propaganda,* 39-40; Popovsky, *Zhizn' i zhitie,* 466-7; Stroyen, *Communist Russia and the Church,* 89-93.

[6]Ibid., 89-94; Struve, 269; Simon, *Church, State,* 94.

[7]At least this was its circulation in 1974. V. Furov, deputy chairman of the CRA, secret (annual?) report to the CPSU Central Committee on the state of the Russian Orthodox Church, printed in *VRKhD,* no. 130 (1979) 328.

chemistry, etc.) should be saturated with atheism . . . the anti-religious thrust of school programs must be strengthened." Indeed, every school textbook subsequently published became even more emphatically assertive of atheism than before, with such declarations as: "Religion is a fantastic and perverse reflection of the world in man's consciousness. . . . Religion has become the medium for spiritual enslavement of the masses."[8]

As often happens in a political system based on coercion and arbitrariness, it was this tougher document of July, rather than the milder one of November, that shaped the future policy toward the Church. As a follow-up, much attention began to be paid not only to a manifold increase of antireligious lectures, the introduction of special obligatory courses on atheism at schools and colleges and the establishment of a central Institute of Scientific Atheism, but to so-called "individual work with believers" as well. The local Communist Party and Komsomol committees, the local sections of the Znanie society, as well as trade union branches, would appoint their atheistic members as personal tutors in atheism to known religious believers, in most cases their workmates. They would visit the believers involved at their homes, try to convince them and, if this did not work, bring their cases to the attention of their union or professional collectives, where their "religious backwardness" and obstinacy would be aired at public meetings.[9] In cases where such actions proved fruitless, they would often be followed by administrative harassment at work or in the colleges, and not infrequently by an appointment to lower paid jobs or expulsions from universities, if the believers happened to be students. Physical harassment of believing school children by classmates, instigated and supported by the teachers, was and still remains quite common.[10]

---

[8]Shafarevich, 50-2. He also notes the moral conflict of a graduating high school student and a university student: both must pass exams in "scientific atheism," citing uncritically all the Marxist attacks on religion whether they believe in them or not.

[9]Richard Marshall, Jr., ed., *Aspects of Religion in the Soviet Union, 1917-1967* (Chicago: University Press, 1971) 140-3.

[10]Ibid., 143-8. Also, Fr. Konstantin Tivetsky's oral testimony to this author (San Francisco, June 1980) regarding the education of his sons as Christians in the USSR in the 1960s and 1970s and their conflicts with the state school; Feliks Svetov, *Otverzi mi dveri*, a *samizdat* novel (Paris: YMCA Press, 1978) 188-91 et passim.

Much attention was applied to induce priests to defect from the Church. Allegedly, about two hundred priests defected, most of them becoming active propagandists of atheism, publishing brochures and books attacking religion, and some of them soon achieving scholarly degrees in scientific atheism and high prominence in their new *métier*.[11]

At least two defections were rather painful for the Church, namely, those of the Very Rev. Prof. Alexander Osipov of the Leningrad Theological Academy and the young lay theology teacher of the Saratov Seminary, Evgraf Duluman. On December 30, 1959 the patriarchate issued an excommunication decree: "The former Archpriest . . . Osipov, the former Archpriest Nikolai Spassky, the former Priest Pavel Darmansky and other clerics who have publicly uttered blasphemy against the name of God, are hereby . . . deprived of all communion with the Church. . . . Evgraf Duluman and all other former lay members of the Orthodox Church who have uttered public blasphemy against God's name are excommunicated from the Church."[12]

The part relating to laymen clearly applied to all those Soviet leaders and Communist Party members who had been baptized in infancy. In essence, this decree publicly reiterated Patriarch Tikhon's 1918 excommunication of the Soviet leadership, to which the latter had been so sensitive at the time because excommunication places a psychological barrier between the believers and the Soviet ruling classes and sustains the attitude of "them" and "us" on a much deeper level for the believers than any antagonism between the rulers and the ruled that may arise on purely social grounds. And the regime responded again in 1960-1961 with a particular intensification of religious persecution. Of the nearly fifteen thousand churches closed after 1959, at least ten thousand fell victim in these two years, and both architects of the postwar church status and policies, Metropolitan Nikolai and Karpov (Chairman of the CROCA) were dismissed in 1960. On January 10, 1960, the CPSU Central Committee called for the intensification of antireligious propaganda, and later in the

[11]For example, Frs. Duluman, Darmansky, Chertkov and Gerodnik. See also books and brochures by renegade priests, e.g.: *My porvali s religiei* (Moscow, 1963), with a circulation of 28,000 copies; and A.B. Yanushkevich, *Razdum'e o vere* (Moscow, 1961). The figure of two hundred is from Struve, 320.

[12]Encyclical no. 23, *ZhMP*, no. 2 (1960) 27.

same month such highly placed leaders as Brezhnev, Kosygin, Suslov and Mikoyan attended a congress of the Znanie society.[13]

The Church did not resign herself to her new fate without resistance. Her strategy was to remind the Soviet public and the Soviet authorities of the Church's important historical contribution to Russian culture as well as to the forging of Russian statehood and Russian national consciousness, and to the patriotic cause of resisting foreign invasions, from the earliest pages of Russian history to World War II. Since 1958 articles on these themes in the *Journal of the Moscow Patriarchate* again became prominent, showing the sensitivity of the Church to the very early warnings of the new storm clouds gathering against her.[14] The church leadership realized that only such secular, state and nation-oriented arguments could impress the atheistic establishment. The most salient of these self-defense actions was Patriarch Aleksii's speech at the Kremlin Conference of the Soviet Public for Disarmament on February 16, 1960. Here are its high points:

Here I stand before you as the mouthpiece of the Russian Orthodox Church, which represents millions of citizens of this state. . . .

As witnessed by history, this is the very same Church which at the dawn of Russian statehood helped to instill civic order in Russia, strengthened . . . the legal foundations of the family, asserted the woman's position as a legal person, condemned usury and slavery, developed the sense of duty and responsibility in man and often, with the help of her own canons, filled in the gaps of the state law.

This is the same Church which has created wonderful monuments enriching Russian culture that still remain the object of the national pride of our people.

This is the Church which in the era of the feudal fragmentation of Russia helped to forge the land into one

---

[13]*Aspects of Religion*, 132-4.

[14]For example, A. Vasiliev, "Polozhenie russkoi pravoslavnoi tserkvi v SSSR," *ZhMP*, no. 1 (1958) 40-7.

whole, defending Moscow's importance as the sole ecclesiastic and civic focus of the Russian land.

This is the Church which in the difficult years of the Tatar yoke pacified the khans, protecting the Russian people from additional raids and destruction.

It was she, our Church, who strengthened the spirit of the people by her faith in . . . freedom, supporting in the nation a sense of national dignity and moral power.

She was the support for the Russian state in its struggle against foreign invaders both during the Time of Troubles and the Fatherland War of 1812. She remained with the nation during World War II, helping it by all means possible to win the war and to achieve peace.

In a word, this is the very Russian Orthodox Church which has all these centuries served primarily the cause of the moral formation of our people. . . .

Since World War II the same Church . . . appealed in 1948 to the Christians of the whole world [to struggle] . . . for peace. . . .

And now our Church, condemns every hostility, every form of antagonism and hatred among nations, stands for disarmament and blesses all peoples' desires to liquidate all forms of weapons; because Christianity, a religion of humility, love and charity, is totally alien to all forms of violence. . . .

[The Soviet government's] appeal "to forge swords into ploughs and spears into sickles" . . . belongs to the prophet Isaiah, whom we Christians call an Old Testament evangelist, because he had foretold the birth of our Savior of the world long before that event.

Thus, the Bible, which is a collection of sacred books of

the Christian Church, proves to be the source of the idea of universal peace, which, because of the growth of the most dangerous weapons, should be recognized as probably the most important idea for humanity of our time.

Yet, despite all this, Christ's Church, whose very aim is human well-being, is suffering insults and attacks from humans. Nevertheless, she does not shirk her duty, appealing to humans to live in peace and to love one another. Moreover, the Church finds consolation in this situation for her faithful: what danger is there in the efforts of human reason against the Church? . . . Jesus Christ himself predicted indestructibility of the Church when he said: "the gates of hell will not overcome the *Church*."[15]

The speech was followed by violent verbal attacks on the patriarch from the floor: "You want to assure us that the whole Russian culture has been created by the Church . . . this is not true!" shouted various representatives of "the Soviet public." A real scandal occurred, confided Metropolitan Nikolai, who added that it was he who had authored that speech. And this was probably the main reason for his enforced retirement in June of the same year from the chairmanship of the Church's Department of External Ecclesiastical Relations. The other reasons were his unpublished church sermons counterattacking the atheists: "The people listen to my sermons and like them. And this is exactly what our [civic] authorities find unacceptable. They want bishops who are silent and who only perform solemn services. They cannot stand those who preach and struggle against godlessness."[16]

Although the patriarch's speech was followed by several laudatory articles in the *Journal of the Moscow Patriarchate*, the 1960-1961 pogrom against the Church and the retirement of the courageous and eloquent Nikolai seem to have caused Patriarch Aleksii, who had never been known as a particularly brave person himself, to submit completely to Soviet pressure[17] and restructure

[15]*ZhMP*, no. 3 (1960) 33-5.
[16]Archbishop Vasily, "Poslednie vstrechi," 209-11.
[17]See, for example, N. Kharyuzov, "K vystupleniyu Patriarkha Aleksiya pered sovetskoi obshchestvennost'yu," *ZhMP*, no. 4 (1960) 50-3. Levitin adds that up to 1960 the patriarch also addressed several letters to Khrushchev complaining

the Church in accordance with Soviet law. The most tragic manifestation of this submission was the amending of the Church Statute, issued in the name of a full sobor of bishops gathered at the Holy Trinity-St. Sergius Monastery on July 18, 1961. The gathering could hardly be called a sobor, however, because the bishops had been summoned by telegrams from the patriarch with no reasons given whatsoever as to why they were being invited. The bishops arrived on the eve of the feastday of St. Sergius, in time for the long Vigil service. The next morning they participated in the long festive liturgy, afterward had dinner and were then ushered into a meeting hall, still unaware of the agenda that was unexpectedly presented to them: (1) enlargement of the permanent Holy Synod by adding the bishop-chancellor of the patriarchate and the bishop in charge of external ecclesiastic relations ex officio to the body of six bishops (the three chief metropolitans ex officio and three bishops elected by the Synod for one session in rotation); (2) amendments to the Statute in the section dealing with the parishes; (3) on the joining of the World Council of Churches by the Russian Orthodox Church; and (4) on the participation of the Church in the World Christian Peace Congress, which had taken place in Prague on June 13-18, 1961.[18]

What interests us here are the changes in the status and organization of the parishes. These deprived the parish priest of all powers over his parish, now to be handed over to the "parish community . . . of at least twenty members," but in actual fact to an executive committee "of three members, consisting of the warden, the deputy warden and the treasurer, elected by the parish community from among the parishioners." The meetings of the whole "parish community" are convoked "when necessary, with the permission of the local city or county soviets." In other words, if the given executive committee of three satisfies the local soviet, the latter may arbitrarily suspend parish meetings in-

about the mounting persecutions and asking for a personal audience with him, but received no reply (Bol'naya tserkov', 5-6). He then resigned himself to the pressures, just like he had done in 1936 when, as Metropolitan of Leningrad, he had issued an order banning the administration of communion to children ("Listening to the Radio," in Patriarch and Prophets, 292). See also chapter 12, note 1.

[18]Anonymous, "Opisanie arkhiereiskogo sobora 1961 g." (samizdat, mid-1960s), AS 701, 1-4.

definitely if it has reason to fear that such a meeting would not approve of the executive's activities and would request its retirement. Such cases became quite common.[19] The interests of a soviet, made up mostly of atheistic communists, and those of the Church are usually at variance, to put it mildly. A secret circular letter addressed to local officials of the CROCA and dealing with the functions of "Commissions-in-aid to Local Governments to Implement the Legislation on Cults" in fact instructs these newly founded bodies to gradually replace the current "twenties" by new ones "formed of citizens . . . who would honestly carry out the Soviet laws and your suggestions and requests. . . . Let the 'council of twenty' . . . elect its executive body. . . . It is desirable that you . . . take part in the selection of members of such an executive body and that [they be] . . . those who carry out our line."[20] All financial, economic and bookkeeping activities and responsibilities, including *voluntary* contributions to the diocese or to the patriarchate for the upkeep of seminaries, etc., are removed entirely from supervision by the clergy and handed over to the executive troikas. The priest remains responsible only "for the spiritual *leadership* of the parishioners . . . for the conscientious and pious performance of all church services, for the satisfaction of all religious needs of the parishioners."

The priest is responsible for the moral discipline of those serving the Church. But how can he fulfil this function when he is not mentioned in the new regulations even as a participant in any meetings of either the community or the executive organ? How can he advise the committee on the Church's position in a controversy that may arise, or advise them as a pastor, when the body exists and meets entirely apart from him and is not responsible to him—i.e., when it is not subject to any church discipline, when it is not in fact subordinate to any orders of the diocesan

[19]Levitin, in *Patriarch and Prophets*, 300-2; Levitin, "A Drop Under the Microscope," ibid., 307-15.

[20]This author's "New Instruction to Soviet Local Officials on how to Treat Orthodox Christians," BBC, Central Research Unit, background note no. 4/67 (February 24, 1967). Nikodim, when shown this document, claimed no knowledge of it but added that it likely was one of those typical secret instructions of 1961 or thereabouts, and that the commissions in question had come into being during the Khrushchev era but by 1968 played a negligible role. However, all the available Soviet legislative documents relating to these commissions belong to 1965-1967. See *Zakonodatel'stvo*, 88-103.

bishop either? It is only on purely liturgical matters and disputes on these questions that may arise between the priest and his executive or the community that the latter bodies are to appeal to the bishop, "to whose competence alone such matters belong." Even the election of a priest for the parish becomes the responsibility of the parish community, in conjunction, however, with "the bishop's blessing" and the proper registration by the civic authorities. All this was presented by the patriarch in his address to the sobor as a return to the Old Russian and apostolic traditions of *sobornost'*, i.e., to the broadening of the autonomy and prerogatives of the community. Indeed this would have been so had it not been for the fact that the community meetings could not take place without the express permission of openly hostile civic authorities for each individual meeting; had it indeed been the community and not an easily manipulated troika that would be running the parish; had the term "community" in fact meant all regularly praying parishioners and not just a group of twenty persons; and, finally, had the parish pastor been the chairman of the church council and thus been able truly to act as its moral and spiritual leader, as the canons stipulate.

It is hardly necessary to elaborate here why this system of parish administration suited the Soviet authorities more than the 1945 one, where the priest, subordinate to his bishop, rather than the church council, de facto subordinate to the Soviets, had been the master of the parish. Still, the question could arise in the reader's mind as to why the patriarch and the bishops obliged so readily. A *samizdat* document, written either by one of the bishops participating in the sobor or by someone personally informed by a participant, throws some light on the matter. Besides the above-described organizational details, which made it impossible for the bishops to familiarize themselves with the agenda and discuss it among themselves in advance, the "proposed" changes had in fact already been decided upon by the Patriarchal Holy Synod in its session of April 18 and published in the *Journal of the Moscow Patriarchate* as adopted. In his opening address, the patriarch made it clear that he did not want any deliberations and arguments, only "ratification . . . of the decisions adopted by the Holy Synod . . . in the spirit . . . of complete unanimity." These words utterly contradicted what he had said a minute earlier, namely: "almost seventeen years have elapsed without a sobor discussion . . . of church matters . . . which according to our Church's rules and regulations are to be decided upon in council. . . . And therefore it is desirable that such long intervals between the sobors of bishops do not occur any more." This contradiction made it clear to every bishop participating in the sobor that this "sobor" was not the place for discussion. This impression was further enhanced by the presence of three laymen, top administrators of the CROCA, sitting silently at a separate little table in the same assembly hall, where bishops alone were supposed to be meeting.

The patriarch claimed that changes were necessary because of allegedly numerous complaints addressed to the patriarchate and to the USSR Council of Ministers. Priests criticized the church councils; church councils criticized the priests; "both complain that the patriarch and the Synod pay no attention to their complaints." The patriarch reminded his listeners that a year earlier the Synod had drawn the attention of diocesan bishops to cases "of abuse of the Soviet laws regarding religious associations." In April of 1961 the government informed the patriarchate that the clerics were continuing to abuse Soviet laws on religion. Indeed, the already cited letter by Fr. Shpiller complained that the abrogation of all administrative rights of the priests over their parishes in the synodal decree of April 18 was explained in terms of the incompatibility of the church by-laws with Soviet laws— with no reference made to the canons. In this respect he saw an improvement in the July sobor of bishops, in the fact that at least lip service was paid to *sobornost'* and to the canons.[21]

But to return to this sobor, it should be added that this was a time of harassment of the clergy, of trials and prison sentences passed on at least two bishops and numerous priests who were fraudulently accused of misusing church funds, of concealing their incomes from the state in order to evade taxes, etc.[22] In these

---

[21]"Opisanie," passim (41 pages); and "Deyaniya arkhiereiskogo sobora russkoi pravoslavnoi tserkvi," *ZhMP*, no. 8 (1961) 5-29.

[22]In 1960 Archbishop Iov (Kresovich) of Kazan was sentenced to three years of hard labor for alleged embezzlement of church funds and evasion of taxes, and Archbishop Andrei (Sukhenko) of Chernigov, who had been imprisoned earlier as a priest, received a new term of eight years. Struve, 312. Nikolai said that the charges in these and similar cases were absolutely fraudulent (Vasily, "Poslednie

conditions, even in the opinion of the caustically critical *samizdat* report, many bishops were hoping that, firstly, divorcing all financial responsibilities from the clergy would protect them from further harassment along these lines[23]; and secondly, the Soviet request to change the by-laws contained an implicit indication that the authorities were not planning an immediate liquidation of the whole Church, as in the 1930s, but only her further enslavement. This gave hope that such times would pass one day and there would be a chance for improvement.

In all fairness, this *samizdat* document, generally hostile to the patriarchate's behavior, reports that the first time the changes were suggested to him by Kuroedov, the new chairman of the CROCA, in 1960, the patriarch protested, and "even fell ill, suffering a nervous shock at the news, and remained inactive for some two weeks. But then, realizing that nothing could be done, he resigned himself, having decided that this concession could delay the approaching end."[24] No doubt, many of the bishops present knew of this and shared the patriarch's resignation.[25]

The particularly disquieting note in the patriarch's address was that he implicitly laid all the blame for church troubles on the clergy by depriving them of most of their canonical rights as the heads of parishes at a time when he was perfectly aware that the government was using all sorts of devious means to subvert and destroy the Church. The antireligious propaganda was fraudulently accusing the victim—the Church and her clergy —of greed, of cheating the believers, of breaking the law and of similar crimes. Church apologists, such as Levitin and the late Boris Talantov, proved most of these accusations unfounded in their *samizdat* pamphlets and letters to newspapers.[26] But none

vstrechi," 214-5). Also in 1960 in the Orenburg diocese alone twenty-six priests were on trial. The number of arrested and sentenced priests may have been in the hundreds. Some were charged with collaboration with the occupiers during the war, although there had been an amnesty in 1956. Struve, 317-8.

[23]In this context Nikodim assured this author in a private conversation that the 1961 decisions were a relief.

[24]"Opisanie," 31-2.

[25]Fr. Borovoi, in a sermon at the Russian Orthodox cathedral in London in July 1978, characterized these years as a time "when it appeared that the string would break any time." If this was a widespread sentiment then the apathy and passivity is understandable.

[26]See the already cited writings of Levitin, and *Patriarch and Prophets*, 69-254.

of these were ever printed either in the official Soviet or the church press. The patriarch implicitly supported the propaganda line, which only too clearly confirmed the accuracy of the fears expressed after Metropolitan Sergii's 1927 declaration: that it would lead to the betrayal of the martyrs.

Some Details of the Persecutions

The most detailed descriptions of the persecutions of the 1960s in the English language are to be found in Nikita Struve's *Christians in Contemporary Russia* and in Michael Bourdeaux's *Patriarch and Prophets,* which is a collection of *samizdat* documents or excerpts thereof and of excerpts of Soviet press articles attacking and defaming religion. Here we shall only summarize some material from these and other books, as well as directly from *samizdat* documents.

Officially, Khrushchev's administration aimed at the restoration of Leninist "socialist legality" after Stalin's abuses. Lenin himself, however, considered that "law must serve the ends of the proletarian dictatorship, which is . . . not restrained by the laws which it . . . creates."[27] The actual persecution of the Church could thus be, and often was, conducted in the name of the restoration of such "legality." Stalin was accused of having abused the Soviet laws on religion.[28] Indeed, the 1945 church by-laws contradicted the 1929 Soviet legislation "On Religious Associations," inasmuch as the former made the parish priest the master of his parish, while Soviet legislation recognized only the lay "twenties." Similarly, a law invalidating all measures instituted by the occupational authorities during the war was invoked to close a large number of churches and monasteries on the former occupied territories. A special instruction of March 16, 1961 emphatically reiterated the 1929 legislation expressly forbidding

See also Talantov's letter to *Nauka i religiya* in response to slanderous attacks on the Church (*samizdat,* Kirov, 1960), AS 703.

[27]A summation of Lenin's utterances on the subject is in Ivo Lapenna's *State and Law: Soviet and Yugoslav Theory* (London: Athlone Press, 1964) 19.

[28]Struve, 295-6; *Aspects of Religion,* 133-4, citing Khrushchev's 22nd Party Congress speech; and Ilichev, the Chairman of the CPSU Central Committee's Ideological Commission, in *Partiinaya zhizn'* (February 1964).

parishes to organize any forms of charity and "religious centers" to "offer financial aid to those parishes and monasteries which do not enjoy the support of the local population."[29] Under this pressure, the Church issued an instruction that parishes that could not pay their way should be amalgamated with neighboring churches. This regulation was locally misused by the CROCA plenipotentiaries and by compliant bishops to close many rural parishes, even those that were quite self-sufficient.[30] Technically, this process was facilitated by the rapid population decline in the villages in the 1960s and 1970s, particularly in central Russia, the Volga, the Urals and in some parts of Siberia. Logically, one should have expected a proportionate increase of churches in the urban areas to which the rural populations migrated, but this did not happen, despite numerous petitions by believers.[31]

The laws banning religious instruction to minors began not only to be more strictly applied, but were logically extended to prevent the frequenting of churches by children and young people. Although no written laws were passed to this effect, oral instructions by the CROCA plenipotentiaries forbidding priests to begin church services in the presence of minors and to give communion to minors were complied with by some bishops and by numerous priests.[32] This was accompanied by a press campaign and appropriate local measures against the use of minors as altar boys, under the pretext that this contradicted the laws banning church work for minors.[33] Religious parents in some instances were deprived of parental rights for what the Soviet authorities qualified as the "fanatical religious upbringing" of their children, the latter being placed in boarding schools.[34] A document protesting the persecutions makes the interesting point that although

[29]See above in chapter 9 on the prior activities of the Church, and the decree banning these in *Zakonodatel'stvo*, 80.

[30]Talantov in *Patriarch and Prophets*, 125-34.

[31]Several Russian clerics informed this author that in many cases rural depopulation was the reason for the continuing decrease of rural parishes after Khrushchev. But they also pointed out the extreme difficulty of opening new parishes in the swelling cities and towns. On the latter see also Shafarevich, 13-8.

[32]Talantov, in *Patriarch and Prophets*, 150; "Letter to the WCC from Odessa," ibid., 160-1; Struve, 317; petition by Feodosia Varavva in *Patriarch and Prophets*, 164-77.

[33]Shafarevich, 48.

[34]Ibid., 53-6.

"two collections of party and state documents on religion" published in 1959 and 1965 make no "mention . . . of the CROCA," "during the period 1957-64 . . . the CROCA radically changed its function [from] . . . a department of arbitration [to] an organ of unofficial and illegal control over the Moscow Patriarchate."[35]

Shafarevich likewise complained in the above-cited report that as many as twenty-nine articles of the 1929 laws on religion were changed by an RSFSR Supreme Soviet ukaz of October 19, 1962, which was not even made public—in other words, "believers were held accountable for them without knowing their contents." Such was the state of the allegedly restored "Leninist socialist legality"!

The situation was to improve somewhat after Khrushchev, when, for the first time, the Statute of the Council for Religious Affairs (CRA) was published in 1966, after the abolition of the separate CROCA and the transfer of its functions to the CRA on December 8, 1965; and when an amended version of the 1929 laws on religion was published in 1975. The amendments were apparently those of the above 1962 ukaz.[36] But their discussion belongs to chapter 12.

Monasteries and Convents

Monastic institutions were most cruelly hit under Khrushchev. Their number was reduced from about ninety in the mid-1950s to seventeen or eighteen a decade later. The process of liquidation began in 1958, when the 1945 tax exemptions on monastic buildings and landholdings were lifted. Henceforth, monasteries were to pay an annual land tax of forty old rubles, or four after the 1961 devaluation, for 0.01 hectares. Thus, the Pochaev Monastery, for instance, would have to pay four thousand new rubles in taxes for the use of its ten hectares (twenty-five acres) of arable land.[37] Moreover, all monasteries but the Trinity-St. Sergius near

[35]Frs. Nikolai Eshliman and Gleb Yakunin, letters to the Soviet government and to the patriarch regarding persecutions (December 15 and 13, 1965, respectively) in *Patriarch and Prophets,* 193 and 195.

[36]Walter Sawatsky, "The New Soviet Law on Religion," *RCL* 4:2 (1976) 4-5.

[37]The Council of Ministers decree of November 6, 1958 (no. 1251), in *Zako-*

Moscow were on territory formerly occupied by the enemy, and many of them had been reopened with the approval of the occupying authorities. This facilitated a "legal" closure of most of them.

A decree of the Soviet Council of Ministers of October 16, 1958 ordered the reduction of tracts of land adjacent to the monasteries (and convents) and used by them for food production. As the decree did not stipulate the actual limits, it invited arbitrary actions. In the case of the Pochaev Monastery, which contained 146 monks in 1961, both its agricultural fields and its orchard were confiscated in 1962 in an abortive attempt to starve the monastery out of existence. The same decree banned the use of hired labor in the workshops and farming operations run by the monasteries. Since this had been accompanied by a secret instruction to the local governments to refuse monastic residence permits to young people and by arbitrary police expulsions, imprisonments and inductions into the armed forces of young monks, the ability of the remaining, largely elderly contingent of monks to provide for themselves and to pay the highly inflated taxes was dramatically impaired. The above decree further stipulated that monasteries enter into special lease agreements with local governments regarding all monastic buildings except the churches. Thus, in the process, the civil authorities were given an opportunity to reduce the number of buildings held by monastic communities or to confiscate all of them. In the case of the Pochaev Monastery, by 1966 all the buildings but the monks' residence building were confiscated: the hostel for pilgrims was turned into a state hospital, and other houses were put to other secular uses. Finally, the already discussed ban on the use of parish or diocesan funds to support poorer parishes or monasteries concluded the process of making monasteries almost totally dependent on the donations of pilgrims. But even the latter were effectively curtailed by the same decree of 1961 banning organized "pilgrimages to holy places," as well as by the confiscation of monastic hostels and by forbidding the pilgrims to stay overnight inside the monastic churches.[38] All these measures combined

nodatel'stvo, 35. Statistics on monasteries are in Stroyen, 80; figures for the 1970s are given by Fr. Yakunin in VS, no. 35-36 (1979) 45-50.

[38]Patriarch and Prophets, 74-116 and 170-7, and other samizdat documents.

could easily render many monasteries insolvent, and then the government could close them for tax evasion.

Our illustrations of the Soviet struggle to close the monasteries in the 1960s have been taken from the case of the great and nationally revered Pochaev Monastery, because here the authorities miscalculated. They had led an open battle against the monastery for five years, in the course of which both the lay pilgrims and several of the harassed monks attracted so much international attention by writing numerous petitions, many of which reached the West, that by late 1966 most of the harassment and violence subsided. The monastery has survived to the present day, although its body of monks was reduced from 146 to some 35.

Besides the already mentioned pressures, direct violence was used in Pochaev. Pilgrims were beaten up by the police in mass attacks. Female pilgrims were in addition raped by policemen, with no prosecution of the violators. One document describes a young woman who had taken vows of chastity and lived in the immediate neighborhood of the monastery and used to go there for the daily cycle of church services. She was dragged out of the house where she resided by the local police, was sexually violated and then pulled to the attic of a house and thrown down from the roof. Several hours later she died in a hospital, where she was taken by local residents who had found her unconscious and bleeding. At least two monks were killed: a thirty-three-year-old monk in perfect health was forcibly put into a forensic mental hospital along with several other monks, where he died within a couple of months; another, twenty-five years old, also perfectly healthy, died under interrogation in prison. When the body was returned to the parents it revealed signs of torture: multiple bruises, blue spots, knife wounds. Concurrently, the Soviet press carried fraudulent reports on the raping of female pilgrims by monks and on alleged illicit mass abortions performed in monasteries to conceal the monks' and nuns' secret sexual activities.[39]

Why were the monasteries subjected to such particular violence? Because they are the traditional centers of national spiritual life and the focal points of pilgrimages. Whereas in the

Allegedly, Aleksii obliged by also issuing a ban on organized pilgrimages (ibid., 152).

[39] See, for instance, S. Bilinets, *T'ma i ee slugi* (Kiev, 1960) passim.

regular parishes real contact between laymen and priest outside the church services is highly circumscribed, not only by the extremely busy schedule of the priests but also by the laws banning religious instruction and "propaganda" outside the church walls, in the monasteries it is much more difficult to control such contacts. People come there especially for spiritual advice and guidance, and many believers and most parish priests try to spend their annual holidays in the monasteries or in their immediate vicinity.[40] In the absence of virtually any church information media, monasteries also act as grounds for exchange of information on church life between the pilgrims, the visiting priests and the monks. All this is highly distasteful to the Soviet regime, with its attempts to atomize society in general and the Church in particular as much as possible.

Parish Churches

The main sources of information on the arbitrary closure of parish churches and the persecution of priests and bishops who resist such closure comes from major *samizdat* documents authored by the late Boris Talantov, a mathematics teacher and an Orthodox believer from the city of Kirov (Vyatka), west of the Urals, and the petitions of Frs. Gleb Yakunin and Nikolai Eshliman of 1965—both reproduced in Bourdeaux's book.

We have already mentioned how "legality" was used regarding formerly occupied territory. In this way, for instance, 210 churches were closed in the diocese of Odessa (out of 400), 180 in Volhynia, 68 in the diocese of Zhitomir, "43 in that of Poltava, 40 in that of Cherkassy, 18 out of 25 in the single district of Lipkan in Moldavia . . . 12 in the diocese of Novgorod. . . . in Kiev only 8 out of 25 churches remain, in Odessa 9 out of 23, in Ismail one out of 5, in Rostov-on-Don 4 out of 12. The cathedrals of Orel, Bryansk, Chernigov, Riga, Kaunas . . . have been closed to public worship."[41] In Belorussia, of 1,250 Orthodox churches

---

[40]Goricheva interview. She herself had spent most of her holidays visiting monasteries.

[41]Struve, 299-300; *Patriarch and Prophets*, 123.

functioning in 1945, a little more than 400 remained open by the end of 1964.[42]

But wanton closure and destruction of churches went on also in territories that had never fallen to the enemy during World War II. In the Vologda diocese, half-way between Moscow and the Arctic, of the eight hundred prerevolutionary parishes all but seventeen were put out of action by the mid-1960s. Over 15 percent of the parishes in the North Ural diocese of Perm were shut down in the early 1960s. Of the seventy-five parishes functioning in the diocese of Kirov in 1960 (in place of over five hundred before the revolution), only thirty-five remained open for worship by 1965, despite the fact that some of these churches had been built by the parishioners themselves and began to function legally as recently as 1956.[43] How was this accomplished?

On some occasions the Soviet laws stipulating that a person's residence registration should be in the same area as his place of employment were applied to declare that a priest had no right to administer parishes outside of his area of residence.[44] In the conditions of the growing shortage of priests caused by the closure of most of the seminaries and the discontinuation of pastoral courses, as well as the growing practice of depriving priests of their registration permits,[45] this resulted in more and more churches remaining without regular liturgical services for long periods. Once six or more months elapsed, the local government, acting on the authority of the local representative of the CROCA, would close the church and, very often, carry out its physical destruction to prevent its reopening in the future.[46]

Contrary to Struve's assertion, priests had never been treated equally with Soviet wage-earners in terms of income tax. Article

[42]F. Kovalsky, "Pressure on the Orthodox Church in Belorussia," ms. in Keston College Archives, SU Ort. 12/1.

[43]Talantov in *Patriarch and Prophets,* 139 et passim.

[44]See our discussion of the 1929 legislation in chapters 3 and 5 above.

[45]Examples of deprivation of registration permits are discussed in many *samizdat* documents, including Talantov (145). Every year in one of its spring issues *ZhMP* lists the names and addresses of all theological schools and conditions of application. Of the original eight seminaries only five are mentioned in the May 1961 issue (the Kievan, Saratov and Stravropol seminaries having been closed in 1960); the March 1964 issue lists only four seminaries (Moscow, Leningrad, Odessa and Volhynia [Lutsk]); but in 1965 only three remain.

[46]Struve, 296-7.

19 of the Income Tax Decree of April 30, 1943 was applied to the clergy during the whole postwar period, which meant that priests were taxed on a par with private entrepreneurs, with the maximum tax rising to 81 percent on income over and beyond 7,000 rubles per annum (the same sum earned by a state employee would be subject to a tax of 13 percent). At best, the tax law could have been leniently applied prior to 1960.[47] Moreover, since 1962 priests were obliged to receive fixed salaries from their parishes in lieu of the earlier practice of payment directly from the believers' contributions for the upkeep of the priest. The fixed salary practice meant that, first of all, a lion's share of the believers' voluntary donations to the church went to the government in the form of taxes. Secondly, poorer parishes that could not afford a fixed financial commitment—and the gross clerical salaries now had to be very high to offset the effect of the taxes—were destined to remain without permanent priests, which facilitated their closing.

In 1960, a press campaign began against the sale of candles in the churches. The press claimed that 75 percent of church income came from the interest earned from the sale of candles. But Talantov, in an open letter to a Soviet newspaper, convincingly calculated that whereas the government earned thirteen rubles in turnover tax from each kilogram of candles bought by a church, the latter's income from the sale of candles to the worshipers depended on the ratio between the candles used by the church for internal lighting and other ritual necessities, and those actually sold to the faithful. When this ratio is fifty-fifty, the church will earn about ten rubles per kilo. But in smaller rural churches, where most of the lighting comes from candles, the churches actually suffer loss on the candles. If the ratio is 75 percent for church use to 25 percent sold to parishioners, the loss is five rubles per kilo.[48] Nevertheless, for a while churches

[47]*Zakonodatel'stvo*, 33-4; *Sbornik po finansovomu zakonodatel'stvu* (Moscow, 1980) 235-40. Writing in 1960 in defense of the priests against accusations of luxury living, Talantov cites 400 postdevaluation rubles as the typical salary of an urban priest, and he pays 50 percent of it in taxes—i.e., there was no leniency by then (AS 703, 6). Fr. Tivetsky confirms the same income tax rate on 400 rubles, but when he was paid 750 a month he had to pay 500 in taxes, and on 600 rubles the tax came to 364.

[48]Struve, 297; Talantov, AS 703, 1-4.

were forbidden to earn interest from the sale of candles under the pretext that this was equivalent to "imposing involuntary contributions forbidden" to the Church by Soviet law.[49] All the above measures were aimed at making as many parishes as possible insolvent, so as to close them under this pretext.

In other cases a general meeting of the village population would be called, and even if, despite pressure from the party officials, it voted against the closing of a local church, the minutes of the meeting would state the opposite and the church would be liquidated.[50] Talantov describes a number of church liquidations between 1960 and 1964 in the Kirov diocese following most of the above patterns, accompanied by the drinking of all the communion wine by the local party bureaucrats and the police, by barbaric physical destruction of the churches (in some cases architectural monuments of the sixteenth and seventeenth centuries), brutal beatings of old women and men and disregard for protest marches and petitions signed by hundreds and even thousands of believers.[51]

In this way, of the 20,000 to 25,000 Orthodox churches functioning in 1958, fewer than 8,000 remained open by 1965. Similar reductions affected all other religious associations.[52] Furthermore, priests were deprived of their Soviet "registration," i.e., the right to function legally, and were even arrested for "trying to attract young people to the church," for deaths of recently baptized babies or simply for being popular and drawing large crowds to their church.[53]

---

[49]Struve, 297. Apparently this request or order was not applied universally and later fell into disuse, because, according to oral evidence of Russian clerics the churches continue to earn interest on the sale of candles.

[50]*Patriarch and Prophets*, 129, and other *samizdat* documents.

[51]Talantov in ibid., 125-40; Struve, 301-2.

[52]Furov gives a figure of 6,694 priests for 1967. The number of functioning Orthodox churches given in the 1966 edition of *Spravochnik ateista* is 7,500. *Aspects of Religion*, 48.

[53]Struve, 318; Talantov and Levitin in *Patriarch and Prophets*, 126-40 and 298-302, respectively. Article 227 of the RSFSR Criminal Code (and similar laws in other republics), which provides for up to five years of imprisonment for religious activities that may be harmful to health, was interpreted very "liberally" to hold baptizing priests responsible for a child's death.

wal of Persecutions?

The imposition on the Church of the changes in the status of the clergy just described is in itself conclusive evidence that the massive campaign against the Church was not merely a matter of abuses of power by local authorities—as church officials sometimes tried to maintain when cornered by sufficiently informed interviewers at press conferences in the West. The persecution was organized and directed from the center. This is further demonstrated by the fact that there were no contemporaneous criticisms of it, and that, concurrently, many official Soviet periodicals overtly condoned it by such statements as "The struggle against religion must not only be continued, but it must be enhanced by *all available means*" (italics ours). Appearing two years after the beginning of the new wave of persecutions, the cited article still recognized the continuing growth of religions. Moreover, it reported that pagan, pre-Christian religions were reappearing and growing in regions that had been converted to Christianity relatively recently—i.e., in Siberia and in the Far North.[54] Whatever form of religious life there was, the foregoing is an admission that the official ideology—Marxism-Leninism—was at least losing its grip on society.

There are several authoritative *samizdat* descriptions of the process of the drifting away of the young Soviet generations first from the legacy of Stalin and then from the whole Marxist-Leninist intellectual and ideological baggage.[55] The two were organically interconnected, not only because Stalin considered himself a Marxist and owed his power position to Lenin, but more immediately because the combination of Stalin's cult and the purges had progressively removed all talent from any influence in Soviet society.[56] The same factors were responsible for the greatest ever

[54]I.A. Kryvelev, "Preodolenie religiozno-bytovykh perezhitkov u narodov SSSR," *Sovetskaya etnografiya*, no. 4 (1961) 37-43. The recently emigrated art critic Igor Golomstock, now of Oxford University, observed similar phenomena of pagan revivals in northern Russia among peasants deprived of priests for long periods of time. Oral testimony to this author (London, summer 1974).

[55]For instance, Abram Tertz (Andrei Sinyavsky), *On Socialist Realism*, any edition; Vladimir Osipov, "Ploshchad' Mayakovskogo, stat'ya 70," *Grani*, no. 80 (1971) 107-36.

[56]This subject is brilliantly exposed in Vasily Grossman's novel *Forever Flowing* (English ed. by Harper and Row) and in Solzhenitsyn's *Cancer Ward*.

isolation of Soviet society from the outside world during the first postwar decade and for the lack of any comprehensive knowledge of its past by the younger generations. If there was anything that prevented total despair at seeing such a depersonalized, gray and shabby social organism, it was the exaltation of the "Great Stalin" and the promise of the achievement of the bliss of communism in the future. Moreover, the latter, in the minds of those who believed, was completely identified with the figure of Stalin: both were great—Stalin was the guiding star of communism—and everything else around was hardly worthy of notice. The death of Stalin and the petty struggle for power among his successors reduced such myths to more realistic proportions, and a general ideological disarray and frustration was the consequence. Khrushchev tried to salvage the situation, to halt the spreading nihilism and ideological cynicism by proclaiming a return to Leninism and promising, in 1959 (at the Extraordinary Twenty-first Communist Party Congress), to build a communist society "in the main" within twenty years. Some of the frustrated intellectuals and youth did indeed turn to the classics of Marxism-Leninism in the hope of finding an alternative to Stalinism within communist ideology. In the course of these searches, their opposition to the continuing arbitrary practices of Khrushchev's reign increased. The regime responded by the only means it had inherited from the totalitarian theory and practice of Marxism-Leninism-Stalinism: repressions and arrests of the critics, which further frustrated beliefs in the possibility of some democratic and more pluralist solution within the Marxist ideological framework and convinced many that Stalinism was not a deviation from but the fulfilment of Marxism-Leninism.[57]

Marxism, however, is a value-oriented, quasi-religious system of thought. Hence, a person brought up on Marxism has an in-built propensity to search for ideational alternatives in a religious-hierarchical context—i.e., for another faith. Hence, it was no accident that along with complaints about a growing nihilism, the Soviet press noted in 1958 that "approximately in the last five years some believers have been showing a more intensive interest in religion; while in some areas there has been an insignificant growth of religiosity in general." The adjective "insignificant," in

[57]See Osipov, 107-36.

an official publication that must not contradict the thesis of the inevitability of the death of religion in a Marxist society, may in fact stand for its antonym.

Moreover, while the above ideological factors stimulated interest in her, the Church was not standing idly by. The same author complains:

> Now not a single church service takes place without a sermon aimed at revitalizing interest in religion. . . . Bishops have lately been touring their dioceses, participating . . . in the services in local churches, much more frequently [than before]; choirs have been significantly increased, many churches have been reconstructed.

The same process, he says, was taking place among the sectarians, Moslems and Jews.[58]

One such episcopal visit, to Kherson, is described by a church source in Russia in a letter:

> The whole cathedral was filled to the bursting point . . . all the galleries, the steps and the garden were crowded with some seven thousand persons. The bishop delivered two to four sermons at each service. After the liturgy the clergy ate at my home; dinner was also served for the choir, visitors, and also for the poorest pilgrims . . .

The crowds threw flowers at the bishop's feet, greeting him with enthusiasm, devotion and love.[59]

Apparently, these festive expressions were not an exception, for they were confirmed in numerous atheistic publications as well. For instance:

> . . . in some churches during the celebration of Easter 100 to 150 children, dressed in specially designed costumes, lead the Easter processions by carrying icons and strewing the path with flowers. . . . Special sermons for children

[58]S.N. Khudyakov, *O preodolenii religioznykh perezhitkov v SSSR* (Moscow, 1958) 47 and 46-7.

[59]Fr. Boris Sartak, dean of the Kherson cathedral, in *Khronika zhizni russkoi pravoslavnoi tserkvi v zapadnoi Evrope*, no. 27 (January-March 1956) 6-7.

are given in churches on certain days. . . . Quite a few priests forbid children to sing Soviet [most probably antireligious] songs . . . to participate in the Pioneer and Komsomol organizations. . . .

Some priests organized youth nature hikes, in the course of which they "led discussions on happiness and virtue." Some priests were imprisoned in these years for attempting to entice youths into the Church.[60] Apparently, such activities prompted the Soviet government's complaints about priests breaking Soviet law—mentioned in the above-cited patriarchal address to the bishops—although in the eyes of the Church these constituted basic pastoral duties, not a crime.

At the same time, reports appeared showing that the majority of monks and nuns, at least in some Soviet monasteries, were not elderly and, at least when tonsured, were under thirty years of age.[61] This must have caused considerable concern for the Soviet authorities—hence, the already discussed antimonastic decree of 1958 and the frantic efforts to close as many monasteries as possible. In fact, the order of October 16 directs the republican governments "to present a report within six months on the feasibility of reducing the number of functioning monastic communities."[62]

Apparently sensing the advent of tougher times, the patriarchate responded with a number of articles in 1960 on the necessity of greater discipline in the church and more dedication and modesty on the part of the clerics. One of such articles cites Patriarch Aleksii's 1953 and other encyclicals calling on the priests and bishops not to emulate the secular practice of annual leave, for pastors cannot take leave from their flocks. Banquets and sumptuous living are condemned for clerics, for the money for them comes from the generous donations of believers for church needs and not for the physical pleasures of the clergy. The clergy are servants, not princes, of the Church. In another

---

[60]A. Valentinov, *Religiya i tserkov' v SSSR* (Moscow, 1960) 30-1.

[61]Bilinets, *T'ma*, 65. He does not give the dates of their tonsuring or veil taking, but all photographs of monastic communities appearing in *ZhMP* show a fair proportion of young people.

[62]Decree no. 1159, in *Zakonodatel'stvo*, 36.

article, priests are implored to instruct the believers in proper church discipline and to cultivate frequent communion.[63]

At the same time, we learn from atheistic brochures that many clerics and parishes engaged in clandestine charity work among the poor and organized free dinners after Sunday liturgy for needy pilgrims coming to church from afar; and priests offended the atheists and atheistic organizations in their sermons.[64] Altogether, atheistic publications began to pay a lot of attention to sermons and their content from the late 1950s. It was stated that, in the majority of churches, sermons were given several times a week, even after weekday services, whereas the old tradition had been to preach only after a full liturgy—i.e., on Sundays and special church holidays. At a time when religious authors (e.g., Levitin, Zheludkov, Talantov) were complaining of the low caliber of sermons, the atheists praised most of the sermons as effectively attracting people to the Church and strengthening their faith. Soviet surveys even made random analyses of topics of sermons in individual cities or dioceses. Thus, a survey carried out in the early 1960s in Astrakhan reported the following topics and proportions: salvation, 33 percent; ecclesiology and the sacraments, 23 percent; apologetics, 11 percent; the Church's teaching on God and Jesus, 15 percent.[65] Apparently, the obligatory topics of defense of peace and of the Soviet social system, very prominent in the sermons published in the *Journal of the Moscow Patriarchate*, amounted to a negligible proportion of the total volume of sermons.

Was this revitalization of the Church a result of the influx into the ranks of the clergy of either clerics released from the concentration camps after 1956 or recently ordained graduates from the revived seminaries, replacing the cowed and demoralized old priests who had survived Stalin's terror because they were no

[63]*ZhMP*, nos. 8 and 9 (1960) 52-8 and 45-51, respectively.

[64]Valentinov, *Religiya*, 40-3. The 1961 ban on charities and pilgrimages must have been the regime's reaction to such activities. Valentinov, in line with the times, constantly accuses the Church and her clerics of breaking the law. See also Bilinets, 65.

[65]V.V. Pavlyuk, *Psikhologiya sovremennykh veruyushchikh i ateisticheskoe vospitanie* (Lvov, 1976) 135 and 116. This tells a great deal about the relative dislocation of talent. Talantov complains that, fearing reprisals for religious propaganda, "many priests . . . from 1960" resort to abstract scholastic moralizing distant from the problems of the faithful. *Patriarch and Prophets*, 147.

threat to atheism? The massive closure of the seminaries in 1960-1964 seems to confirm our supposition that the regime was not happy with the new priests.

But while priests in general were so closely watched and circumscribed in their activities by the state that most of them limited all their activities to the confines of the church building, laymen continued to carry on most of the missionary work of attracting people to the Church, according to both Soviet atheistic sources and statements by Soviet clerics.[66] One author, on the basis of a sociological survey of believers in the Ryazan diocese, argues that one of the stimuli to the Church was Khrushchev's introduction of the first realistic pension system in the USSR in 1956. This allowed masses of people to retire (at age sixty for men and fifty-five for women) "without further worries about jobs and careers," and then to become active in church life. This is a tacit admission of religious persecution in the USSR, because it implies that going to church can be detrimental to one's professional opportunities. The author continues: "pensioners have significantly enlarged the number of Orthodox believers . . . the replenishment of the church *aktiv* on account of the pensioners cannot but cause concern in Soviet society [*obshchestvennost'*] . . . permanent parishioners . . . by their influence and authority assist in the dissemination of vestiges of religion among the youth and children." This contradicts her earlier assertion that the church *aktiv* consists predominantly of old, semi-literate women. In the highly meritocratic Soviet society, such women would hardly have sufficient "influence and prestige" to attract young people to the Church. But there are more contradictions in the same article when the author says that the most numerous group of practicing members of the Orthodox Church in the diocese in 1961 were "between forty and forty-five years old and, partly, youth."[67]

Whatever the contradictions in the Soviet studies of religion, the picture that emerges is not that of a dying institution, to say the least. And this was incompatible with Khrushchev's promise of building communism, for a thriving Church had no place in

---

[66]Testimony to this author by several Soviet Russian clerics and by Goricheva.

[67]Z.A. Yankova, "Sovremennoe pravoslavie i antiobshchestvennaya sushchnost' ego ideologii," *Voprosy istorii religii i ateizma*, no. 11 (1963) 73-80.

a communist society. Consequently, according to unofficial information of the time, a secret decision was adopted by the Communist Party Presidium after the Twenty-first Party Congress in 1959 to wipe out the Church "in the main" in the course of the seven-year plan of economic and social development adopted at the same congress. All that was probably expected to remain of the Church by 1966 was a patriarchate, with its external affairs department to aid Soviet foreign policy, and a few practicing churches to placate foreign visitors and tourists.[68] To achieve this in such a short time, force, coercion and direct persecution had to be applied, of which some illustrations have already been given.

But there was also another innovation, as it was realized that mere verbal attacks and insults against religion were achieving very little. To be sure, these continued, and included even subversive attacks. For instance, a certain Alla Trubnikova, pretending to be a pilgrim, managed to infiltrate on separate occasions different Orthodox and sectarian religious groups. She subsequently published reports on her "findings" and observations in the most Stalinist literary monthly, as well as in separate booklets. In these she fraudulently depicted religious believers as hypocrites, greedy moral degenerates, etc. But this was too much even for the antireligious monthly *Science and Religion* to stomach. The journal attacked her for doing more harm than good for the atheistic cause: firstly, because her character assassination of the believers contradicted the fact that these people were ready to suffer for their beliefs, i.e., they must be sincere, not hypocritical; secondly, because her exploits confirmed the believers' suspicions that the communists were installing secret agents to subvert the Church from within, and such suspicions made any dialogue and face-to-face contact between believers and atheists impossible.[69]

But what was new was the renewal of systematic field surveys and studies of the religious situation in the Soviet Union. Such surveys had ceased to be taken since the late 1920s, and atheistic authors complained that they were struggling with the unknown—

[68]Oral testimony to this author by an informed Moscow priest (Moscow, May 1964).

[69]D. Ushinin, "Novye veyaniya v ateisticheskoi propagande v SSSR," *Grani*, no. 60 (1966) 201-4. Also, Alla Trubnikova, "Tainik v taburetke," *Oktyabr'*, no. 9 (1964) 161-77; and *Komandirovka v 13-i vek* (Moscow, 1965) passim.

their writings had to be based on stereotyped assumptions, with no real figures and facts concerning the contemporary believers, their mentality, age, educational level or their categories of faith.[70] Such studies and surveys appear to have begun anew in 1959, but detailed publication of the data obtained in these and later surveys began only in the 1960s, generally after Khrushchev's fall. Primitive, crude attacks predominated as long as Khrushchev was in power, for he had no patience for scholarship, however a priori antireligious and biased it may have been.

To the mass closure of churches and the fear of many believers of "unpleasant consequences" for attending services, the Church responded with what the Soviet religion-watchers would soon term "modernization." This included a new practice of prayer by correspondence: funerals in absentia after a civilian burial, weddings in absentia, private prayer for a person or even confession by correspondence. One Soviet source reports that in one church as many as 63 percent and in another as many as 89 percent of all private religious rites were performed in 1963 in absentia, on the basis of a letter or a confidential petition. The other innovations, enforced by the growing shortage of churches and the persecution of youngsters and their parents for serving in the altar, included the performance of two and more liturgies per day in the same church and the use of nonworking women, mostly pensioners or secret nuns, as acolytes.[71] The reasons for these practices were obviously the fear of repercussions and the long distances to the nearest church, the number of churches being inadequate. At the same time, these reports imply that the administrative attacks have not reduced the numbers of believers, especially since their estimates of infant baptisms remain high: between 40 and 60 percent of all the newly born.[72] Other reported

[70]See, for example, V.F. Elfimov, *O prichinakh i usloviyakh sushchestvovaniya religioznykh perezhitkov v SSSR* (Vologda, 1971) 4-9. Among other things, he criticizes Soviet authors for automatically defining religion only as "a remnant of the past," for this presupposes its ability to exist "outside of conditions, time and place"—i.e., it implicitly rejects Marxist environmentalism and historical determinism.

[71]N.P. Andrianov, et al., *Osobennosti sovremennogo religioznogo soznaniya* (Moscow, 1966) 208-15; Yankova, "Sovremennoe pravoslavie," 73-80.

[72]V.D. Kobetsky, "Issledovanie dinamiki religioznosti naseleniya," in *Ateizm, religiya, sovremennost'* (Leningrad, 1973) 170-1. His sample is that of children in one of the most prestigious Soviet youth camps, mostly of highly placed and

innovations included priests giving introductory remarks to the
faithful to explain the more difficult parts of the liturgy before
performing them, and the actual performance of many parts of
the service in the middle of the church rather than in the sanctuary, to enable the faithful to participate more directly.[73] This,
of course, harkens back to the liturgical experiments of the Renovationist Bishop Granovsky.

Soon after the fall of Khrushchev, Soviet professional atheists
began a cautious reassessment of the five years of persecution.
Their general conclusion was that it had not payed off: the civic
and political loyalty of many believers had been badly undermined
by these methods. Deprived of registered churches, believers
went underground. And it was admitted that concealed, uncontrolled religious practices were socially more dangerous than an
overt and hence controllable Church. Moreover, the privations
and suffering of Christians had drawn "unhealthy" sympathetic
attention toward them and toward religion in general from people
who would otherwise have remained outside of the religious
sphere. And the great efforts to gain renegades from the ranks of
the clergy had failed to produce the desired effect on believers,
who argued that such rascals had served the Church only for
pecuniary reasons, and therefore they would now serve the atheists
for the same reasons. Thus, the more of them that left the Church,
the better off she would be. Generally, after the fall of Khrushchev, the campaign of direct persecution subsided, although very
few of the 10,000 to 15,000 closed churches have ever been
reopened.[74]

On November 10, 1964, the Central Committee of the CPSU
issued a declaration "On Errors Committed in the Conduct of
Atheist Propaganda." The declaration reaffirms that actions of
administrative interference in the affairs of the Church are unacceptable.[75] There is nothing new in such decrees and declarations
either by the Soviet government or by the Party. They have been
published after every wave of particularly harsh persecutions or
at the time of a change of leadership (several times in the 1920s,

party-card carrying parents. Over 52 percent of these children were found to be
baptized—hence, the average should be even higher.
    [73]Yankova, 73-80.
    [74]Ushinin, "Novye veyaniya," 198-221; Shafarevich, 13-26.
    [75]Shafarevich, 70.

1930, 1954, etc.). However, it testifies to the fact that the ideological leadership of the Soviet Communist Party had once again admitted defeat in its head-on attack on the Church.

Metropolitan Nikodim and the External Relations of the Church

Those who were aware of the magnitude of Khrushchev's attack on the Church were particularly appalled by the statements of the leaders of the patriarchate at press conferences abroad or in interviews granted to foreign correspondents in Moscow. It has to be kept in mind, however, that even the late architect of the patriarchate's foreign policy, Metropolitan Nikolai, despite the fact that he had fallen from power in 1960 because of a head-on collision with the state, defended the fraudulent assurances made by his colleagues to the effect "that the Church in Russia is free and that there are no persecutions." Nikolai once said with a sad smile: "If I had been in their place . . . I would probably have said the very same thing."[76]

But the old Nikolai was not "there." Although considerably younger in age than the patriarch, he had been forced to retire from both of his key positions in the Church in the course of 1960. In a private conversation only some three weeks after his retirement (on June 21) from the post of Chairman of the Church's Department of External Ecclesiastical Relations, the metropolitan said that this was the state's retaliation for his active sermons against the wild antireligious propaganda, full of insinuations and lies, that had then just begun. Characteristically, he still believed in the ability of the patriarch and the bishops to resist direct state interference into the internal affairs of the Church, assuring his interlocutor that the Soviets could remove him only from the above position, as it was a political rather than an ecclesiastical appointment—although officially it was he who requested the Synod to relieve him of the post. One of the Synod bishops at first said he would never agree to sign Nikolai's resignation. But Nikolai responded: "This is necessary." The patriarch confirmed it, and the question was settled. Nikolai was certain, however, that the Soviets would not and could not force

[76]Vasily, "Poslednie vstrechi," 216.

the Church to retire him from the post of Metropolitan of Krutitsy, the most prestigious position in the Church next to that of the patriarch. Nikolai said, "They would not dare. And the Synod would never agree." But they did dare. The following September, Nikolai was removed from this post as well. And less than a year later he died, ostensibly of a heart attack (although persistent rumors maintain that he was murdered).

A person close to Nikolai thought that the reason why Nikolai had agreed to petition the Synod for retirement was that the Soviets "had demanded of him concessions that his conscience did not allow him to accept."[77] Was one of the concessions that was demanded of him a pledge that under no circumstances, in any conditions, would he admit that the Church was persecuted in the USSR? Judging by the behavior of the man who soon replaced Nikolai as head of the Department of External Ecclesiastical Relations—the thirty-one-year-old Archimandrite Nikodim (soon to be consecrated bishop, then elevated to archbishop and eventually to Metropolitan of Leningrad)—this could very well have been the case.

Indeed, Nikodim (Rotov) tread his ground very carefully, making no hint of any persecutions in any of his official statements, and even in private tête-à-tête conversations admitting only individual cases of persecutions, and only when pressed hard and when facts were laid before him that he could not deny. But his administration ushered in a new era in the whole conduct and context of the external policies of the Moscow Patriarchate. Nikolai had followed Soviet foreign policy commands and made the necessary gestures, such as the vicious and fanciful attacks on the US during the Korean War (so fanciful in fact that one often wondered whether he made them deliberately, feeling that no person in his right mind would believe him and it would be clear that he was forced to behave in such a way). Nikolai had been a reluctant, if loyal, servant of the Soviet state, not its partner. Nikodim, a Soviet man through and through, a son of a Ryazan provincial party secretary and a neophyte who had joined the Church as a teenager, had the characteristics of the new generation of bishops described above by Fr. Shpiller. (Only he was much more intelligent than most, hence he probably appreciated

[77]Ibid., 216-7.

the essence of Shpiller's argument.) In his foreign policies he behaved more creatively than did his predecessor, and he appeared to be much more independent a partner with the Soviet regime. Nikodim's policies, of course, responded to Khrushchev's policies of peaceful coexistence, of enlarging and strengthening the contacts of the Soviet Union with the foreign world—in short, of attempting to come out of isolation. It was Nikodim who led the Moscow Patriarchate into the World Council of Churches (although the decision to do so had been made under his predecessor).[78] It was Nikodim who cofounded and joined the Prague Peace Conference, as well as a number of interconfessional dialogue undertakings in the West. It was he who discontinued the attacks against the Vatican and established very close links with it. It was eventually under him and on his initiative that the Orthodox Church in America was granted autocephaly. It was he who established a special section for Afro-Asian students at the Leningrad Theological Academy and began an active theological student exchange program with the Vatican and with the Roman Catholic Church in general. In contrast to Nikolai, who would visit a foreign country or Church, make a few attacks in support of Soviet foreign policy interests and return, only further isolating the Russian Orthodox Church from the rest of the world and from world Christianity, Nikodim aimed at establishing permanent ties and contacts with as much reciprocity as was necessary for the Church to exist *within* the Soviet organism, *not outside* it—so the Church would be ready to play an active role in society the moment the state would realize its need for her services, and thus eventually win a return into the fulness of Russian life. He strongly believed that such a moment would come, even "if in the meanwhile we shall be reduced to two or three open churches in the whole country."

As to fraudulent statements by the Church's bishops (including himself) in public appearances, he once remarked to this author with a sad smile: "It is you in the West who react so readily to untrue statements . . . The Soviet public has got used to them. . . . I am not saying that this is good or bad, I am merely stating the fact that what shocks you here does not evoke a similar response in our country." Whether this assessment is accurate or whether

[78]Oral testimony of Very Rev. Prof. John Meyendorff.

it merely reflects the experiences of the milieu in which he grew up (party members), the circumstances of the conversation were such that they left little doubt that he believed in what he said. Moreover, as a neophyte, a man who had embraced Christianity in a world of militant atheism, he was much less sensitive to the importance of theological differences between Orthodoxy and other Christian persuasions, particularly Roman Catholicism. As he once put it to this author, explaining the reasons why the Moscow Patriarchate (under his direct pressure) resolved to admit Roman Catholics to the chalice in case of the absence of Roman Catholic clergy, "In our contemporary world of atheistic agression, the differences dividing Christians are much smaller than the things we share vis-à-vis atheism and materialism, and we should stress our unity, rather than our differences."

It may perhaps even be argued that Nikodim's party-family background attracted him toward Roman Catholicism, with its centralized, authoritarian power structure. He might have seen in it an effective counterpart to the totalitarian, centralized force of the Communist Party. Nikolai, on the other hand, because his family originated from Belorussia, where contact and conflict with Roman Catholicism were so acute, could never have felt that way about Western Christianity, particularly about the Roman Church. Hence, Nikodim's policies and contacts with the West had a ring of sincerity and free will in them, while those of Nikolai were obviously enforced. This difference must have been an important factor in winning for Nikodim an extreme popularity and prestige in western church circles, including the World Council of Churches—although he himself was very disappointed with the secularization of that body.[79]

The contacts and prestige Nikodim achieved obviously also raised the international prestige of the Church he represented, and this forced the Soviet government, in its turn, to show more respect for the Church. Whereas persecutions of individuals, particularly young members of the intelligentsia, for practicing religion have not disappeared after Khrushchev, attacks against the patriarchate and the Patriarchal Church as a body have become very rare.

[79]See our "Mitropolit Nikodim i ego vremya," *Posev*, no. 2 (February 1979) 21-6.

Otherwise, as far as sycophantic confirmations of Soviet foreign policy statements and aims, etc., are concerned, all that continued under Nikodim as actively (if not more actively) as under Nikolai. It is hardly worth the while to cite details. Most of them are presented and analyzed in Fletcher's already cited *Religion and Soviet Foreign Policy.*

CHAPTER 11

The Catacombs: The "True Orthodox" and Other Currents

The "catacomb" Church (or movements within Russian Orthodoxy that refuse to associate administratively, sacramentally, or both, with the Moscow Patriarchate because of its subservience to the Soviet regime) is predominantly a by-product of Metropolitan Sergii's 1927 Declaration of Loyalty. The catacomb phenomenon is also commonly known as the "True Orthodox Church" (IPTs) and/or the "True Orthodox Christians" (IPKh). In the specialized Soviet atheistic press the debate on whether the True Orthodox Church and the True Orthodox Christians are one movement or two different ones has not been fully settled. The most convincing view is that there is one and the same movement, but that the appellation True Orthodox Christians is commonly used by those communities that have no priests. As there is very little replacement for deceased or liquidated catacomb priests, more and more communities have changed from churches into lay groups of True Orthodox Christians. The authors stress that dogmatically and ritually there are no differences between the two groups—nor does either of them differ in any of these characteristics from the regular Orthodox Church—and there are no "initiation rituals" of any kind for members of the Orthodox Church entering the "True Orthodox," and vice versa.[1] These,

[1]For the different views see A.I. Klibanov, "Sovremennoe sektantstvo v tambovskoi oblasti," *Voprosy istorii religii i ateizma* 12 (1961) 96; and Fletcher, *Church Underground*, 180-229. These authors, as well as Yankova, Nikolskaya and others, treat the IPTs and IPKh as separate movements. Among authors

however, should not be confused with the "True Orthodox Christian Wanderers" (IPKh-S), who are a catacomb branch of the Old Believers, in all other respects paralleling the IPKh.[2] It appears from the findings of Soviet field surveys (1959-1961 and 1971-1972), as well as from the materials of police investigations and trials of both the postwar and prewar days,[3] that the two groups and the multiple sects associated with them go much further back in time than 1927. We have discussed this subject to some extent already in chapter 5. Specialized Soviet publications, cleared of ideological and propaganda rhetoric, add more information and make it possible to reconstruct a more or less consistent story of their development and dissemination.

One of the early "semi-sects," which later became one of the branches of the catacomb Orthodox, appears to be the *Ioannity* (Ioannites), so named after Fr. Ioann (John) of Kronstadt. As has been mentioned, he is widely considered a saint and was recently uncanonically "canonized" by the émigré Synodal Church. Several hundred miraculous deeds resulting from his prayers were recorded in his lifetime. The Ioannites idolized Fr. John already in his lifetime, exceeding the acceptable levels of veneration of saintly people in the Orthodox Church. Yet they never broke with the Orthodox Church, while the Church, although criticizing them, has never reached a decision on whether they were a sect or an extremist current within the Church. Fr. John allegedly predicted the forthcoming fall of the monarchy and the coming of an era of the Antichrist upon Russia (he died in 1909). Hence, the Ioannites never reconciled themselves with the Soviet regime and never accepted any form of civic loyalty to it, thus directly and actively contributing to the post-1927 opposition to Metropolitan Sergii. According to survey interviews:

> there are neither any ritualistic nor dogmatic distinctions between the Ioannites and the True Orthodox. The only original difference . . . the deification of John of Kronstadt . . . has withered away owing to the particular vene-

regarding the IPKh as but a priestless continuation of the IPTs, both remaining theologically Orthodox, see Demyanov, and N.F. Zybkovets, *Natsionalizatsiya monastyrskikh imushchestv v sovetskoi Rossii* (Moscow, 1975).

[2]Demyanov, 92-4, etc.
[3]Ibid., 18-9 et passim.

ration of John's cult by all branches of the True Orthodox without exception. . . . Many of them possess a manuscript called *Visions of John of Kronstadt;* in many of their dwellings, portraits of this priest of the Black Hundreds appear next to the icons.[4]

Marxist "religiologists" try to explain the fact of the main concentration of the True Orthodox in the Central Black Earth region (the Voronezh, Tambov, Kursk, Lipetsk, Michurinsk areas) by the sociomaterialistic peculiarities of the region: the higher than average rural character (90.5 percent of the population in 1927 were rural dwellers); a particularly sharp decline of living standards and agricultural yields after the end of the Civil War (the cultivated area decreased by 44 percent in comparison with the prerevolutionary era); a low literacy rate (the national average was 39.6 percent in 1926, while the Central Black Earth area's was 37.8 percent); the particular failure of the Renovationists in the area (7,778 Tikhonite parishes to 259 Renovationist in 1925); and the stubborn resistance of the local population to Soviet power, reflected in the mass peasant rebellions of 1921-1923 under Antonov, Kolesnikov and others. It is highly questionable, however, whether the latter two phenomena can be seen simply as by-products of the other socioeconomic factors. Firstly, Civil War operations and White Army offensives reached the area in 1919. Secondly, this area had been less affected by serfdom than most other parts of European Russia: there had simply been no serfdom there until the late eighteenth century, and even in the nineteenth most of the peasants were state peasants—i.e., they were freer than private serfs and continued to enjoy forms of elected rural self-government.[5] Hence, their opposition to the Soviet regime may at least as legitimately be explained by a deeper tradition of freedom and independence.

It was there that a religious-monarchist movement of "Fedorovites" arose in the 1920s. They were the followers of a local monk, Fedor Rybalkin, who was prophesying the return of the Whites and the imminent fall of Soviet power. In 1928, according

[4]Their icons also include portraits of not yet canonized martyrs of the twentieth century—i.e., Christian victims of the Soviet terror. Ibid., 14 and 113-5.

[5]Ibid., 16-7; Klibanov, "Sovremennoe sektantstvo," 60-9.

to Soviet sources, the movement was largely liquidated in the Voronezh province when their activists were brought to a mass trial. But the Fedorovites and similar movements managed to spread to other regions and to proliferate across the whole country in the 1930s and again after the war. In 1930 a similar movement appeared in the northern Caucasus, the Kuban region and the Ukraine—the very areas of concentration of the Whites as well as of other anti-Bolshevik forces during the Civil War. This movement preached that the tsar's family had miraculously survived and presumably would return to power. These extremist anti-Bolshevik religious movements were not confined to the more peripheral areas, however. Similar sects, and groups already assuming the appellation "True Orthodox," allegedly appeared in the mid-1920s in the Tatar and Mordva republics on the Volga and in the Bryansk, Vologda and other provinces. Their common features include claims that the Soviet regime represents the reign of the Antichrist and general eschatological beliefs. But in the 1920s, prior to Sergii's Declaration of Loyalty, they formed merely an extremist branch of the Tikhonite Church, were led by some monks and priests of that Church and continued to be communicants of that Church. It was only after Sergii's declaration that they formally broke with the overt Tikhonite Church as administered by him, while the legalization of Sergii's Synod made all these movements illegal—i.e., it pushed them into the "catacombs."

Thus begins the story of the "Leningrad Autocephaly" headed by Metropolitan Iosif, discussed already in chapter 4. There was also a similar temporary autocephaly in the Yaroslavl diocese headed by Metropolitan Agafangel. Similar autocephalies arose and existed for a while in the areas of the Urals, the lower and central Volga, Gorky, Ivanovo, Barnaul (Siberia), Kursk, Irkutsk (Siberia) and other dioceses. All these self-declared autocephalies based themselves on Patriarch Tikhon's encyclical of November 20, 1920.[6]

But the most influential anti-Sergiite autocephaly was evidently the so-called *Buevshchina* (Buevism), named after a vicar-bishop of the Voronezh diocese, Aleksii Bui. Soviet sources indicate that it spread not only across the whole Central Black Earth

[6]See above in chapter 4.

area but also to the Ukraine, Kuban, the Don and the northern Caucasus. Allegedly, clerics belonging to this movement told peasants to boycott collective farming and induced many to quit collective farms. The sources associate many anti-collective farm riots with "Buevite propaganda." Although a Soviet author maintains that this schism was liquidated in 1932, obviously by OGPU terror, a few lines later he writes that "thanks to the arrests of their leaders and preachers there was a lull in the activities of the True Orthodox . . . toward the end of the 1930s, but they were on the rise again toward the end of the 1940s. Some of their followers continue to be active even today." The author admits that the arrests helped to suppress the movement only temporarily, for they were normally compensated for by its reappearance in another part of the country. In general, there was "an enhancement of anti-Soviet activities of all groups and variants of the True Orthodox in the 1930s," but the author maintains that as long as there still remained reliable Tikhonite priests, trusted by the "True Orthodox," most of the latter continued to frequent these Patriarchal churches until their closure. When the churches began to reopen in the 1940s with new contingents of priests, the "True Orthodox" did not return to them.[7]

Indeed, their opposition to the Soviet system expressed itself even in avoiding the state school system, or allowing their children to attend it only up to grade three or five, in order to achieve the minimum literacy necessary "to read religious literature." It is claimed that this attitude has been lately modified and their children have at last begun to attend the full secondary school. But the literacy and educational level of the IPKh communities remained very low, owing to the former practice.[8] Moreover, the communities consisted almost entirely of peasants, for most of those priests' families that used to be in their ranks deserted for the official Church (this apparently relates to the period of the post-1943 legalization of the Church). Most of the IPKh peasants

[7] Demyanov, 18-30. He gives no information on the numbers arrested and sentenced and on the sentences passed.

[8] Ibid., 46-9. It should also be noted that expulsions of practicing believers from higher and even secondary educational establishments are quite common, and there have been periods in Soviet history when an overtly practicing Christian was excluded from the Soviet school system, at any rate above the primary school. Thus, illiteracy of believers is not necessarily their own fault.

continued to refuse to join collective farms, at most agreeing to sign work contracts with them as hired laborers.[9] However unreliable the Soviet categorization of believers into "fanatics," "convinced believers," "believers by tradition" and "waverers," it may be of interest that while some 80 percent of the surveyed IPKh members were women, the largest category among them was that of "believers by tradition" (almost 44 percent), the second largest category being "fanatics" (30 percent). Among men the largest category was "convinced believers" (nearly 38 percent), while the second largest was "waverers" (23 percent).[10]

Much remains unsaid and undiscovered or undisclosed in all Soviet official writings on the "True Orthodox." On the one hand, both Soviet and independent sources indicate that the IPTs and even the IPKh are dying out; on the other hand, as late as 1975 some Soviet authors spoke of dozens of secret clandestine "True Orthodox" monasteries and convents in the Siberian Taiga, complete with pastoral and missionary courses.[11]

It appears that, among the catacomb Orthodox, either returning or not returning to communion in the revived Patriarchal Church once the churches began to reopen is the criterion that separates all forms of internal opposition from that which became known as the IPKh. We have already mentioned the effect of Bishop Afanasy's return to the Patriarchal Church in 1945.[12] Hence, the postwar "True Orthodox" appear to represent only a part of the original catacomb Church. The following document shows that the prewar "catacombs," despite all their intransigence, still left the door open to reconciliation with the Patriarchal Church, at least by implication (presumably under different conditions).

In 1937, whether by accident or by divine design, two metropolitans, four bishops, two priests and six lay activists of the catacomb Church found themselves grouped together for several hours in a transitional detention center near Irkutsk in Siberia. The group saw this as a unique opportunity to hold a secret sobor.

[9]Ibid., 40-5 and 92-141.
[10]Ibid., 50-1.
[11]Zybkovets, "Natsionalizatsiya," 111-2; Fletcher, *Church Underground,* 226-7. Also oral testimony to this author by the monk mentioned in chapter 4 (p. 162).
[12]See above in chapter 4, pp. 161f.

One of the lay participants was proceeding from this point to internal exile rather than to prison. Therefore, he was instructed to memorize the decisions of the sobor and to pass them on to the catacomb Christians. Among the decisions of the sobor were:

(1) The sobor forbids the faithful to accept sacraments from the clergy legalized by the anti-Christian government. . . .

(4) All church branches growing from the ecclesiastic trunk—. . . the trunk is our prerevolutionary Church—are living branches of Christ's Church. Let there be prayerful and liturgical communion between the clergy of all these branches. . . .[13]

The document, if it is genuine, shows a very ambivalent and contradictory position. On the one hand, the "sobor" condemns that part of the Church which has been legalized by the state; on the other, it calls it one of the branches of Russian Orthodoxy and supports intercommunion. Although it further condemns those who think of themselves as the Russian Church rather than as one of her branches (this presumably refers to Sergii), the document can also be interpreted as opening a road to an eventual reconciliation with the Patriarchal Church, once certain conditions are met.

But to return to the Soviet descriptions of the remaining "True Orthodox," they record even an appearance of a youth movement among them in the postwar 1940s. Hence, the rather high proportion of young people in the movement found in the late 1940s and up to the surveys of 1959: 40 to 60 percent under thirty years of age. These young Orthodox sectarians appear to have been even more intolerant of the established Soviet order than the older members: "Most of them swore to remain celibate and considered service in the Soviet armed forces a deadly sin. In many respects they revised the more moderate policies of the older members and took over leadership in some groups of the

---

[13]"Vazhnoe postanovlenie katakombnoi tserkvi," reprinted in *Pravoslavnaya Rus'*, no. 18 (1949), from an article by B. Zakharov in the Paris Russian newspaper *Russkaya mysl'* (September 7, 1949).

True Orthodox. . . . some of them engaged in terrorist acts."
They preached the approaching end of the world and several
times announced its date. The Khrushchev seven-year plan,
promulgated in 1959 (and accompanied by a planned destruction
of the overt religions), was interpreted as the beginning of the
Antichrist's final reign prior to the last judgment. From "1955
the preaching of celibacy spread over the entire organization. . . .
[Consequently] the birth rate among the 'True Orthodox' declined
sharply."[14]

Allegedly, on August 30, 1953, these IPKh fanatics, deciding
that it was the beginning of the second coming, burned down
fourteen houses and murdered or wounded six collective farmers.
These fanatical currents evolved into such extremist sects as the
Molchalniki (silencers) and the *Sedmintsy* (seven-dayists). They
refused either to contribute to or to accept the products of the
Soviet economy, surviving by picking berries and mushrooms in
the summer and sewing and knitting in the winter. For a while
they accepted only food produced prior to the 1959 "Devil's"
population census and broke relations even with those IPKh
members who continued to participate in the national economy.
Their preaching of the imminent end of the world resulted in
the swelling of their ranks by some 50 percent. The most extreme
members of the sects starved themselves to death, while others
began to leave them when the predictions failed to materialize
and the pre-1959 food disappeared.[15]

It is also possible that, just as in the 1930s, the intensification
of Khrushchev's attacks on all religions drew Orthodox Christians
of all hues together again. The persecution of the official Church
must have raised her prestige in the eyes of the "True Orthodox"
and their offspring sects.

However skeptical our attitude toward Soviet religiologists
may be, we may not totally discard their assertions based on the
repetition of the 1959-1961 survey in 1971-1972. According to
these, during the decade the "True Orthodox" declined to less

than one-half of their 1959 strength, and of that remnant 70 percent were over fifty years old.[16] The decline and aging was likewise confirmed by a recent emigrant from the USSR, Alexander Chernov, a former IPTs-IPKh activist and a deadly enemy of the Moscow Patriarchate. In his story, however, he paints a picture of a very extensive, well-organized and extremely efficient network of underground religious communities that managed to keep him out of sight from Soviet organs for some fifteen years. While declining in numbers, the movement, according to him, is growing more and more radical. He admitted that the movement is now almost without priests.[17] This lack of regular and theologically educated clergy is in itself likely to breed more fanaticism. Thus, one of the latest outbursts of rebelliousness in the provincial areas of the Russian republic has occurred in 1981 in connection with the exchange of internal passports. Masses of religious believers have been boycotting the new passports on the grounds that the new wording of Soviet citizenship, "CITIZEN OF THE USSR" (*grazhdanin SSSR*), somehow coincides with the apocalyptical beast's number—666. The refusal on the periphery to accept the new passports has taken such mass proportions that the provincial Soviet-Russian media has been threatening that those who refuse would be subjected to legal punishment and deprived of their retirement pension rights.[18]

The role of priests among the IPKh, according to Soviet sources, has lately been performed more and more often by elderly women, known as nuns or "blackies" (*chernichki*), whose secret monastic communities form the core of the IPKh. It is not clear who veiled them (or are they some sort of "self-veilers"?). They bury and baptize, and even on occasion hear confessions and perform marriage ceremonies.[19] Thus, as often happens with schismatics, a movement that began as most conservative has

---

[16]Demyanov, 42-5.

[17]Interview with Alexander A. Chernov, an official of the Russian émigré organization NTS, kidnapped from Bulgaria in 1944 and in 1978 allowed to leave the Soviet Union after two spells in concentration camps and some fifteen years of activities in the catacomb Church, in *Posev*, no. 10 (1979) 40-6. In fact, he expressed the hope that the émigré Synodal Church would secretly ordain priests for the catacombs.

[18]"Khronika," *Posev*, no. 12 (1981) 4-5; and oral testimony by an informed clergyman of the Russian Orthodox Church.

[19]Demyanov, 40-6.

evolved into a most radical sect: female clergy, uncompromisingly opposed by the whole world of Orthodoxy on canonical and theological grounds, has been well nigh established by the "True Orthodox."

Soviet sources are rather vague on the numerical strength of the IPTs-IPKh. On the one hand, even for the Central Black Earth region they estimate only some 3,000 IPKh adherents for the 1950s and fewer than 1,500 for the 1970s; on the other, they call them the third largest religion in the area.[20] Surely, this would imply higher figures than the above in an area with a total population of over eight million in 1972! They admit, however, that the IPKh, and particularly their numerous apocalyptic-eschatological sects and branches, are not communicative, shunning in particular all contact with any representatives of the Soviet establishment. This precludes even distantly approximate estimates of their numbers by the Soviet atheistic surveys.[21]

The above-cited Chernov estimates that the total number of catacomb Christians runs into the millions, and he refers to a 1972 or 1973 unpublished speech by a high-ranking party official at an in camera conference of teachers. The official allegedly claimed that 52,000,000 persons belonged to the official Orthodox Church and 48,000,000 to the catacomb Church.[22] But this estimate stands completely alone and isolated. Surely, had there been such huge numbers of organized Orthodox Christians outside the official Church, other practicing contemporary Russian Orthodox Christians would have come across them, no matter how clandestine their behavior. This is not the case, except for those who have been to prison, where they do come across imprisoned members of the IPKh, mostly old people.[23] The only other Soviet

[20]Ibid., 42-3; Klibanov, "Po tomu zhe marshrutu: 1959-1971," *Nauka i religiya*, no. 3 (March 1972) 55.

[21]*Konkretnye issledovaniya*, articles by Klibanov (29-30) and Z.A. Yankova (112-3). Demyanov contradicts himself when he says that by having interviewed 1,360 IPKh members in 1972 he succeeded in surveying "about 90 percent of the IPKh membership" in the Central Black Earth region (125-30). If the IPKh avoid contacts with Soviet representatives, how does he know how many constitute 90 percent?

[22]The lecturer was allegedly E.N. Klimov, a CPSU Central Committee inspector. Chernov interview, 45.

[23]Testimonies to this author by Vladimir Telnikov (Munich, spring 1972), a dissident who had been in a concentration camp from 1957 to 1963 and who had even been baptized there by an IPKh layman prisoner for faith; and of the

citizen this author encountered who had known the "catacombers" rather intimately was a monk of the Patriarchal Church who had himself spent many years in the catacombs and remained quite sympathetic to them. His story sounded much more plausible than the above Communist Party estimates. He claimed that in the late 1960s there were still at least as many "catacomb" priests as those officially registered. But even he admitted that the former were mostly elderly and because of their clandestine character had tiny congregations (sometimes half a dozen people). Owing to their "deep underground" state, they do not engage in any dissemination of the faith and hence practically attract no "new blood." Because of the last catacomb bishops' refusal to consecrate new bishops, in order to preclude a perpetuation of this schism, there was no way for the "catacombers" to obtain new priests other than those ordained by bishops of the Patriarchal Church. This would be unacceptable to the more intransigent elements of the IPKh, who deny even the sacramental validity of the official Church; and the reduced remnant of the "catacombers," according to the above evidence (including Chernov's), tends to be the radical or the more extreme one.[24] Yet, there must have been a compromise on this issue, for if our monk's testimony is accurate, the increased numbers of catacomb priests in the 1960s should be seen as a direct result of Khrushchev's attack and of the deprivation by the state of close to twenty thousand priests of their registrations. Obviously, the most conscientious of these "de-registered" priests preferred to go underground rather than secularize.

But perhaps the "catacombs" are to be interpreted more broadly than just the IPKh-IPTs and related sects. Even Chernov

writer Andrei Sinyavsky (Paris, spring 1974). A case in point is Vladimir Osipov, a neo-Slavophile dissident released in 1982 after completing his second concentration camp term of eight years. Although claiming to be an ardent Orthodox Christian, he refused to marry in church because of the subservience of the official Church to the atheist regime. He wants to be married by a catacomb priest, but despite his prominence as a dissident, apparently all these years he has not been able to find one. The inconsistency of his position is that at the same time he has accepted sacraments, apparently, in the official churches. Mikhail Kheifets, "Russkii patriot Vladimir Osipov," *Kontinent*, no. 28 (1981) 137-8.

[24]Chernov interview, 44. This tallies even with the statements of Soviet religiologists that while some of the IPKh have lately become more moderate and have lately begun to accept the services of the Patriarchal clergy, "others are for all intents and purposes becoming real sectarians." Demyanov, 63-7.

admitted this when he said that there were different degrees of catacombs, from the IPKh to those who partly accepted the official Church—attending services in the open churches but not taking the sacraments.[25] The accounts of the above-mentioned monk about clandestine monasteries, described in chapter 5, revealed that he meant many different things by the term "catacombs." According to him and other sources, thousands of clandestine nuns have been veiled by the "registered" bishops and blessed by them to form secret communities in regular apartments while earning their living by work in hospitals—for the canons permit monastics to miss services only when rendering vital help to fellow men or saving human life. These nuns, obviously, remain within the Patriarchal Church and attend services in the officially open churches, yet they are in the catacombs as far as their monasticism is concerned.[26]

Other independent sources testify that the usual practice for a priest of the Patriarchal Church when he is deprived of registration by an arbitrary action of the local plenipotentiary of the Council for Religious Affairs is to move to another diocese. But if the plenipotentiary chooses to persecute him even beyond the borders of his jurisdiction by alerting his colleagues in other provinces, the cleric becomes an unofficial "wandering priest," visiting the faithful in those settlements where there are no open churches and/or performing baptisms and other rites without registering them, which suits those who are afraid of the consequences of officially registered church participation. Likewise, these priests as a rule do not break their liturgical ties with the patriarchate, although they function as catacomb clergy.[27] In fact, a Soviet source gives an even more precise illustration of such an ambivalent interpretation of the term "catacombs." According to him, the Autonomous Republic of Komi in the extreme northeast of European Russia, which had several hundred churches before the revolution, retained only three officially registered Orthodox parishes by the mid-1960s. But, in addition, there were also twenty

[25]Chernov interview, 45.

[26]The already cited Goricheva confirmed that many of her women friends, young Leningrad intellectuals, have taken vows before ruling bishops of the Patriarchal Church to live as nuns in the world in secret monastic communities.

[27]Fr. Tivetsky's testimony. *VRKhD*, no. 132 (1980) 211, contains a report on the arrest of one such wandering priest, Fr. Savva (Kolchugin).

unregistered Orthodox communities with "unofficial priests," who were, however, not members of any schismatic groups, because he mentions them in addition to the above two IPTs/IPKh communities in the same republic.[28]

That there is a distinction between the IPKh and unofficially functioning Orthodox communities that do not break their canonical connections with the patriarchate (although, most probably, they remain administratively unconnected to it) is further illustrated by the different attitudes of the patriarchate to clandestine Orthodoxy in official statements and in reality. On the one hand, Fletcher cites examples of attacks by Patriarchal bishops against "people who call themselves Christians but in fact . . . are self-ordained. . . . [they] slander the contemporary Orthodox Church and spread obloquy about the Holy Patriarch."[29] On the other, he also quotes testimony from Metropolitan Sergii (Voskresensky), the Baltic exarch, on the catacombs in the 1930s, according to which the latter were but an underground branch of the official Church, or at any rate appeared to have been so treated by her.

> There was in general a very active secret religious life—secret monks and priests, catacomb churches and liturgies, baptism, confession, the Eucharist, weddings, secret theological courses, secret stores of utensils for divine service, icons, service books, secret relations between congregations, dioceses, and patriarchal [sic!] administration. In order to destroy a catacomb patriarchate as well, it would have been necessary to execute all bishops. . . . And if one imagines the impossible, that complete destruction of the entire Church organization was successful, faith would remain nonetheless, and atheism would not have won a step.[30]

This attitude tallies with the testimony of the above-cited monk of the contemporary Patriarchal Church. He said that Patriarch Aleksii had a deep admiration for the "catacombers." When the late Metropolitan of Kiev, Ioann (Sokolov), once complained

[28]Yu.V. Gagarin, *Religioznye perezhitki v Komi ASSR* (Syktyvkar, 1971) 73-6.
[29]*Church Underground*, 186-7.
[30]Ibid., 82.

to the patriarch that the catacomb Church was particularly active in his archdiocese, the patriarch responded in the monk's presence: "You should not complain but thank God that there are so many courageous Christians in your diocese who have not bent their backs to the atheists as we have done. Their prayers will save our Church one day." Had the "catacombs" consisted only of the militantly anti-Patriarchal IPTs/IPKh, the patriarch would hardly have been so benevolent toward them. In view of all these facts, the above-cited Communist Party secret inside figures only mean that there are about 100 million practicing Orthodox Christians in the USSR (i.e., more than three times as many as claimed in the published Soviet statements on religion), of whom 52 percent are taken care of by the registered parishes and 48 percent belong to unregistered parishes and communities. Of these, a small percentage may actually belong to the IPKh/IPTs and their sects.[31]

Catacombs or Sects?

So, perhaps the Soviet authors, either deliberately or out of ignorance, confuse two different issues: the intransigent and, by now, sectarian "True Orthodox," and catacombs in general. The latter, in terms of the cited evidence, appears to be but an umbrella term that includes not only the IPTs/IPKh, but also: (1) Orthodox Christians who fail to gain permission from the state to function as an official church community and thus are forced to resort to illegal religious activities; (2) those who feel that the relationship between the patriarchate and the state is too fragile and the status of the former too uncertain to rely on that overt institution of the Church alone, and therefore may keep some form of undercover church life just in case, if it should become necessary to preserve the Church in the underground once again, as in the 1930s; and (3) those who may be in total disagreement with the official policies of the patriarchate yet accept the sacramental validity of its clergy, and thus resort to those pastors of the official Church whom they personally trust.

[31]As Chernov does not say whether he was present at that conference, he may have heard the story from someone else in a distorted form—perhaps the speaker said simply 52 to 48 percent and the figures became distorted to 52 to 48 million.

Such are the impressions one gains on reading the following major catacomb document of 1970, which begins with the following epigraph:

At a certain time the Faith will fall in Russia. The glamor of terrestrial fame will blind the reason: the Words of Truth will be violated. But people unknown to the world will rise from the midst of the commoners, and they will restore that which had been violated.

> Porfiry, a monk of the Glinskaya Hermitage, in *Pravoslavnaya Tserkov' o pochitanii Imeni Bozh'ego i o molitve Iisusovoi* (St. Petersburg, 1914)

This *samizdat* document, authored by anonymous members of the "Catacomb Church," as the authors identify themselves, condemns the Moscow Patriarchate as a new Judas betraying Jesus and his message while giving him a kiss.[32]

Most of their arguments are theologically valid. First of all, they claim that Sergii's 1927 declaration proclaiming full loyalty to "the new political, social and economic system of the state . . . ignores . . . the significance of ideology in the new state." The authors quite rightly argue that the attempts in the official statements of the Moscow Patriarchal clergy to separate the Soviet state from the Communist Party are wholly artificial, for the Party rules and dominates the government, and its ideology is militantly atheistic. Therefore, loyalty to the regime without specifying its limits means loyalty to an ideology whose aim is the destruction of the Church.

Secondly, every believer, especially a neophyte, in the Soviet Union lives with an acute sensation of conflict between the teachings of Christ, on the one hand, and the policies of the Moscow Patriarchate and the behavior of its clergy, on the other. This leads either to his disappointment in the Church or to the accept-

---

[32]"Rossiya i tserkov' segodnya" (apparently written in 1970 because it mentions Aleksii as dead—he died in 1970—and Pimen as metropolitan—he was elected patriarch in the spring of 1971), AS 892.

ance of a life of duplicity, which is incompatible with the Christian conscience.

Thirdly, because the bishops are foremost in making fraudulent declarations about freedom of religion in the USSR and appeals to the laity to support the Soviet regime in its "humanist" struggle for peace, etc., therefore "the flock . . . often does not trust its bishops." The clergy respond by overt appeals in their sermons to the faithful: "It is none of your business to judge the bishops. . . . Your business is to pray, that's all." This contradicts the basic canons of Orthodoxy, which have "always emphasized active participation *of the laity* in the life and direction of the Church."

This duality, moreover, pervades even the upper clergy of the patriarchate. While declaring their total loyalty and practicing complete submission to the regime, they vehemently reject such terms as "Soviet Church" or "a Soviet bishop," maintaining that they are *Russian* bishops of the *Russian* Church—thereby confirming the dichotomy and the incompatibility between a Church and the Soviet state.

The authors of the document also argue that by maintaining in official declarations that there is no persecution of the Church in the Soviet Union, the patriarchate is actively betraying the martyrs of the Soviet era, and hence Christ himself, in defense of whose name people have suffered martyrdom.[33]

In 1927, receiving a Leningrad delegation of believers, Metropolitan Sergii arrogantly told them: "Yes, I am saving the Church." The document challenges this statement on two grounds. First, it is not an organization of bishops but Jesus Christ himself who is saving the Church in Russia, because the very survival of religion and the appearance of believers among the young generation is nothing short of a miracle. This repeats the old controversy between the Sergiites and their opponents. Sergii saw the necessity of at least a skeleton central organization for church survival, while his opponents argued that the Church has survived by the strength and purity of faith of her believers and by the will

---

[33]See the same accusations against Sergii in 1927, in chapter 4 above. Lately, however, some clerics of the Moscow Patriarchate have made public statements on the "sixty years . . . of suffering . . . and trials" resulting in "thousands of new saints." Fr. Borovoi, sermon at the London Russian Orthodox cathedral (July 1978), in *Russkoe vozrozhdenie*, no. 9 (1980) 40-2.

of God—she could survive without any central body, organization-
ally destroyed but consolidated in the believers' unity in the faith.
This is the crucial point made by the catacomb Church. The
second argument is that in the conditions of complete submission
to the secular authorities and their orders, aimed at the destruction
of the Church, the clergy does not fulfil even minimal pastoral
duties. For example, they often refuse to baptize children brought
to the church by collective farmers over a distance of hundreds of
miles, only because the parents or godparents have no passports,
which must be recorded in the church book according to the
Soviet laws.[34] Owing to the existing laws, the Church and her
clergy are precluded from any religious-educational or enlighten-
ing activities to the extent that "the average Soviet citizen today
does not even know who Christ is; as to the Trinity, he has never
even heard of it." Far from saving the Church, "the duplicity of
the patriarchate is a barrier preventing many a pure soul from
joining the Church." And groups of lay believers "write innumer-
able complaints and requests to open churches for worship . . . but
has there been at least a single case when the patriarchate supported their pleas?"

Finally, representatives of the patriarchate, according to the
document, justify their double-dealing by saying that "if everybody went underground, who would cater to the faithful?" The
document argues that, in practice, this

> hierarchy, having refused to join the "catacombs," has
> become . . . isolated. It is alien to the people. . . . The
> modern Soviet man, doped by vodka and political indoc-
> trination, looks at the churches indifferently, not expecting
> anything out of them which might give him some warmth
> and disclose the truth to him. Such a voice is absent when
> man thirsts after it, tired of the lies surrounding him.

This isolation of the clergy from the people and the policy of

[34]"Rossiya i tserkov' segodnya," 9. Collective farmers are the only category of
the Soviet population without regular passports—they may receive them only by
the will of the farm administration when, with its permission, they leave the farm
for any length of time. The authors, obviously, refer to extreme cases because the
practice of unofficial, unregistered baptisms is very widespread, according to all
our sources.

submission leads to serious theological incompatibilities. The Church is identified with the hierarchy, i.e., with the concept of *organization;* and this hierarchy justifies its inaction when the Church is attacked by saying: "Our Kingdom is not of this world." But, "when objections are raised against the compromises with the prince of this world, the response is that this is necessary to preserve the hierarchical succession, open parishes, etc.—i.e., the external organization of the Church."

The document says that even representatives of the official Church justify the duplicity of their hierarchs as but a bridge that will allow the Church to cross over into the eventual conditions of freedom. But, the document maintains this duality cannot last long: "Either there will be a triumph of an integral religious consciousness, or church consciousness as such will disappear." The authors believe that the Church will survive to the day of freedom, when both the Moscow Patriarchate and the catacomb Church will present their cases to an all-Russian sobor.

The arguments and erudition of this document do not fit into the standard Soviet propaganda depictions of the True Orthodox Church as a bunch of illiterate and fanatical obscurantists dreaming of the monarchy. In fact, the document emphatically states that "we are not idealizing either the synodal Church [i.e., the tsarist past], the Church of Muscovy or the Byzantine Church . . . the Church and the state are different by nature and will always remain as alien to each other as the Church and the world. Therefore, every alliance between the Church and the state is unnatural."

However, there are some marked inconsistencies in the document as well. On the one hand, its tone is one of no compromise with the Patriarchal Church. On the other, it says that had not the Communist Party been restrained by the necessity to impress the world with its tolerance, it would have "annihilated in a moment . . . [even] Metropolitans Pimen and Nikodim." In other words, despite all their compromises, bishops of the official Church work *for the Church,* not for the communists. Then it admits that there are decent bishops in the official Church, that "the church consciousness tries to find its true spokesmen among the higher clergy" and that neophytes join the Church by seeking baptism and spiritual guidance from priests in the official Church who: "On the one hand . . . pursue the patriarchate's loyal policy toward the state. . . . On the other hand, subjecting themselves to all sorts of dangers . . . secretly help to bring people to the Church, lend religious literature to them. Therefore, a truly religious life in fact always takes 'catacomb' forms."[35]

Thus, contrary to the rest of the text, these lines testify that the official Church cannot be reduced to the appellation of a Judas, that in search of religion the seeking person does turn to the clergy of the official Church (as the only salient one?) and that at least some such clerics reciprocate. In other words, the document implicitly grants the Sergiite Church a positive role in society. Moreover, in its extended interpretation of "catacombs" it turns the term into a qualitative, not an institutional, term, granting its applicability also to the more pastorally conscientious clergy of the Patriarchal Church,[36] in agreement with what has been said earlier.

We have also seen that by the 1960s, owing to the growing shortage of clergy in the catacomb Church, her adherents were advised by a bishop of apparently Metropolitan Kirill's persuasion to seek out honest and dedicated priests in the official Church and accept them as their spiritual fathers and pastors.[37] Thus, nearly two decades after Bishop Afanasii's (Sakharov) exhortation to catacomb Christians to return to the Patriarchal Church under Aleksii, the anonymous catacomb bishop offers the same advice, although in a somewhat more cautious form. The "catacombers" are told, as it were, to retain their underground cells and groups, but to accept the sacraments from the Patriarchal Church as individuals. In other words, the implied suggestion is to keep the underground group in case of need, in case of another wave of persecutions against the visible Church, and/or perhaps to retain informal embryonic Christian communities in lieu of the needed genuine parish life, which is impossible in the overt churches under the current Soviet laws.

[35]"Rossiya i tserkov' segodnya," 8 and 10-1. Metropolitan Pimen is, of course, the current patriarch.

[36]Fresh from the Soviet Union, the Russian Christian writer Vladimir Maksimov stated that insofar as a clergyman of the Moscow Patriarchate conscientiously fulfils his pastoral duties, he works in the catacombs—because he inevitably breaks the Soviet law that allows him no pastoral functions other than the performance of the liturgy. Interview by Gleb Rahr in *Posev*, no. 4 (1974) 11.

[37]Regelson, 192-3. The letter is dated 1962.

The above-cited document implicitly, if reluctantly, testifies to the fact that in the early 1970s such a partial fusion or inter-penetration between the catacombs and the official Church was continuing. Another illustration of this process is three *samizdat* letters, two of them addressed directly to the émigré Synod, or the "Russian Orthodox Church Abroad," as it officially calls itself. In fact, these are the only catacomb documents treating the Synod as their supreme ecclesiastic authority known to this author. This fact in itself casts doubt on the overoptimistic estimates regarding the size of the catacombs and, even more so, regarding the alleged canonical connection between the catacombs and the émigré Synod.[38] But to return to these documents, one of them is signed by "Christians of the Russian Orthodox Church," by which is clearly meant the contemporary Patriarchal Church, because the signatories speak about the Patriarchal episcopate as *their own,* although they criticize its weakness vis-à-vis the atheistic regime. They mention the Moscow Theological Academy as an institution of *the* Russian Orthodox Church. There is no mention in the document of any separate clandestine Church, but the position is that the Patriarchal Church in Russia and the "Russian Church Abroad" constitute one single Russian Orthodox Church.[39] Another letter lauds the émigré Synod and its episcopate as *the* episcopate of the Russian Church. But then it maintains that there is only an "external break between the 'Karlovtsy' and the 'Patri-archal' churches," and further: "Not only the martyred and sincere Sister, the catacomb Church, looks with love and gratitude at the Russian Orthodox Church Outside Russia, but also some lay people as well as clerics of the Moscow Patriarchate."[40]

A document similar in tone, although not addressed to the émigré Synod, signed by a "Group of Russian Believers" and written on the eve of the sobor of 1971, demands that the patri-

[38]Chernov says that "The catacomb Church looks up with hope toward the Russian Church Abroad'" (44). The above-cited monk likewise said that those of the catacombers who categorically refuse to recognize the validity of the Moscow Patriarchate regard the émigré Synod as their authority.

[39]The letter is dated 1966 and is addressed "To the Archpastors of the Russian Church Abroad." See AS 726.

[40]The authenticity of this letter is somewhat suspect, for it was disseminated by the "Department of Foreign Relations" of the émigré Synod and has never been mentioned in any *samizdat* documents. It was published in *Russkaya mysl'*, no. 3143 (March 17, 1977).

arch be elected in accordance with the procedures and canons of the 1917-1918 Sobor. Thus, the authors act as a voice from within the official Church. On the other hand, not inconsistently with the above, they criticize Western Christians for finding excuses for the Sergiite Moscow Patriarchate's policies and for supporting the patriarchate.[41] This is a dichotomy typical of the borderline "catacombers." But all these documents indicate that the majority of the catacomb Christians are within the official Russian Orthodox Church in the USSR, forming an internal opposition to the patriarchate's policies rather than one from outside it and wholly separated from it.[42] It could not be otherwise, for no matter how clandestine the catacombs were, had they really been an institution apart from the Patriarchal Church in the proportion claimed by Chernov (52:48), close to half of all the practicing Orthodox Christians among the current emigration wave from the Soviet Union would have been members of that institution. In actual fact, to the best of our knowledge, of the several thousand Orthodox Christians who have recently emigrated, Chernov is the only one who belonged to the real underground Church. Others vehemently reject even the existence of such a "catacomb Church," or at least maintain that they have never heard of it in the USSR.[43]

Lately, however, apparently under the influence of events in the Baptist Church—where the existence of an unregistered parallel church organization forces the authorities to be more lenient and permissive toward the registered, official Baptist Church than, in fact, toward the incomparably larger Orthodox Church[44]—there has developed within the Orthodox Church a school of thought in favor of setting up just such a parallel,

[41]AS 891.

[42]This tallies with our earlier conclusion, but contradicts the official claims of the émigré Synod. See chapter 8 above, pp. 267f, 275f.

[43]Among them is Goricheva, who had lived in the "political underground" and traveled far and wide to monasteries and other places of popular pilgrimages across the country in the years 1975 to 1980. She had never heard about a "catacomb Church" until her arrival in the West.

[44]On the split in the Baptist Church see Michael Bourdeaux, *Religious Ferment in Russia* (London: Macmillan, 1968). On the "privileges" enjoyed by the official Baptists, see our article "The Forty-First All-Union Congress of the Evangelical Baptists of the Soviet Union," *St. Vladimir's Theological Quarterly* 19:4 (1975) 246-53.

unofficial branch of Orthodoxy in the USSR. Advocates of this idea point to the precedent of Patriarch Tikhon, who shortly before his death consecrated many clandestine (substitute) bishops and priests as candidates to replace those who would be arrested. They understand that the registered bishops of the official Moscow Patriarchate would be jeopardizing the fate of the whole official Orthodox Church in the country if they engaged in such massive clandestine activities. So, what is being suggested is that some of the foreign visiting bishops, particularly those of the Orthodox Church in America, should, while in the USSR, ordain or consecrate unofficial (unregistered) clergy. This clergy, free from any control by the CRA, could then engage in missionary activities banned to the official clergy and, in particular, take care of the needs of Christians who live in areas where the Soviets have not permitted the reopening of churches—e.g., large stretches of Siberia and the Far East, especially Kamchatka, where there has not been, as of 1980, a single functioning church, despite repeated petitions from believers. It has been confided to this author by a priest of the Moscow Patriarchate that this idea and hope has lately gained considerable currency in the Soviet Union. Its advocates hope that the appearance of a parallel hierarchy would force the state to be more responsive to the needs of the official Church in order to weaken the raison d'être for such a parallel church organization.[45]

Only the future will show whether these ideas are realizable. But it is quite clear that they have nothing to do with any rejection of the Moscow Patriarchate and do not question the spiritual and canonical validity of that Church.

---

[45]Fr. Gleb Yakunin, "O sovremennom polozhenii russkoi pravoslavnoi tserkvi i perspektivakh religioznogo vozrozhdeniya v Rossii," a report to the Christian Committee for the Defense of Believers in the USSR, in VS, no. 35-36 (1979) 5-78. The other cited source believed that another reason for the greater Soviet tolerance of the Baptists was that the Orthodox Church, as a national historical organism, presents a much greater threat to the communist monopoly of power than does the fringe sect of the Baptists.

CHAPTER 12

The Russian Orthodox Church, 1965-1982

In a formal sense, the most important event in the post-Khrushchev era of the Church was the death of the ninety-two-year-old Patriarch Aleksii in April 1970 and the election of the sixty-one-year-old Metropolitan Pimen (Izvekov) of Krutitsy and Kolomna as the new patriarch at the All-Russian National Sobor of May-June 1971. It was the first time since the revolution that the deceased patriarch had not named a preferred heir in his will. In this sense, Pimen's election was the first formally canonical one since the election of Tikhon in 1917.

Not much can be said on the late patriarch's activities in the last five years of his life. Although direct persecutions subsided after Khrushchev's demise, there is no evidence that the octogenarian patriarch or his Synod in any way overextended themselves to win back the positions, parishes, seminaries and monasteries lost in the preceding five years. In 1967, Metropolitan Pimen, in confidential conversations at the Council for Religious Affairs, described the patriarch as having totally fallen under the control of his private secretary, Daniil Ostapov—a son of a former household serf of the Simanskys (Aleksii's aristocratic parents) who had been a devoted butler to the future patriarch since the days the latter was a college student. According to Pimen, it was Ostapov rather than the patriarch who was now running the Church, making appointments, etc. Pimen described him as an uncouth, arrogant and dishonest man, who had nevertheless subordinated the patriarch to his will, controlled all visits to the patriarch and was almost always present at such visits. "Hence, it is often impossible to have a tête-à-tête conversation with him."[1]

It was hoped that such lethargy in the center would end with the patriarch's death and the convocation of the national sobor. The latter, it was hoped, would be more than a mere formality. Letters and petitions were addressed to the preconciliar commission requesting revision of the 1961 Church Statute amendments so as to return some authority to the parish priest. The best known of these was offered by the then Archbishop of Irkutsk, Venyamin (Novitsky), who even presented a full revised draft Statute on parish administration, which differed from the one imposed on the Church in 1961 only in the following respects: (1) ". . . parish clergy have the right to be members of the 'twenty' and to cosign agreements. They may be elected to parish councils and to its auditing commissions." (2) "The executive organ of the parish community is responsible for its activity to the general parish meeting together with its priest," the connotation being that the priest presides over these meetings, for (3) he is responsible for the "spiritual leadership of the parishioners," and (4) "The executive organ does not interfere" in the spiritual and liturgical activities of the priest, and may forward complaints regarding these only to the diocesan bishop. Finally (5) the hiring and firing of parish employees by the parish executive organ must be coordinated with the parish dean.[2]

[1]Cited by A. Plekhanov (a CRA official), in an internal report on Pimen's visit to the CRA on February 21, 1967, ms. in Keston College Archives, 4-5. Aleksii was so devoted to Ostapov that when he was arrested soon after the war (according to rumors, it was the work of some churchmen surrounding the patriarch who wanted to get rid of Ostapov's influence on him), the patriarch telephoned Stalin and threatened to resign immediately if Ostapov was not released. Stalin complied (!). In 1973 Ostapov, in his eighties by then, was arrested once again on charges of corruption. This time it was Academician Andrei Sakharov who raised a letter campaign on behalf of the old man and secured his release. Levitin, *Ruk tvoikh zhar,* 200-1; "Late Patriarch's Secretary Arrested," *RCL* 2:4-5 (1974) 57. In 1962, when the Orthodox cathedral in Riga was confiscated by the state, this author's informant, an influential Moscow priest, tried to plead with Aleksii to save it, reminding him of his effective action on behalf of Ostapov. But the patriarch refused to make an issue over the cathedral, saying that physical church structures are state property and their closure is the business of the state.

[2]"Proekt redaktsii IV razdela 'Polozheniya ob upravlenii russkoi pravoslavnoi tserkov'yu,' " *VRKhD,* no. 120 (1977) 297-300.

Fr. Yakunin forwarded a petition to the same commission to reinstate him as a priest. This letter was the result of his earlier petition to the then locum tenens Pimen, to which the latter had replied that since it was the late patriarch who had banned him, only a patriarch could restore him to the priesthood; and it was futile to address such a petition to the sobor since it was not a sobor that had interdicted him to start with. Pimen reminded Yakunin that he and his colleague, Fr. Eshliman, in accordance with the patriarchal decree of 1966, would be restored as priests on their repentance. To this Yakunin responded that he had nothing to repent for, and since the ban had not been a canonical measure but a purely administrative one, it should therefore be resolved in an administrative manner.[3]

One of the most controversial petitions to the commission requested a theological scrutiny of Metropolitan Nikodim's concepts of ecumenism, social Christianity and apology of socialism, which the authors—a young priest, Nikolai Gainov, and three laymen (Regelson, Felix Karelin and Viktor Kapitanchuk)—saw as heretical. According to later information, this letter caused the greatest sensation and liveliest discussions between sobor sessions.[4]

In one respect the sobor was modeled in practice on all such formal "democratic" conferences in the USSR (e.g., sessions of the Supreme Soviet, party congresses, etc.): very little more than plain rubber-stamping of unanimous decisions took place at the *open* sessions of the sobor. But it would be wrong to conclude that the sobor was entirely insignificant, or that the unanimous, open election of the patriarch, with only one candidate permitted

[3]*Veche*, no. 5 (May 25, 1972), reprinted in *VS*, no. 9-10 (1973) 65-70.

[4]Along with Nikodim, they also criticized Fr. Vitaly Borovoi and his theory of revolutionary Christianity and Christian social action. See *Veche*, no. 2 (May 19, 1971), AS 1020, 33-47. Among other addresses to the sobor was one signed by a young Moscow priest, Georgy Petukhov, Hierodeacon Varsonofy (Khaibulin) and a layman, which treated the Soviet persecution of religion as one phenomenon with the materialistic and anti-Christian offensive in the West— both of which were unleashed by the "forces of broad Zionism and Satanism." The constructive part of the letter demanded the reopening of churches, seminaries and monasteries, the right to teach religion to willing children and adults and broad rights for Christians in the Soviet Union to publish and preach Christianity, which alone could save the country from moral decay. *Veche*, no. 3 (September 19, 1971), AS 1108, 62-7.

at the sobor itself,[5] was an essentially meaningless formality.

First of all, there was at least some probing of the ecclesiastical public opinion by the Soviet government prior to making its choice known to the bishops. Apparently, the government at first had three candidates in mind: Metropolitans Nikodim of Leningrad, Pimen of Krutitsy and Iosif (Chernov) of Alma-Ata and Kazakhstan. It seems that Nikodim (as the above-mentioned petition illustrates) was perceived as too controversial a figure to command undivided authority among the church people.[6] According to a reliable Russian church source, Nikodim at first was a very serious candidate, but then, after negotiations (apparently with the CRA), he decided to decline the honor. Unaware of a rapid decline in his health, he was hoping to achieve more for the Church by remaining at the head of her foreign relations and by building up new cadres of well-educated clergy through the seminary and academy of his diocese, leaving the largely ceremonial post to the less-controversial Pimen. Indeed, the consecrations of most of the new bishops in the 1960s and 1970s were performed by Nikodim, and a majority of them had gone through the Leningrad theological schools.

The then seventy-eight-year-old Iosif (1893-1975) turned down the offer, made by the Kazakhstan CRA, on the grounds that he was too old and possessed only a primary education. As he put it, "I don't want to be the object of criticism in the Synod for ignorance, and to be forced to accept their opinions simply because they are theologians, while I am uneducated and must obey them." This bishop had spent some twenty years in Soviet prisons and concentration camps, eleven of them for having functioned as the ruling bishop of Rostov-on-Don under the German occupation, although he had constantly been in trouble with the Germans for his loyalty to Metropolitan Sergii of Moscow and for offering public prayers for him even after Sergii had

[5]Archbishop Vasily (Krivocheine), "Interview," *Episkepsis,* no. 35 (July 20, 1971) 10-1.

[6]Evidence of such probing is presented by the "confidential" CRA report on a conversation with Aleksii, Archbishop of Tallin and Estonia (February 20, 1967), in which he says that Pimen is an inactive conservative bishop, while Nikodim is very active and powerful but his ways are too radical for the conservative bishops of the older generation and the laity. These elements, as well as the patriarch, would prefer to see Pimen as the future patriarch.

been elected patriarch and had issued a condemnation of bishops collaborating with the Germans. To the very last day of his life, Iosif commanded tremendous popularity among the faithful, and showed considerable independence in running his huge diocese, removing morally unsuitable clergy and supporting popular priests. Over two thousand Moscow believers and clergy had allegedly signed a personal petition begging him to accept the patriarchal candidacy and admonishing him that he would answer before God at the last judgment if he refused, but all in vain.[7]

All this represents sufficient evidence that the secular Soviet authorities did take the popularity of a bishop positively into account when considering candidates for the patriarchal see— Iosif, with all his past martyrdom and ecclesiastic intransigence, could not have been too endearing to them. We do not know if any other candidates were considered by the secular powers. Most probably not. Their criteria must have included a certain measure of spiritual popularity, so the candidate would not arouse suspicions in the eyes of the flock as to his religious integrity and would not be dubbed a KGB agent. Other criteria must have included a certain malleability and educational or personal defects, which would make the candidate "bendable." In the case of Iosif, there was little malleability, but the Soviet authorities must have hoped that, being very old and uneducated, he could be pressed by the weight of the erudition of his "advisers," who were controlled by the CRA.

In the case of the then sixty-one-year-old Pimen, there was what even those Russian churchmen who have spoken kindly of him term "excessive fear of the Soviet government authorities." Behind this fear is a checkered and controversial past of prisons and exile and rumors of having an illegitimate family and affairs with women on the side. These, however, appear to be nothing more than rumors, for smuggled out, confidential inside CRA documents, based on oral reports to the council by Archbishop (now Metropolitan) Aleksii (Ridiger) of Tallin present this information as rumors, and there is no direct evidence of any further investigation.[8]

[7]See Archbishop Vasily's obituary on Iosif, "Pamyati episkopa-ispovednika," *VRKhD*, no. 116 (1975) 225-9.
[8]Ibid. Aleksii of Tallin stated that Ostapov may have been using these rumors against Pimen. Should they be accurate, it would be fair to remember that in the

What is more surprising is that a biographical note on Pimen by the same council is full of inconsistencies. It says that in the 1930s Pimen had spent three years in Soviet prisons, followed by two years as a sanitary instructor in Uzbekistan, apparently in post-prison exile, and three years in the Soviet armed forces during World War II, where he rose to the rank of major. Then, allegedly, he spent the years 1944 and 1945 in prison again, returning to the priesthood and monasticism in 1946. The obvious incongruency is that the document claims that his last imprisonment was for desertion and that in 1945 he was released under a general amnesty. This is complete nonsense, for the only punishment for deserters, particularly a senior officer, in wartime was execution. Moreover, the 1945 amnesty did not cover deserters.[9] It is indeed surprising that this fantastic story could appear and remain uncorrected in an internal state document. However, what is really compromising to Pimen in this document is the allegation that over the years Pimen had given different and contradictory information about his past in various *vita* forms he had to complete on different occasions, revealing attempts to conceal some biographical facts from the state.

It was apparently these facts that made it possible for the CROCA-CRA to "hook" him. A CRA report, written apparently around late 1963 or early 1964, complains that Pimen shuns all contacts with the CROCA (in contrast to Aleksii Ridiger, who appears to have been the CRA's regular informant on internal church affairs), but the very next day after Archbishop Aleksii's report of February 20, 1967, Pimen "visited the council on his own initiative," assured it of his most sincere loyalty, gave the most detailed information on inside life and human relations in

1930s Pimen had no access either to a monastery or to service in the Church, being haunted and alternating between prisons and internal exile. Only a man of steel, endowed with a martyr's spiritual powers, would be able to preserve monastic chastity in these conditions.

[9] A. Plekhanov, "Spravka na M. Leningradskogo . . . Pimena," CROCA internal information on Pimen, then still Metropolitan of Leningrad (1964?) 1-2. According to Levitin's oral testimony to this author, Pimen had served in the Political Department of the Soviet Army in World War II, rising to the rank of major before the authorities discovered who he was. What was scandalous and led to his expulsion from the armed forces and incarceration was that a monk and a priest could become a Soviet *political* officer.

the patriarchate and expressed readiness to cooperate fully.[10] Archbishop Aleksii characterized Pimen as a man without will, initiative or administrative talents, lazy and easily influenced by other people's opinions. At the same time, he said, Pimen was a very impressive liturgist and was liked by the flock for his prayerful services. It was, apparently, these priestly qualities, combined with some blemishes in his biography and the lack of personal leadership qualities, that made him an "ideal" nominal patriarch in the eyes of the Soviets. Their caution in nominating a patriarchal candidate acceptable to the believers may be illustrated by the words of one Russian monk very negatively inclined toward the regime. He said to this author: "We chose Pimen for his piety and religious sincerity, not for any intellectual or leadership qualities." In other words, the selection appeared to him so natural that he thought of it as the real choice of the faithful.

The sobor, as we have said, was a rubber-stamping show of unanimity fully in accord with the Soviet tradition. Indeed, how could the authorities permit real democracy at a church council? Would not the Church then appear much more attractive to the nation than the state, the Party and their forums? But, according to Archbishop Vasily (Basil) of Brussels, who participated in the sobor, what it rubber-stamped were decisions adopted at the council of bishops that had directly preceded the sobor and at which real debate and discussion had taken place. Only bishops were present at that council, and the discussion was relatively free.[11]

[10]A. Plekhanov, "Spravka o besede . . . s Pimenom," a report on a conversation with Pimen held on February 21, 1967 and dated March 31, 1966 (Keston College Archives).

[11]The disgraced bishops Pavel (Golyshev) and Ermogen (Golubev) were prevented from attending both the council of bishops and the national sobor. Both had criticized the 1961 decisions and had given written support to the Eshliman-Yakunin memoranda of 1965. Both had run afoul of the local CROCA and CRA plenipotentiaries, whereupon Pavel was moved from the Novosibirsk archdiocese to Vologda, and Ermogen from Tashkent to Kaluga and eventually into forced retirement in the Zhirovitsy Monastery. Pavel had protested his appointment to the tiny diocese of Vologda with its seventeen parishes and requested the right to return to France (he was a postwar repatriate), which eventually was granted. In 1967 Ermogen had stated to Archbishop Aleksii that as a retired bishop he had the full right to participate in the future sobor, and that in this opinion he was supported by other bishops. See *Spravka* (April 1967); Archbishop Ermogen's

Some bishops (mostly from the West, but not exclusively so) insisted on a secret ballot for the election of the patriarch, saying that this alone would give the newly elected patriarch the necessary authority and credence. But most of the Russian bishops responded to this that *in the given circumstances* Pimen was the only appropriate candidate available in the over-fifty age group of bishops, and the people of Russia simply would not accept a patriarch of a younger age. Therefore, even a secret ballot would result in the election of Pimen, while open voting would give, according to them, more popular confidence in the unanimity of the church leadership. This, however, was a "doctored" opinion, because originally most of the bishops, in particular the members of the Synod, had strongly opposed Pimen's candidacy, suspecting him of being a CRA agent.[12] This must have been the ultimate reason why no secret ballot was allowed.

memorandum of December 25, 1967, "K 50-letiyu vosstanovleniya patriarshestva" (AS 751), in which he argues that the 1945 Sobor had illegally changed a number of very important regulations of the 1917 Sobor, and requests frequent convocations of *regular sobors*. On Pavel, see *VRSKhD*, no. 103 (1972) 173-4 and no. 104-105 (1972) 166; on Ermogen, see *VRSKhD*, no. 86 (1967) 61-5 and no. 87-88 (1968) 8-14. Ermogen's obituary in *ZhMP* (no. 11 [1978] 21) only mentions that he died in retirement, omitting any of his actions from 1963, when he was removed from Tashkent, until his death in 1978. The other gap in his *ZhMP* biography, from 1931 to 1945, indicates that he had spent most of those years in prisons and/or punitive exile. There was, however, a report in *ZhMP* (no. 4 [1969]) on a July 1968 Synod session at which Ermogen was present and was subjected to criticism for "activities harmful to the . . . Church."

[12]See Fridrikh Neznansky, "Taina patriarkha," *Novyi amerikanets*, no. 98 (December 25-31, 1981) 18-21. While the paper, America's only Jewish Russian-language weekly, is rather sensationalist, the author, a former Soviet criminal investigator, has proved himself rather responsible in his other publications in the West. His story is about alleged corruption and the disappearance of hundreds of thousands of rubles from the patriarchate's treasury, which he was ordered by the state procuracy to investigate. The aim of the Soviets was to accuse Bishop Pitirim, who at the time allegedly had been the Synod's choice for the patriarchal throne. But as soon as Neznansky's investigation led him away from Pitirim and straight to Pimen, then Metropolitan of Krutitsy, he was ordered by no lesser a body than the CPSU Central Committee to stop his investigation, and the whole case was hushed up. At the Central Committee he was informed that Pimen was their choice for the patriarchal see, but the Synod was resisting this, when he was suspecting the metropolitan of being an agent for the regime. The CC official assured Neznansky that this was not so—although Pimen was a 100 percent friend of the Soviets, and hence they preferred him to Pitirim. It was necessary to compromise Pitirim in order to force the Synod to give in to Soviet pressures to have Pimen nominated as the candidate in case of the death of the ninety-year-old Aleksii. The story leaves a shadow of doubt. First, Neznansky does not mention the

The other issue discussed at the bishops' council at great length was the 1961 Statute and the possibility and desirability of its abrogation or revision. The leading bishops, however, responded that although the Statute was far from ideal, and indeed some provisions contradicted the canons, it had not caused as much harm as anticipated, thanks "to the wisdom of the priests and of the laity." Moreover, it corresponded to the state laws on religion of 1929 and therefore the state would not permit any amendments, viewing all such attempts "as hostile to the state." What surprised Vasily was that the bishops who were known to have been critical of the 1961 Statute, including Venyamin (Novitsky), remained silent during these debates. Venyamin later confided to Vasily that he and other authors of memos suggesting amendments to the 1961 Statute had been deceived by the preconciliar commission, having been told that there would be no debate on the subject, because since the Statute corresponded to the state laws, it could not be changed. Kuroedov's deputy, Makartsev, warned: "Whoever tries to resist the decrees on the parishes will get his leg broken." To the question why the archbishop did not join the discussion once he saw that it was taking place, the seventy-one-year-old Venyamin replied: "I had spent twelve years in the concentration camps of Kolyma. It is beyond my powers to repeat the experience at my age. Forgive me!" Venyamin, however, added that the situation in the parishes was often almost catastrophic, owing to the virtually limitless powers of the lay executive councils over the priest and the parishes. At their last encounter (Archbishop Venyamin died in 1975), two years after the sobor, Venyamin confided to Vasily that the situation in the parishes was "becoming worse and worse . . . [the civil authorities] are interfering everywhere, appointing their people to all positions."[13] Thus differed the sincere opinion of this

date of the event; and second, Pitirim has recommended himself from the beginning of his episcopal service to the present day as exceptionally docile and subservient to the regime. Hence, it is doubtful that the Synod really wanted him that much, and it is equally unclear why the regime would have put up such a fight for Pimen over Pitirim.

[13]Vasily in *Episkepsis;* and "Arkhiepiskop Venyamin (Novitsky), 1900-1976," *VRKhD,* no. 120 (1977) 289-94. It is surprising that Vasily accepts the argument of the nonavailability of other likely popular candidates among bishops over fifty years of age, apparently ignoring Archbishops Mikhail (Mudyugin) and

highly revered and experienced martyr-bishop from the optimistic assurances Archbishop Vasily had received from other bishops at the council sessions.

The other issues that were debated at the pre-sobor council were the degree of permissible participation of the Moscow Patriarchate in the peace campaign and the necessity of any new measures against the Karlovci schism. On the former issue, some criticism was expressed of "the political coloring" of the patriarchate's role in the peace campaigns.[14] On the Karlovcians, Metropolitan Anthony (Bloom) of England made an impassioned appeal for moderation at the main sobor, effecting important changes in the final sobor documents in relation to the originally militant attack on the Karlovcians by the late Metropolitan Nikodim[15] and restraining the sobor from issuing a final condemnation of the post-Karlovcian Synod. This was as close as the sobor ever approximated any expression of differences in the open.

One of the most important decisions of the preparatory council of bishops, the initiative of which, according to rumors, came from Nikodim, was the lifting of all interdicts (excommunication) from the Old Believers. No doubt, on this issue the unanimity at the bishops' council and the national sobor was genuine.

Archbishop Vasily stressed that it was stated that the decision to have only one official patriarchal candidate and to elect him by an open ballot related to this sobor alone and was not meant as a precedent-setting event binding on future sobors. The implication of this was that the participants had no choice this time, but were hopeful of better times to come, when proper *sobornost'* could be reinstated in the Church.

The Status of the Church in the Brezhnev Era

The first ever publication of the CRA Statute in 1966 and of the amendments to the state laws on "religious associations" in

Mikhail (Chub), or Leonid (currently Metropolitan of Riga), to name but a few. It seems that they were simply politically unacceptable to the CRA.

[14]Vasily, in *Episkepsis.*

[15]*Dokumenty: Pomestnyi sobor russkoi pravoslavnoi tserkvi* (Moscow, 1972) 179-80. Characteristically, Anthony's speech was not published in the selected proceedings of the sobor that appeared in the relevant issues of *ZhMP.*

1975 showed that Khrushchev's harsh oppression of the Church was not meant to be discontinued by the Brezhnev regime, only to take more civilized forms. One of the expressions of this was published laws in place of secret instructions. The CRA Statute turned that body from a liaison agency between the Church and the government, as allegedly formulated by Stalin,[16] into "an organ . . . of control over the Moscow Patriarchate," as exemplified by the following excerpts from its articles:

(3) The CRA . . .

   b. Supervises the observance of the legislation on cults by religious organizations or servants of the cult . . .

   e. Examines and decides . . . questions connected with the activities of religious organizations in the USSR . . .

(4) The CRA has the right:

   a. To make decisions . . . on registration and removal of registration of religious associations, on opening and closing prayer houses . . .

   b. To verify the activity of religious associations in their observance of the Soviet legislation on cults and to issue compulsory orders for eliminating violations of them."[17]

Undoubtedly, it was helpful for the Church that the official prerogatives, functions and responsibilities of the CRA had at last become known to her. Unfortunately, however, as the 1962/1975 amendments to the legislation on religious associations confirm, the transfer of many of the controlling functions over religious bodies from the local soviets to the CRA has made it more difficult for the believers to fight for their rights. Earlier, when only the soviets could withdraw registration and close a religious community, the latter would appeal for help to a *differ-*

[16]See above in chapter 6.
[17]Walter Sawatsky, "Statute of the CRA," *RCL* 4:4 (1976) 31-4.

ent body, the CROCA/CRA, an *intermediary* between the Church and the state—i.e., at least technically a neutral body. Now they have to appeal to the same body that has been persecuting or oppressing them.

When the amendments to the laws on religion, which aligned the laws with the CRA Statute prerogatives, were at last made public in 1975, one of their most negative aspects became apparent: they made the procedure of opening a new house of prayer much more bureaucratically cumbersome. In the past, a religious association had to apply to a local soviet, which had to either grant the permission or give a written refusal within one month (article 7). Now, to begin with, a religious association may not even begin to submit any applications to the local soviets before the CRA has given it permission to register (article 4). The new article 7 gives no time limit to the local soviet, which, however, cannot make the final decision—it must forward the petition to higher state authorities, which must, within one month, "make their recommendations to the CRA." The final decision belongs to the CRA, which again is under no time limit. Formerly, articles 37 and 44 gave religious associations the right to appeal. This is no longer mentioned in the 1975 legislation. Now only the CRA has the right to make a decision to close a church, and it is to this body again that a religious association may appeal. The right of the state to remove individual members from the executive body of a religious association and the old limits on church activities remain unchanged. The new revisions specifically forbid even voluntary church collections among parish members outside church walls and require "special permission from regional or city soviets for services held outside and also in . . . the homes of believers."

The positive points for the Church in these revisions are the approximation of the Church to the status of a legal person and the removal of regulations on how delegates to ecclesiastical conventions are to be elected. As Walter Sawatsky, the Keston College authority on religious legislation in communist states, points out, "Procedures for electing delegates are now left to the canonical rules of religious bodies, although the law specifies that participants must be persons of good will." As to evolution toward the status of a legal person, the new articles 3 and 20 omit the phrase stating that religious associations do not have the rights of a legal person, and specifically add that they "have the right to acquire church utensils, cult objects, means of transport; to rent, construct and purchase buildings for their needs in accordance with established legal procedure." This revision had been preceded by the 1945 letter of the then head of the CROCA, Georgy Karpov, to Patriarch Aleksii (mentioned in chapter 6) granting religious associations certain property acquisition rights, which is now confirmed and extended to parishes as well in the newly revised article 3.[18] The irony of these revisions is that the Church and the individual parishes have acquired the right to own any houses except the houses of prayer—i.e., the church buildings themselves, which remain the property of the state, on lease to religious associations. The logic behind this limitation is perfectly clear: to prevent a large-scale reopening of churches and to retain for the state the right to close and confiscate them at any time.

As we shall see later, Fr. Gleb Yakunin has taken a totally negative view of the 1976 legislation's centralizing thrust. But the general opinion of the Russian clergy is that in practice, with the growing decline of centralized party discipline and with the proportional growth of arbitrary rule by local party officials, the real status of the Church varies from diocese to diocese, and very much depends on the personalities of the local bishop and even of the parish priest, on the one hand, and of the local party and CRA officials and on the personal relations between them and the clergy, on the other. Hence, it seems, both the pessimistic assessment of the situation by the late Archbishop Venyamin and the more optimistic assurances at the council of bishops were correct.

[18]See the full text of these amendments in *Vedomosti verkhovnogo soveta RSFSR*, no. 27 [873] (July 3, 1975) 487-91. See also appendix 6 below, pp. 493ff. In the text above, we have used Sawatsky's excellent summary translation of the amendments and his elaboration on them (4-10). As of 1981, we have been informed by a Moscow Patriarchate source that the Church is actively engaged in negotiations with the state, pressing for full legal person status. In his lectures on the Church under the Soviets delivered at the Leningrad Theological Academy, the late Metropolitan Nikodim always stressed that as long as the Church did not enjoy the status of a legal person, she remained without any effective rights, completely at the mercy of the state. The implication for his students was that their primary aim as churchmen would be to struggle for such a status, without which all forms of protest were quite futile. This facet adds an important corrective to Fr. Shpiller's above-cited observations on the submissiveness of the new bishops.

A general complaint of both the dissidents and the clerics of the Moscow Patriarchate concerns the general docility of the bishops and their tendency to excuse their passivity by attributing everything to "God's will." But the very same sources make a distinction between such passive bishops and the ones who really put up an externally invisible struggle for the Church. They warn, however, against drawing attention to the positive bishops, except for those who have died or whose activities have become generally known. Otherwise, publicity can harm them, because most of their work is done quietly, either in informal personal dealings with state officials or in instructing the laity on how to fight for their church or strive for permission to open a new one. Legally, bishops and priests have no right to give such instructions, let alone initiate the formation of a group of twenty or engage in charity or youth work. All initiative must come from the laity. Yet, for instance, the late Metropolitan Nikodim of Leningrad engaged in all these activities. He instructed laymen how to form groups of twenty and how to fight for the opening of churches. He readily received young people in search of God, and he generously gave financial help to those in need, particularly theology students and their families, but also needy believers. This is how the Leningrad churchmen explain the fact that, on his death in 1978, the forty-nine-year-old metropolitan left the diocese nearly half a million rubles in debt. This information is indirectly confirmed by V. Furov, the CRA deputy chairman in a 1978(?) secret report to the CPSU Central Committee on the state of the Church over the preceding decade. A considerable part of the report deals with the ruling bishops of the Russian Orthodox Church, mentioning by name and categorizing fifty-seven of them.[19]

Russian clerics indicate that all such reports and information have to be taken with a grain of salt. After a bishop has been

[19]We date the report as probably 1978 because, although the information given covers roughly the period from 1967 to September 1975, it mentions both Mstislav and Bogolep as ruling bishops of Kirov. Mstislav died in 1978, and the next incumbent was Bogolep. The sloppiness of the report is remarkable. See VRKhD, no. 130 (1979) 275-344, particularly 278-9.

Yakunin says that at his death Nikodim was found to possess one million rubles in cash (taken by the state bank and thus most likely lost for the Church) and left the archdiocese over 300,000 rubles in debt. "O sovremennom polozhenii russkoi pravoslavnoi tserkvi," 24.

consecrated and appointed to a diocese, he is informally advised by the patriarchate that, on arrival at his diocesan center, he should pay his first visit to the local CRA plenipotentiary and tactfully present some valuable gifts to him. His whole future career, as well as his ability to serve the interests of the Church, may depend almost entirely on the relations he establishes with the plenipotentiary: on how tactful, discreet and at the same time generous he will be in bribing him. If the relations are cordial, the diocese may prosper, new parishes may open, new ordinations of good priests may take place, while the plenipotentiary will report the opposite to his superiors: that churches are being closed, atheistic work is effective and the bishop cooperates with or does not resist the activities of the CRA and of the atheists. Conversely, negative reports on a bishop do not automatically mean that the given bishop is particularly effective in his work for the Church (although more often than not there may be an element of truth in them)—they may just as well simply reflect a quarrel between the plenipotentiary and the bishop, the refusal of the latter to properly bribe or gratify the plenipotentiary or his lack of tact and discretion in doing so.

For the same reasons, no church statistics are reliable in the USSR. The patriarchate has no way of protecting its files from the eyes of CRA agents, and hence a good bishop would rather not submit detailed and wholly accurate information on his diocese to the patriarchate. Meanwhile, it is in the interest of each local plenipotentiary and of the CRA as a whole to report a general decline in the numbers of active parishes, in attendance at services, etc.[20] This accounts for great differences in the various reports on church statistics.

For whatever it is worth, the 1972 inside figures of the patriarchate claimed 6,850 officially registered churches and 6,180 officially registered, functioning Orthodox priests across the USSR. According to our source, since then, because of the rapid decline of the rural population and the near impossibility of opening additional churches in the swelling urban areas, there

[20]Fr. Tivetsky's oral testimony, confirmed by other Soviet Russian clerics. It has been reported that in order to be received by Trushin, the CRA plenipotentiary for the Moscow province, his deputy must be generously bribed. See L. Sergeeva, "V tiskakh sistemy," *Posev*, no. 7 (1981) 32. Unscrupulous bribe-taking by Trushin and other CRA officials is confirmed by Neznansky (see n. 12 above).

may have been a further slight decline in the number of open churches in the course of the 1970s. The number of priests, however, has been steadily growing since the second half of the 1970s. The figure for total priestly ordinations in 1979, for instance, was at least 276, but it may have been as high as over 400, depending on the criteria used for calculation. Since then the figure for annual ordinations has continued to grow. To calculate the minimum figure the data shown in table 12-1, supplied by members of the Russian Church, have been used.

TABLE 12-1
NEW PRIESTS ORDAINED IN 1979

Leningrad Seminary and Academy	76
Moscow Seminary and Academy	approx. 100
Odessa Seminary	over 50
home-educated	at least 50
Total	at least 276

A dissident source, however, claimed that in the same year some 200 persons of secular-intellectual background, with numerous Jewish converts among them, were ordained priests without having gone to seminaries.[21] Should this be true, it would augment the "home-educated" from 50 to at least 200 ordinations, and the total to at least 426. A well-informed Russian clergyman thought both figures—the 200 home-educated and over 200 seminary-trained new priests—to be realistic. The typical age, according to Russian sources, of new priests is around thirty (younger for seminary graduates, older for the home-educated). In other words, if the current figure remains steady, over the span of one priestly generation the total number of priests should rise to somewhere

[21]Letter of December 20, 1980 to this author from a thirty-two-year-old Muscovite intellectual who had emigrated in 1980, but prefers to remain anonymous as a source. She and her convert husband were active in Russian Christian intellectual circles, and both are of a Jewish background.

According to CRA reports, it was around 1970-1974 that the Church experienced the most acute clergy crisis—a demographic echo of the suppression of seminaries and ordinations and the deprivation of masses of clergy of registration in the Khrushchev years. See the CRA's report for 1970, "Krizis kadrov russkoi pravoslavnoi tserkvi," ms. in Keston College Archives (10 pp.), and the Furov report (see n. 19).

between 12,000 and 14,000, or double the 1972 figure. But, according to all information, the numbers of ordinations, theology students and candidates per seminary place continue to rise.

While the regime at the moment refuses to permit even the reopening of the five seminaries closed under Khrushchev, it has reluctantly permitted some building projects on the grounds of the existing three. In Leningrad in 1977 two additional buildings in the courtyard of the seminary-academy building were returned to the Church for student dormitories, thus freeing the current seminary-academy building entirely for classes. This allowed the institution to almost double its intake and open choir directors and readers courses at the academy. This latter three-year course, attended mostly by girls, has grown from sixteen students in 1978 to over seventy in 1981.[22] In addition, Archbishop Kirill, the rector of the Leningrad theological schools, was at last granted a permit to take over the whole large building of the present seminary and academy on the condition that another building is to be constructed at church expense elsewhere in Leningrad to house the students of a secular college that had been occupying the other half of the seminary building. The completion of that building, for three million rubles, will allow the theological schools of Leningrad once again to double their student body. The Moscow (Zagorsk) theological schools managed to practically double their space by a subterfuge, as it were. Their administration had gained permission from the state to carry out extensive renovations on the old building, but when the scaffolding was removed (in 1980?) there was a new building adjacent to the old. The civil authorities protested: the monastery is a historical landmark and no new buildings are permitted on its territory. But eventually the tempest subsided and the seminary has additional room for growth.[23]

[22]According to a 1982 Russian church source, in the academic year 1981-1982 there were sixty-two girls attending these courses, representing one-sixth of the applicants. The aim of the course was to train not only choir directors but also potential church wardens, so that these powerful offices would be occupied not by ignorant persons often hindering proper pastoral work of the priests, but by theologically trained lay assistants to the pastor. The choirmaster trainees are to make tours of parishes during summer holidays, giving concerts of liturgical music and thus helping to raise the religious-musical culture in provincial churches.

[23]On the increasing frequency of reconstruction and expansion of existing church facilities, see *ZhMP* for 1979-1981, esp. no. 3 (1978) 15-7; no. 1 (1979)

This form of enlarging church facilities has lately become quite popular. Attempts to gain permission to either build a new church or to reopen a closed one very rarely succeed. For instance, despite the fact that in the city of Gorky, with its 1.5 million inhabitants, there are only three small churches open for worship while more than 1,700 people have signed petitions to all sorts of state agencies over the past fifteen years to open additional churches, no such permission has so far been granted. The authorities told the petitioners to organize out of their midst groups of twenty and let each group address itself to the relevant city district soviet. Five such groups were subsequently organized in 1978 in five different city districts, but none so far has gained anything.[24] Similarly, there have been numerous petitions from the huge Kamchatka peninsula, where not a single parish remains open, but they have fallen on deaf ears.[25] Even on the basis of the very limited data available through *samizdat* many similar stories could be reported.

Indeed, there have been a number of cases of enforced, vandalistic and brutal closures of churches even in the post-Khrushchev period. But except for the brutal blowing up of the Holy Trinity Church in Leningrad on November 15, 1966 and a couple of suburban churches in Minsk, the other known cases have occurred in smaller, distant provincial towns and rural districts,[26] and, according to Russian churchmen, they are isolated relapses of Khrushchevism in local officials who are mentally decades

16-8; and no. 5 (1980) 13-5. Additional information from oral testimonies of Russian clerics.

[24]*Documents of the Christian Committee for the Defense of Believers' Rights in the USSR*, 1 and 2 (San Francisco: Washington Research Center, 1979-1980), *samizdat* reprints, contain these and numerous other petitions for the opening of churches. See also *RCL* 6:1 (1978) 45; 7:4 (1979) 258-61; 8:2 (1980) 152; and above, chapter 6, n. 27.

[25]Yakunin, "O sovremennon polozhenii," 65-6.

[26]On Leningrad, see *Russkaya mysl'* (January 26, 1967). In 1973, the Cathedral of the Resurrection in Chernigov was closed by force, leaving the believers only a small wooden church on the city's outskirts (*Christian Science Monitor* [July 2, 1973]), and the Epiphany Church in Zhitomir was closed and bulldozed on the pretext that it was adjacent to a school and thus had a bad influence on the pupils (*VRKhD*, no. 111 [1974] 241; and no. 116 [1975] 230-1). In addition, there were reports of the brutal closure and destruction of two village churches in the Rovno and one in the Lvov provinces in the Ukraine and one in a Belorussian village. See *Khronika tekushchikh sobytii*, no. 53 (August 1979) 129-30; and no. 54 (November 1979) 99-102.

behind the times. The trend, nevertheless, seems to be reversing. At least since the late 1960s a tiny number of churches have been either reopening or even built anew. Patriarch Pimen, in his fifteen-thousand-word report reviewing the history and life of the Russian Orthodox Church since the revolution—presented at an international conference of churchmen organized by the Moscow Patriarchate in May 1978 to mark the sixty years since the reestablishment of the patriarchate—revealed that "in the last few months" seven new parishes began to function in the USSR and four churches were built "recently."[27]

It may be of interest that of these eleven churches only three are in European Russia, the remaining eight being in the Far East, Siberia and Central Asia, all relatively close to the Chinese border. It is true that these areas are particularly short of churches, but this cannot be the sole answer to the puzzle as to why all of a sudden, in the space of a few months, several churches were opened in these areas—particularly in view of the fact that further to the north in Kamchatka there is not a single church and only three functioning churches in the whole huge republic of Yakutya. The answer, to my mind, should be sought in the proximity to China and also in the Moslem-nationalist revival in Central Asia, as well as in the need to placate Russian patriotism, which at least on the popular level always goes hand-in-hand with a religious perception of one's country.

Browsing through the *Journal of the Moscow Patriarchate* for the three years that have elapsed since the patriarch's report, one notices reports of another ten churches either newly reopened or constructed.[28] This, however, hardly covers all churches opened over this period of time, for reasons already discussed, and also because the *Journal* simply has no space for reporting all events across the country. For instance, none of the issues reported the opening of the first Orthodox church in the far eastern port city

[27]"Doklad . . . Patriarkha Pimena . . . (25 maya 1978 g.)," *ZhMP*, no. 8 (1978) 3-31.

[28]This includes a second church in Volgograd and Pyatigorsk, a basement church under the Novosibirsk cathedral, a new church at the diocesan center of Minsk and two churches in addition to the single functioning one in Suzdal, an ancient city of churches and monasteries. See *ZhMP*, no. 2 (1979) 18; no. 3 (1979) 22; no. 7 (1979) 21; no. 1 (1980) 28; no. 5 (1980) 22; no. 6 (1980) 18; no. 8 (1980) 20 and 24; no. 5 (1981) 30.

of Komsomolsk-on-the-Amur (built by the Komsomol in the 1930s). A peculiar twist in this case is that allegedly it was the local Soviet authorities who proposed to the believers to build a church there, in order to somehow offset the uncontrollable growth of the most extreme sects in the city.[29] The incompleteness of the reports on church life in the *Journal* can be illustrated by the fact that only seventy priestly ordinations are reported for 1979, while the realistic estimate, as we have seen, is closer to four hundred.

Be it as it may, the number of newly opening churches is insignificant in proportion to the total churchgoing Orthodox population, particularly in view of the marked rise in the ranks of urban believers—partly as a result of migration of the rural population to the cities, but also because of the general religious revival, which will be discussed below. What occurs much more frequently than the actual building of new churches or reopening of churches that had been confiscated is the enlargement of the existing facilities by building additions to the churches under the guise of repairs and reconstruction, as well as by building special large baptismal chapels. The latter are occasionally reported in the *Journal of the Moscow Patriarchate,* while the fact of enlargement of the existing facilities can be discerned in the numerous reports therein on the consecration of new altars by bishops in churches after "extensive repairs."[30] Dissident émigré artists, many of whom are iconographers, have reported frequent cases of decorating such rebuilt and greatly enlarged churches all over the USSR, from Siberia to central Russia and elsewhere.[31]

[29]See the letter to the editor in *VRKhD*, no. 33 (1981) 298. There have been reports both in the official press and by dissident sources of a revival of paganism in areas where Orthodox churches have not been functioning for decades—e.g., in the area of Kargopol, which used to be one of the monastic centers of northern Russia. See Gennady Russky, "Kleima: K ikonam severo-russkikh svyatykh," *Kontinent,* no. 22 (1980) 9; and above in chapter 10, n. 54. A 1982 source confirmed that the closure of churches in Siberia has resulted in a colossal growth of all types of sects there, particularly the Jehovah's Witnesses, which has begun to worry even Soviet authorities.

[30]The first eleven issues of *ZhMP* for 1980 report at least seventeen cases of reconsecration of churches or of additional altars (permitting extra services), of churches built to replace old structures, of basement churches constructed under the main ones and of independent baptistries built adjacent to the main churches.

[31]One such artist we interviewed was Lydia Georgieva (Rome, June 1981), a

But to return to the seminary issue, the third seminary, that of Odessa, should be mentioned as well. It was likewise granted a permit in 1976 to construct an additional building, doubling the educational and dormitory facilities. Consequently, the seminary, which had had around 120 students in 1974, grew to 260 students by 1980.

Altogether, in 1977 there were 788 intramural seminary and academy students and 814 correspondence students in the USSR. By 1981 the figure had grown to a total of at least 2,000—1,100 in the correspondence division and over 900 in the day division.[32] It is generally recognized in church circles that, owing to the close control of the seminaries by the CRA—which includes rejection of so-called religious fanatics, constant KGB attempts to recruit seminarians and policies of extreme loyalty and subservience to the state on the part of the seminary administration and some professors—the priests graduating from the seminaries are on the average less dedicated to their vocation than those who prepare for ordination outside any institutional framework, under the guidance of a bishop or a priest.[33] The regime's "laxity" in permitting the seminaries to more than double their student body over the last decade and a half may be a sign of its desire to reduce the number of ordinations outside this institutional framework, because in the latter case the ordaining bishop pre-

professional restorer and iconographer. She carried out numerous fresco assignments in such enlarged churches, particularly in Siberia, in the last few years.

[32]"Russian Churchman Reports Plenty Clergy Recruits," *OC* 17:2 (February 1981) 1. The total number of students in the Leningrad schools of theology in the 1981/1982 academic year, according to another church source, included four hundred in the day division, which in itself would considerably increase the total student body over the figure of the preceding year. Only 20 percent of applicants to the seminary and academy could be accepted, owing to a shortage of space—which hopefully would be ameliorated on the return to the seminary of the other wing of the building by 1983 and the completion of a construction program in the yard of the seminary that would roughly double the present teaching and living space. Currently, on the average, fifteen students live in each room at the seminary dormitory.

[33]Yakunin, "O sovremennom polozhenii," 53-4. According to this report, charismatic professors who stir up religious enthusiasm in their students are particularly subjected to removal from teaching posts and from contacts with the seminarians. Archimandrite Tikhon (Agrikov), formerly of the Moscow theological schools, for example, was even removed from the Holy Trinity-St. Sergius Monastery for the same reason. Furov (317) likewise writes: "The CRA plenipotentiaries . . . have continued to take measures to prevent the admission of fanatics . . . to the theological schools."

sents a list of his candidates for ordination to the local CRA plenipotentiary often literally on the eve of the ordinations. The plenipotentiary then has no time to do "proper" investigations on the candidate's background, particularly if he is an outsider to the given province.[34] One of Furov's complaints against Archbishop Chrysostom is precisely that he often ordains friends arriving for ordination from other areas of the country, "some of whom have a seriously compromised past."[35] This concern by itself indicates a rise in the number of young men eager to take holy orders, thus testifying to a religious revival among the Soviet youth.

However, if the already discussed figure of over two hundred extrainstitutional ordinations per annum is accurate, the regime should permit more seminaries to reopen to protect itself from such "untamed" clergy. Obviously, the existing facilities cannot expand indefinitely. Yet, in the words of Russian clerics, at the given moment this is entirely out of the question. This inconsistency on the part of the authorities seems to indicate that they cannot be sure of the reliability of their own cadres as well as of the prospective clerical teaching and administrative personnel on the periphery. Hence, they are afraid to allow the expansion of theological education to cities other than the three where the machinery of control and supervision has achieved more satisfactory standards from the Soviet point of view over the thirty-five years of their unbroken existence. Some evidence of this is Furov's boastful assertion:

> The [Patriarchal] Synod is under CRA control. The selection and distribution of its permanent members has been and remains entirely in the council's hands; candidates for the rotating positions in the Synod are likewise coordinated with the responsible officials of the council. Patriarch Pimen and the Synod's permanent members coordinate with the leadership of the CRA . . . all issues to be discussed at the

[34]Yakunin, 52-3; also, testimony of Fr. Tivetsky and of several clerics of the Moscow Patriarchate.

[35]Furov, 286-8. In a conversation with the CRA, Chrysostom complained that the seminaries were accepting insufficient numbers of candidates and refusing former Komsomol members.

Synod sessions, as well as the final "Resolutions of the Holy Synod."

Even if this statement contains no exaggeration, that is where the full control ends, according to the report itself. First, it subdivides the fifty-seven bishops it mentions into three categories: (1) Seventeen bishops (eight young ones, and nine of the prewar generation[36]) "in word and in deed confirm not only their loyalty but also a patriotic devotion to socialist society." (2) Twenty-three bishops (of them only seven of the prewar generation) are "loyal to the state . . . observe the laws on religious cults, but in their daily administrative and ideological activities aim at activizing the clergy and the parish activities, preach the enhancement of the role of the Church in personal, family and social life . . . select young people and enthusiasts of Orthodox piety for clerical ordinations." (3) Seventeen bishops (ten of them of the "young" category) "try to evade the laws on religious cults. Some of them are religious conservatives, others are capable of falsifying the situation in the dioceses [in their reports][37] and the relationship between them and the Soviet officials; still others try to bribe the CRA plenipotentiaries and to slander them, as well as other local Soviet officials."[38]

It may be of interest that the second and third categories are made up predominantly of the post-Stalin generation of bishops, as well as some who come from the territories incorporated into the USSR since World War II—i.e., who have no memories of Stalin's horrors. These dynamics seem to suggest that the Church would struggle for more independence with the assumption of all leading positions by the post-Stalin generation of bishops. Another noteworthy point is that among the bishops of the first, i.e., most

[36]By the prewar generation we mean those born before the revolution who had lived in the Soviet Union through the thirties. Most of them had been through jails and/or internal exile. The category of "young" bishops also includes those of any age who had not lived in the Soviet Union in the prewar years and also did not go through Stalin's prisons and camps of the 1940s-1950s to the best of our knowledge.

[37]This would seem to imply that "conservatives" are honest, and the "falsifiers" are not conservatives by definition—an interesting "Freudian" slip in a communist official's report.

[38]The report is blatant in its disregard for logic and accuracy. Why should a bishop slander a plenipotentiary after having bribed him? One defeats the other.

loyal, category are Patriarch Pimen and the late Iosif of Kazakhstan. The former, as we have seen, was pressed into obedience by some type of blackmail; the latter was known as a very dedicated and active bishop and should have been placed in any but the first category.[39] Most probably it was good relations with the Kazakh plenipotentiaries, to which Iosif had referred in his interview with Archbishop Vasily,[40] that were responsible for his inclusion in the "most loyal" category.

Another case in point, confirming the decisive factor of informal relations with the plenipotentiaries, is Bishop (now Archbishop) Chrysostom of Kursk and Belgorod, whom the report singles out in particular for attack. The bishop, who was forty years old in 1975, is accused of behaving too independently from the local plenipotentiaries and of being at loggerheads with them. According to unofficial church information, this young bishop is of a rather short-tempered, frank and energetic disposition. Moreover, he arrived in his new diocese holding another position: that of deputy head of the Church's Department of External Ecclesiastical Relations. This, apparently, had given him a sense of independence from the local plenipotentiaries, owing to which he probably ignored the customary "gifts" to them. His "crime" was that, on arrival in the dual diocese and finding that of the 175 parishes some 60 were not active owing to lack of priests, he undertook "ardent actions to reactivate religious life." In a talk with the CRA officials in Moscow he said: "I don't want people to call me an atheist or a *chekist,* things which are often heard about us. I want to have a clean record as a bishop, both in the eyes of believers and of foreigners. . . . I don't go around calling on the believers to solicit for the opening of new parishes. It is they who come to me." He complained that, in 1975, a local CRA official had tried to ban infant baptisms on weekdays—a regulation that the bishop overruled as illegal—and that he was

[39]The other more prominent still living bishops in category 1 are Aleksii of Tallin, Yuvenaly, then of Tula and now of Krutitsy, Sergii of Odessa, Nikodim of Kharkov, Pitirim of Volokolamsk, Meliton of Tikhvin, Leonty of the Crimea and others. Of these, only Yuvenaly would appear to belong to category 2. He behaves with extraordinary loyalty in his external and policy declarations, but he has proven himself a zealous protector and patron of the Church in both the Tula and the Krutitsy (Moscow) dioceses.

[40]Vasily, "Pamyati episkopa-ispovednika," 227-8.

constantly being insulted by the atheists as an ardent believer. But the latter did not bother him too much, for "such are the times." The CRA reports that he in fact got busy finding clerical candidates for the inactive parishes, ordaining at least twenty-two new priests in the course of his first year in the diocese. In one of his sermons he dared to ridicule the atheists' claims that there was no God because the cosmonauts had not seen him. He argued that all fundamental things were based on belief: religious believers know in their hearts that God exists; atheists believe the scientists that the universe is infinite. The CRA reprimanded him for the sermon, which, allegedly, led to rumors that he had attacked the Soviet system of government. Such are the "Procrustean" limits within which a senior clergyman has to function in the USSR!

The young bishop has in fact recommended himself very well even in his foreign contacts. During a visit to the US, he frankly admitted serious frictions between the Soviet atheistic state authorities and the Church. He said that there were many young religious people willing to dedicate their lives to the Church, but that the existing seminaries could accommodate only one-fourth of all applicants. Therefore he alone ordained 120 new priests without any formal theological education during the six years of his episcopal tenure in the dual diocese, with its 175 functioning churches, none of which remained without a priest by 1980. He admitted that churches were indeed closed in the USSR, but he confirmed that none of them were ever closed by the Church or by the believers, thus implying that the closing was not voluntary, contrary to the frequent allegations by the state (supported even by some bishops, including Metropolitan Sergii Stragorodsky, as has been shown earlier) that churches close for the lack of believers or in response to petitions of the believers. In this respect, Chrysostom saw his Church in a spiritually better position than, for instance, the Anglican Church in England, where he witnessed some churches converted into restaurants by the clergy themselves. Hinting at the futility of the antireligious struggle, he said that in the last few years Orthodox churches were opened in two cities "specifically founded as communist strongholds." His estimate of the active Orthodox Church membership in the USSR was between thirty and forty million. Of his own diocese, he said that the attendance was steady, but with a marked increase of young people in the last few years.[41]

His independent behavior did cost him the deputy chairmanship of the Department of External Ecclesiastical Relations in 1981.[42] But Chrysostom is not the only bishop who worries the CRA. It is concerned in general "with the activities of some young ruling bishops, who have performed certain duties abroad [apparently satisfactorily from the CRA's viewpoint], but at home demonstrate a religious zeal, ignoring the instructions of the CRA and of the local soviets."[43]

The CRA reports confirm the considerable dissatisfaction of the bishops and priests with the 1961 amendments to the Church Statute: "Bishop Pimen [of Saratov] has in private conversations criticized the 1961 reform, saying it was imposed on the Church by the state, that it goes against the interests of the Church and infringes on the priesthood not only materially but also morally and legally, subordinating it to parish wardens." The "crimes" of Archbishop Nikolai, then of Vladimir and Suzdal, were that while

intelligently representing the Church in encounters with foreigners . . . at the same time he tries to extend his influence over the parish executive organs, to build up good church choirs, to rejuvenate the membership of the "twenties" and of the auxiliary church personnel, and to remove the limitations on church bellringing.

[41]"Russian Churchman Reports," 1 and 5. Russian church sources add that by 1981 he had over 200 priests serving the 175 parishes in both of his dioceses and that he trains and freely allows priests ordained by him to go to any diocese they want—saying he does not care where they serve as long as they serve the Russian Orthodox Church.

[42]"Opredelenie svyashchennogo sinoda," *ZhMP*, no. 10 (1981) 4.

[43]In addition to the already mentioned bishops who do not satisfy the CRA, Furov names Archbishop Nikolai, then of Vladimir; Bishop Mikhail, then of Astrakhan; Pallady, then of Zhitomir; Aleksii of Kuban; Metropolitan Nikolai of Lvov; Iosif of Rostov, whom he describes as "a fanatical and cunning monk"; and Bishop Bogolep, then of Nikolaev (285-95). In 1975 the latter had defrocked an immoral priest who apparently was working for the CRA/KGB, and the Church was forced to temporarily retire him (Yakunin, 22-3). Later he was appointed to head the distant Kirov diocese. Russian clerics confirm that most of the young bishops are highly dedicated to the Church.

Archbishop Nikolai is particularly attentive to the enhancement of the clergy cadres . . .

Acting within the law, he has carried out a number of measures which have activized the believers:
—increased the frequency of episcopal services . . .
—requested of the clergy to give frequent sermons . . . and the number of these has significantly increased . . .
—provided parishes with priests, thus preventing gaps in regular services.

It was owing to his "exceptionally high religious activity" that "only a few years ago" the bishop was removed from Rostov-on-Don on the petition of the local CRA organs. Now, says the report, it is high time he were moved somewhere else. Indeed, in 1976 he would be transferred to the diocese of Kaluga for supporting the Vladimir believers' protests over the temporary closure of the twelfth-century Dormition Cathedral in that city for major fresco restoration work. The believers feared that the church would never be returned to them, as so frequently happened with other churches and monasteries, including the Kiev Monastery of the Caves.[44] Apparently, Archbishop Nikolai shared these apprehensions, although most of the money for the restoration came from the church. In this case he proved wrong: the cathedral was returned for regular services in 1979 after the completion of the extensive repairs and restoration.[45] But had the believers made no noise, would this have happened?

Another *enfant terrible* is Archbishop Mikhail (Mudyugin), then of Astrakhan. This man has an unusual biography and a history of conflicts with the state. Born in 1913, he had received two degrees: one in foreign languages, and a graduate degree in metallurgical engineering, which he subsequently taught for a number of years in a Leningrad engineering college. With Metropolitan Nikodim's help he signed up for a theology correspond-

---

[44]"Soviet Religious Samizdat," *RCL* 6:3 (1978) 213; Furov, 285-95.
[45]An unfriendly *samizdat* report on Nikolai in connection with the Vladimir cathedral affair is in Ratmirov, "Restavratsiya ili diskriminatsiya?" 16-8. On the restoration and return of the cathedral to the believers see *ZhMP*, no. 4 (1977) 121-5; no. 12 (1978) 17-9; no. 3 (1980) 17-8.

ence course. Completing this, he resigned from his former employment, was tonsured a monk and ordained priest. This caused an uproar in the Leningrad Soviet press. To calm things down, Nikodim temporarily removed him to the provincial city of Vologda. When the passions had subsided, Nikodim brought him back to Leningrad, consecrated him bishop and appointed him rector of the Leningrad Academy, with the assignment of teaching a course on the Soviet Constitution. A year later, the Soviet authorities forced his removal for teaching a course on comparative antireligious legislation in different communist countries under the guise of the Constitution course. In the late 1960s he was posted to Astrakhan,[46] where, according to the report, the bishop continued to show independence of mind. He supported "the extremist view that it's about time to change the Constitution by giving wider rights to religious organizations, which should be made equal with other social organizations in terms of electoral rights, giving them the right to offer their candidates for the elections to the soviets on all levels." He is said to be openly dissatisfied with the 1961 legislation, and tries to check the functions of the plenipotentiary and to increase the role and responsibilities of the priest by rebuffing the parish organs.

Thus, we see that some bishops are actively trying to change the formal status of the Church in Soviet society, paralleling similar activities in the 1930s, when many clerics interpreted the 1936 Constitution as granting "social organization" rights to the Church.[47] Moreover (western observers, take note!), overzealously loyal political behavior and declarations by Russian bishops, particularly when abroad, are not tantamount to a total "sell-out"—they may in fact be the price the bishop has decided to pay for

[46]Private information sources.

[47]See the relevant material in chapter 5 above. While ZhMP reported special diocesan clergy conferences at which local CRA plenipotentiaries and Znanie spokesmen delivered lectures on the excellence of the new Brezhnev 1977 Constitution, samizdat sources revealed letters from Christians to the Soviet government protesting the further limitations of the rights of religious believers implied by articles 6 and 25. The former identifies the Communist Party and its aims with those of Soviet society, while article 25 declares that all educational institutions are to serve the needs of the "communist upbringing"—which automatically excludes Christian families from the ranks of legitimate Soviet citizens and makes Christian education an antistate activity. See, for instance, the Christian Committee for the Defense of Believers Rights' in the USSR's address to Brezhnev, document no. 11, in VS, no. 28 (1977) 33-7.

the opportunity to truly serve the Church at home. Perhaps the most striking illustration of this is the behavior of the late Metropolitan Nikodim, who, despite his active promotion of Soviet foreign policy at international church conferences and repeated public denials of persecution of the Church at home, has been placed in the second category by Furov, as a man zealously dedicated to Christ and his Church. As an illustration of this, Furov cites with displeasure the following theses from a lecture by Nikodim:

(1) Jesus is One, and there is nothing better than he.

(2) Try to gather together as often as possible for the eucharist and for the glorification of God . . . [whereby] the power of the Satan . . . and his works are destroyed.

(3) Unity in Christ links into a tight union not only the terrestrial Church but the celestial one as well . . .

(4) The main purpose of the Church is the sanctification of the people within her gates. But she must concern herself also with those remaining without.

(5) St. Paul wrote: ". . . had he ceased to seek God's blessing and aimed at serving people, then he would not be a servant of Christ."

Furov does not like this concentration on things divine and spiritual. He even criticized Patriarch Pimen for having dared to insert into a speech full of civic loyalty to the Soviet social system a few words of criticism of the World Council of Churches for having reduced the Christian message to "social issues alone" and for reminding his foreign audience that the essence of Christianity is to "witness Christ to the contemporary world." On Nikodim, Furov says, by disseminating ideas like the ones cited he was leading the youth away from contemporary social issues and toward Christ and Christocentrism.[48]

Furov's report cites several other examples of "errant" bishops and priests. But what is its vision of the "ideal cleric"? To begin

[48]Furov, 283-4. Nikodim also taught church history of the Soviet period at the theological academy. What worried Furov was that he expressed similar views to his Soviet students.

with, the report states what kind of work the CRA and its local plenipotentiaries perform to assure for themselves the desired type of bishop: "In the last few years we have developed a clear and comprehensive system of [political] education [*vospitanie*] of the episcopate and the priesthood through the episcopate." The positive results of this "education" are Patriarch Pimen's sycophantic letters to Kosygin, cited in the report, and (which for Furov appears to be particularly important) a lukewarm attitude of some bishops to the Church, to the services, sermons and other genuinely pastoral duties. Several bishops, mostly of the older generation, including Metropolitans Pallady of Orel and Serafim of Krutitsy and Bishop Iona of Stavropol—all deceased since the report—as well as the patriarch, are praised for these "qualities" and for staying in their diocesan sees rather than circulating within their dioceses. Pallady, in addition, is praised for particularly generous donations to the Peace Fund—i.e., for arbitrarily handing over to the state hundreds of thousands of rubles donated to the Church by the laity out of their meager earnings, and this in addition to the enormous taxes levied by the state on the churches and the clergy, which are paid from the same generous donations of the flock. This, in Furov's view, is just and fair, while Archbishop Ioasaf of Rostov is attacked in the report for receiving in addition to full board one hundred rubles a month as salary and three hundred for expenses.[49]

The late Metropolitan Serafim of Krutitsy is, moreover, praised for full cooperation with the CRA, disciplining his priests on the first demand from the council. The report even cites an abbreviated version of Serafim's circular letter to the heads of parish deaneries of December 13, 1974. The degree of correspondence between Serafim's circular, Furov's complaints in the cited report and the CRA officials' complaints regarding the behavior of priests in earlier reports available to us is so remarkable that it leaves the impression that the metropolitan was an employee of the CRA, not of the patriarchate. The CRA reports contain concrete cases of priests breaking the 1961 and other Soviet regulations in such matters as: administration of the parish, where some priests allegedly subordinate the executive

---

[49]The extremely modest salary of 100 rubles, compared to the 300 for expenses, is obviously meant to evade the exorbitant taxation levels on clerics' incomes.

organ to themselves and control the parish, including its finances, for their own gain; delivering sermons critical of atheism as a doctrine or of some aspects of social and human relations in the USSR; baptizing adults and children without registering them in the parish documents—i.e., without exposing the parties concerned to harassment from the state; engaging in charity, or helping the neediest parishioners; visiting groups of old and ill people in their homes and administering communion and extreme unction to them; submitting some believers to ecclesiastic disciplinary measures (deprivation of the chalice for a certain time, etc.); and concelebration with other priests in other churches without the express permission of the bishop. All these acts, which in any normal ecclesiastical life are usual functions, duties and rights of the priests, are banned, as we have seen, by Soviet law. As soon as such breaches of discipline by his parish priests were reported to Serafim, Furov boasts, he responded with the strict circular forbidding all these activities to the priests (stating, inter alia, that sermons should be purely theological and apolitical—although he himself has made many sermons praising the Soviet government and its alleged peace efforts, which, apparently, are not deemed to be political) and entrusting the district deans with new police functions of ensuring that the circular is strictly enforced.

Luckily, there is a *samizdat* commentary by Fr. Gleb Yakunin that shows that Serafim fulfilled the CRA request without even bothering to investigate the accuracy of the allegations. For instance, three priests are accused in the circular of abusing power and the parish funds. In actual fact, one of the priests had spent five thousand rubles of his own money to help finance major repairs of his church. The parish was very grateful to him and produced official documents clearing the priest of all accusations of misuse of funds. Yet, "Fr. Nikolai Afonsky was forcibly retired." The other priest's "crime" was that he had supported the struggle of his parish against an arrogant and dishonest warden, who was imposed on the parish by the civic authorities. Under parish pressure the Soviets were forced to agree to the warden's retirement and his replacement by a popular person elected by the parish, but in vengeance they falsely accused the parish priest of embezzlement. The effect of this accusation was such that the priest, Fr. Alexander Korobeinikov, landed in a mental asylum with a nervous breakdown. Later he received an appointment to another parish, thus proving his innocence. In another case, the parish priest and all the members of the parish executive organ were sacked by the Soviets because they dared to build a beautiful iron fence around the church, whereas, allegedly, the local soviet permitted them only to build a wooden one. The chairman of the soviet was enraged by the prospect that the church fence would be the most beautiful structure on the collective farm. The story really tells a tale on the "extent" of the rights of a parish: even with its own money it has no right to build a fence on its own territory without special permission, and then it has no right to choose the material and style it likes!

Fr. Yakunin comments that the worst part of the story is that Metropolitan Serafim took the plenipotentiary's words at face value, believing him rather than his own priests and parish administrators. The other tragedy of the situation, as noted by Fr. Yakunin, is that the Church in the USSR is deprived of the right to have an ecclesiastical court. Therefore, the clergy and civilians serving the Church are entirely at the mercy of arbitrary commands, orders and decrees of the bishops. This becomes particularly unbearable in the cases of such weak and cowardly persons as the late Serafim. In his case the arbitrariness was not his own, but was simply transmitted via him from a body with aims diametrically opposed to those of the Church.[50]

One accusation, however, which even Serafim dared not bring forward against his priests, was the practice of unofficial charity. Condemnation of charity would go so blatantly against basic Christian precepts that with all his subservience[51] even this weak

[50]See "Tsirkuliar . . . Serafima," no. 900 (December 1974), along with Yakunin's commentaries, in *VRKhD*, no. 118 (1976) 287-97.

[51]At the time of Solzhenitsyn's expulsion from the USSR in 1974, Serafim made a statement for the Soviet press approving of the expulsion. This caused an uproar, including protests from the patriarchate's own most prominent bishops abroad, Anthony of London and Vasily of Brussels. Serafim had a heart attack very soon after. In 1977 he retired for health reasons and in 1979 he died at the age of seventy-four. Fr. Dudko depicted him as a sincere man but so weak as to be almost senile. See E. Ternovsky and E. Shteinberg, "Otkrytoe pis'mo m. Serafimu," *VRKhD*, no. 111 (1974) 132-3; also *RCL* 6:1 (1978) 45; and *ZhMP*, no. 6 (1979) 16. When Serafim forbade Dudko to deliver his sermons in the form of answers to believers' questions the latter went to see him and pointed out Serafim's wrongdoing. The latter's response was: "It's high time I retired, but

but still religiously sincere metropolitan could not bring it forward as a reproach. Perhaps the CRA did not dare to reproach the priests in its reports to the bishops for the same reasons.

But the CRA's internal reports are full of instances of this illegal charity engaged in by priests and bishops, interspersed with stories of corruption of the priests, as if to suggest that both belong to the same category. Comparing these different CRA reports, one cannot fail to notice glaring contradictions between them, which throw additional suspicions on the reliability of the data contained. For example, while the 1978 Furov report praises Metropolitan Pallady of Orel for his total subservience and his CRA-approved lukewarm attitude to his pastoral duties, a 1968 report singles out Pallady's diocesan administration, along with several others, as engaging in charity on a large scale. The same Pallady is singled out in a 1970 report as active in finding dedicated individuals and ordaining them outside of the seminaries, and saying: "In the spiritual field it is not formal education that is most important, but dedication to the Church."[52] Among other charity "crimes" mentioned are free dinners organized on Sundays and feastdays for hundreds of needy pilgrims coming to church from some distance; financial support for the nine poorest members of one parish, amounting to a total of 350 rubles over one year; and curtailed payments by a parish in the Crimea to the Peace Fund, caused by charity donations to its neediest members.

The widespread dissatisfaction of the clergy, the bishops and the laity with the 1961 Statute is reported in all CRA documents—which contradicts their tendency to present conflicts between laity and priests in the parishes over administrative and financial control as a common situation.[53] Had this been true, the laity would

how will I take this burden of sins with me to the other world?" See Fr. Dudko's press conference of April 27, 1977 in response to the articles in *Literaturnaya gazeta* of April 13 and 20, AS 3003, 11.

Archbishop Pitirim (Nechaev), however, the *ZhMP* editor, even surpassed Serafim, giving an interview to the Soviet press agency Novosti in which he said that the teaching of religion to children would be a violation of their conscience and charity was unnecessary because of the excellent Soviet welfare system. Archbishop Vasily bitterly criticized him for this in a Russian BBC broadcast. See *VRKhD*, no. 114 (1974) 268-70.

[52]"Krizis kadrov v RPTs," in the 1970 report "Iz otcheta za 1970 g.," ms. in Keston College Archives, 1.

[53]Ibid., 2-4. A similar earlier report cites multiple instances of both believers and priests evading the 1961 strictures and collections by believers to support

not have shared the "greedy" priests dissatisfaction with the post-1961 status of the parish priest.

Despite all bans, churches continue to hold a special service for school children at the beginning of the school year.[54] The CRA is likewise worried by the fact that, in the poorer parishes, voluntary, unpaid work for the church is practiced by members of the church committee and by readers, choirmasters, cleaners and other auxiliary parish workers.[55] Obviously, they would rather present all work for the Church as materially motivated. Widespread unregistered baptisms, marriage ceremonies, extreme unctions and other private services, many of them performed at the homes of believers, are likewise a constant object of concern for the CRA and a frequent reason for punishment by the state. Far from always, but quite often, these unregistered rites, and even whole liturgical services performed secretly in private homes, are carried out by priests deprived of registration by the state. In reporting these cases there are also inconsistencies. For instance, we are told that a certain priest was deprived of his parish registration "for lechery and drunkenness." But in the first year since his dismissal he performed ninety-seven unofficial baptisms in the same village.[56] Surely, had he been punished for the above reasons, he would not have enjoyed the popularity and confidence of his former parishioners, which are the obvious preconditions for such illegal activities.

In conclusion, one of the reports warns against a complacent view, according to which "Orthodoxy has been tamed and rendered harmless." It cites long excerpts from Patriarch Aleksii's speech of 1960 in defense of the Church, and calls it a "militant speech . . . made use of by the western propagandists as well as by the most active and fanatical circles inside the country."[57]

their priests. In the Lvov province alone 180 members of parish organs were deprived of registration for such collusion with the clergy (1968 report, 7). See also Yakunin's commentaries in VS, no. 28 (1977).

[54]The above 1970 CRA report cites such practices in the Altai region in Siberia (8). Fr. Tivetsky informs us that services for school children are generally and widely practiced across the USSR.

[55]The 1970 report, 8.

[56]From the 1968 report, 3.

[57]The 1970 report, part 2: "Tserkovnaya propoved'. Stremlenie k modifikatsii i obnovleniyu," 16-7. It also cites Metropolitan Nikodim's 1968 address at the Leningrad Theological Academy on the needs and aims of contemporary theology.

Although, according to the report, the total circulation of the *Journal of the Moscow Patriarchate* was only fifteen thousand in 1970, the report talks about a dangerous Christian influence of the journal and its articles on the population. How ineffective must the millions upon millions of official antireligious publications be if a single monthly with such a meager circulation is a threat to them! Good choral singing, the reports say, is also a way of attracting people to the Church. At the time there were allegedly a total of 40,914 permanent members of church choirs in the country, nearly 23,000 of whom were receiving no remuneration at all.[58]

As we have just mentioned, much is made in the reports of alleged priestly corruption and irreligiosity. One report even cites a priest who allegedly stated that the majority of the contemporary Orthodox priests are nonbelievers. Yet, another report quotes the remarkable Archbishop Ermogen (forcefully retired to a monastery for his opposition to the 1961 Statute, for constant conflicts with the CRA plenipotentiaries and for his support of the Eshliman-Yakunin 1965 action) as saying that the regular priests were much more religiously conscientious and dedicated to the Church than the bishops.[59] Levitin, who is very critical of the policies of the Moscow Patriarchate and the behavior of much of its clergy, also approvingly quotes a Russian Orthodox priest as saying: "I have known negligent priests, lecherous, drunken ones, but I have never met a single nonbelieving priest."[60] But the CRA's Plekhanov remains faithful to the canons of Soviet atheism in his report. These require "nonbelieving" priests as evidence that the Church is only a source of income for the clergy, a business to draw money from the believers.

Ermogen's just quoted statement was made in relation to the then anticipated sobor, regarding which he allegedly said that there was little hope of independence of action on the part of

(*ZhMP*, no. 12 [1968] 63). Its orientation toward the future rather than the past displeased the CRA. For Aleksii's speech, see above in chapter 10, pp. 333f.
   [58]The 1970 report, part 2, 18-20. Fr. Yakunin gives the 1978-1979 *ZhMP* circulation figure as "about 20,000" per issue. "O sovremennom polozhenii," 60.
   [59]A. Plekhanov, "Spravka," confidential document of April 1967, in Keston College Archives.
   [60]Volume 3 of his memoirs, *V poiskakh novogo grada* (Tel Aviv, 1980) 16.

the bishops, and only regular parish priests could be expected to voice a genuine choice of patriarchal candidates. On the general clergy situation an informed Russian cleric privately confirmed that the bishops, owing to the isolationist "microclimate" to which they are largely confined by Soviet legislation, assuage their consciences (concerning their inactivity and passivity) by blaming everything on the "will of God." It is, he said, "precisely among the parish priests that steadfast opponents of the regime can be found. But the most irreconcilable critics of the 'godless power' are among the laity . . . especially the older women, who constitute the majority of active churchgoers."[61] Here we see the reasons for the CRA attempts to slander and besmear the priests and to create divisions between them and the laity. These characteristics of the laity and the lower clergy must have been the main reason why no really controversial issues were allowed on the floor of the main part of the sobor, in which the priests and laymen participated, let alone any free discussion of candidates for the patriarchal throne.

The Pimen Era: An Interregnum?

The general consensus of Russian churchmen is that the post-Khrushchev era is marked by the growing senility of the party and government leadership, by their lack of dynamism and by

[61]The same opinion is expressed in the above-cited Yakunin report (25-36)— namely, that the parish priest is closer to the flock and its spiritual life, needs and grievances. The "flock is his social base and his defense" both against the Soviet authorities and from the hierarchy, cowed by the CRA. "The more dedicated the pastor, the bigger and the more active his flock and the stronger and more independent the pastor's position." But then he says that because of the legal restrictions on the priest's prerogatives, "despite its sincere religiosity, the contemporary clergy is nevertheless reduced to the status of a caste of 'high priests' . . . performing the rites." Regarding the bishops, whom Yakunin sees as particularly subservient, he cites the case of his and Eshliman's 1965 memoranda, which at the time received the support of an episcopal letter signed by ten bishops, headed by Ermogen and Pavel (of Novosibirsk), requesting the convocation of a sobor and the abrogation of the 1961 stipulations. Of these only the French-educated Pavel and the former Polish citizen Venyamin (Novitsky) supported the letter to the end. Even Ermogen gave up the leadership of this movement as soon as he was retired to a monastery (19-24). As to the older women, it should be borne in mind that by now they belong to the generations born and brought up under the Soviets.

the growth of "unofficial decentralization"—i.e., actual insubordination of local officials to the center. These factors, in the words of one such cleric, are at the core of "a more liberal attitude of the Soviet administration toward the Church," although there is no change in "the principles" of the Soviet political or ideological system. There is also a widespread belief that there is an element of conscious internal policy changes in the attitudes of the regime toward the Church—namely, a general anticipation of the inevitability of a major war, probably with China, which would force the regime to appeal to national sentiment, which in the Russian context inevitably includes some concessions to the Church. This is how they explain the regime's permission to reopen and even build a few churches and baptistries in Siberia and Central Asia. If the latter opinion is correct—i.e., if the "liberalization" is part of a conscious policy—then the concessions have been very meager, indeed uneven, and often were paralleled by acts of continuing brutal suppression and even persecution of believers and of independent religious activities.

In actual fact, there may be a combination of mutually exclusive trends at work. Some elements in the leadership may be consciously courting nationalism (and the national culture and religion as a part of it) in view of the extant ideological vacuum caused by the bankruptcy of the official ideology and the need to replace it with ideas that have roots in the nation and yet would not automatically conflict with an authoritarian system of government.[62] Others (mostly the older generation, i.e., the current leaders of the first rank) may still be clinging to the old Marxist rhetoric, for lack of imagination or daring and for fear of unleashing nationalistic centrifugal forces in a multinational empire. Along with this goes the continuing active hostility toward the Church. Still others want to enjoy the material pleasures of their privileged status to the last, suppressing any signs of independence and initiative from below, whether it be religious or otherwise (hence the suppression of religiophilosophic circles, etc.), but being quite willing to entertain "magnanimous concessions," such

[62]See our articles and papers on the interrelationship of nationalism and religion in Russia, including "Ethnocentrism, Ethnic Tensions and Marxism-Leninism," in *Ethnic Russia in the USSR*, ed. Edward Allworth (New York: Pergamon Press, 1980) 124-36; and "Russkii natsionalizm, marksizm-leninizm i sud'by Rossii," *Grani*, no. 111-112 (1979) 406-47.

as the opening of a church here and there or permitting the enlargement of, say, seminary facilities. Be it as it may, the seeming inconsistencies are typical signs of a political and personal *interregnum*.

In the opinion of several churchmen, much in this situation depends on the personality of the bishop. Much more would depend on the personality of the patriarch. Thus, the new forty-nine-year-old (in 1982) Patriarch of Georgia Ilya has achieved much in a mere five years on the throne: he nearly doubled the number of functioning churches, repaired and reopened a number of monasteries, doubled the number of students in his seminary, began publishing a regular journal, restored all the dioceses of the Georgian Church, consecrated additional bishops and achieved a considerable revival in the Georgian Church and an influx of youth into it. As to Patriarch Pimen, a source said, "he is simply frightened of everything and spends his leisure embroidering miters and baking little pies—which are his two hobbies." Thus, the Church's current era is also an interregnum. But perhaps the source was a little too severe on Pimen? The Georgian situation is quite different. There is a rising Georgian nationalism, and the Church is seen as the national Church, very much like Roman Catholicism in Poland or Lithuania. The Russian Orthodox Church has to function in a much more heterogeneous area, both nationally and religiously, which gives the Soviets a much greater opportunity to divide and control, if not to rule.

The much better position of the official branch of the Baptist Church, reflected in the net increase of almost 170 registered communities between 1974 and 1978 and in more frequently convened general assemblies, at which some real debate and secret ballot elections take place, is determined by several factors, in the opinion of Russian Orthodox clergy. First, the existence of the illegal Baptist movement forces the Soviets to be much more lenient to the legal Baptists, in order to undermine the arguments of the illegal ones. Also, because of the existence of the option, the most intransigent Baptists join the underground movement, and consequently the official Baptist Church is much "purer" than the Orthodox Church, which contains within herself both the docile and the more radical elements. Hence, Soviet authorities find the legal Baptists to be politically more reliable than the adherents of the Orthodox Church.[63] Secondly, in terms of struggle for the Church and for the opening of parishes, the Baptists have a greater tradition of individual activism than the Orthodox, and, on the average, they have more young people in their "twenties" groups than the Orthodox. The Orthodox neophytes rarely join the "twenties," either limiting themselves to a spiritual participation in the Church or, if they do become active, expressing their activism more often in a religious, religiophilosophic or human rights *samizdat* and leaving the real struggle for the Church in the "twenties" to the least educated and the elderly.[64] Finally, and perhaps most importantly, no matter how active, the Baptists and other sectarians remain on the fringes of Russian culture, while the Orthodox Church is seen by the Soviets as a potential threat to their monopoly of power.

Nevertheless, despite all these odds against the Orthodox, the Church's gains under Patriarch Pimen have not been entirely negligible, especially in the dioceses administered by capable, energetic and dedicated bishops. Some of these achievements have already been mentioned. As to the 1975 amendments to the state laws on religious associations, they are a controversial issue. Fr. Yakunin argued that it had been easier for a local religious group to deal with and appeal against a local soviet; but there is no appeal against a decision of the central office of the CRA in the both geographically and hierarchically distant Moscow. Understandably, Kuroedov, the CRA chairman, praises the new legislation for having streamlined procedures for the believers and because "the principle of centralization has been stressed,

---

[63]Michael Rowe, "The 1979 Baptist Congress in Moscow," *RCL*, no. 3 (1978) 188-200; David Kelly, "Nairobi: a Door Opened," *RCL*, no. 1 (1976) 4-17; Pospielovsky, "The Forty-First All-Union Congress of the Evangelical Baptists," 246-53.

[64]In the words of one Russian cleric, the dissidents joining the Church would do much more good for her if they concentrated their struggle within the "twenties" for such concrete aims as the opening of a church. The old and semiliterate church activists get bullied and brutally threatened by the Soviet authorities, who would not allow themselves such blatant brutality and disregard for law in relations with the intellectuals. He cited two cases in which an Orthodox and a Baptist "twenty" both began to struggle for the opening of a church (Sestroretsk near Leningrad and Kaliningrad in the former East Prussia). In both instances the Baptists got their church and the Orthodox failed. For attempts to overcome this handicap see n. 22 above.

giving greater powers to the Council for Religious Affairs."[65] In reality, the legislation may be a double-edged sword. While giving more property rights to existing parishes, diocesan centers and bishops, it makes the procedure for the opening of a new parish more difficult, and it makes even the temporary existence of a religious society prior to registration illegal. Nevertheless, in this era of crumbling of the central authorities, where there are cases of the central CRA assuring petitioners of the survival of their church but the local authorities disregarding the instructions from the center and destroying or closing the church,[66] granting more power to the central CRA office may do more good than harm. Working closely with the Church, and especially with her Department of External Ecclesiastical Relations, should make it more sensitive to issues that have reverberations abroad—e.g., oppression of believers, closing of churches, etc. (This is assuming that the written laws do have effect on the Soviet administrators, which is far from certain.) As to the greater rights of the hierarchs and parishes, they still do not amount to a legal recognition of the Church as a whole, as an institution. Now registered with the state and enjoying greater rights of possession (rather than property) are the individual group of "twenty," the individual bishop, the diocesan center and the patriarch as an individual functionary. But all of them do not add up to an organization or institution in the eyes of the law.[67]

The Church has already made use of the law. In September 1980, in the village of Sofrino, not far from Moscow, the patriarch officially opened a large plant with modern technology for the production of candles, incense, chalices and all the other necessary utensils and symbolic objects used by the Orthodox Church and individual Christians. The story is a long one. The

[65]*Izvestiya* (January 31, 1976); and "Torzhestvo leninskikh printsipov svobody sovesti," *Nauka i religiya*, no. 1 (1978) 3-4. English translation of the former in *RCL*, no. 2 (1978) 41-6. See also Yakunin's critiques, "Obrashchenie chlenov khristianskikh tserkvei SSSR," *VS*, no. 28 (1977) 58-78; and "Pis'mo Gen. Sek. VSTs F. Potteru," *VS*, no. 24 (1976) 20-62.

[66]This occurred, for example, in Balashovka (Rovno province), where the local soviet ignored the CRA promise to reopen the local church (closed under Khrushchev) and had it formally liquidated by a fraudulent trick. See *Khronika*, no. 54 (November 1979) 100-1.

[67]Conversation with a leading Russian Orthodox cleric, and L. Sergeeva, "V tiskakh sistemy," 30.

patriarchate had fought for the right to possess such a plant or plants since 1946. In 1957 the Church was granted the right to establish several small enterprises in some individual dioceses. The patriarch had petitioned for the right to build a larger one attached directly to the patriarchate, and this right was finally granted. But, according to reports, no sooner had the plant been launched than the Soviets suppressed most of the other workshops, making the new patriarchal factory virtually the only such enterprise for the whole Church of Russia. This, given the endemic Soviet shortages of raw materials, irregularities with supply and communications, is certain to result in periodic shortages of needed objects in individual parishes and whole dioceses.[68]

In 1981 the offices of the publishing house of the Moscow Patriarchate were moved from their cramped premises in the former Novodevichy Monastery in Moscow to a new building built especially for this purpose in the same city. It is too early to say if this will result in more church publications. So far, the Church does not possess her own printing base and has to resort to state printing enterprises, paying the highest possible tariffs and taxes as a private enterprise. However, she has in the last few years increased the volume of church publications somewhat, printing a new edition of the Bible and another separate New Testament, a Prayer Book, a Psalter, a Horologion or book of permanent church service prayers of the twenty-four-hour cycle, and a Priest's Service Manual, the first volume of which appeared in 1977. It contains some theological notes explaining the meaning of certain prayers and rituals to the priest, some notes on church history and the history of certain services and other necessary information for the priest and the layman on ecclesiology, including some sermons of church fathers. The same year saw the publication of a service book for the yearly cycle of services, the first since 1958. But the most important publication of recent years has been the Menaion, which began to be published in 1970 and is apparently intended to consist of at least twelve volumes. It contains services to all saints of the Russian Church and to most other saints recognized by the Orthodox *oikoumene,* and includes musical scores for prayers and some hagiographic material. This is the first ever such complete publication, as it includes material

[68]*ZhMP*, no. 11 (1980) 12-5; details in Sergeeva, 31.

from previously unpublished local manuscript texts of akathists to locally revered saints and iconographic models for the painting of icons of these saints. The text draws to a great extent on the work of the late Bishop-martyr Afanasy (Sakharov), who had contributed greatly to the task of Russifying the Slavonic texts of the old menaia to make them comprehensible to the modern Russian. The currently published Menaion keeps the Slavonic texts, with some minimum Russification of the least understandable terms. Each volume is restricted to the saints of the given month.[69]

Will the expansion of office space mean at least an increase in circulation figures for the *Journal of the Moscow Patriarchate,* i.e., its availability on subscription to the average Orthodox Christian believer in the USSR? The *Journal* has substantially improved in quality in the last decade. It contains a more detailed chronicle of the lives of individual dioceses, albeit almost exclusively in the form of diocesan episcopal visits to the peripheral parishes, many of which include ordinations of local priests and consecrations of reconstructed or repaired churches and additional altars and chapels in the existing churches, etc. Among these, information on the patriarch's services is conspicuous by the absence of Pimen's visits to peripheral diocesan centers and churches, in contrast to the late Patriarch Aleksii.

Allegedly, Pimen wanted to make several such journeys but was advised by the CRA that this was undesirable from their point of view. Although this was not an order, and, surely, the patriarch could have shown some independence, nevertheless he fully complied. We are told that, when the late Metropolitan Nikodim took a summer cruise down the Volga on a passenger steamer, he would go ashore every time the steamer docked, and he would be met by the local clergy and laity and proceed to celebrate a religious service of one sort or another. In contrast, the patriarch, when taking a similar cruise, isolated himself on the upper deck. In the words of one Russian Orthodox bishop,

[69]The New Testament was apparently issued in two editions, one in 1976 (with a circulation of 75,000) and another in 1979. These were the first editions since 1968. *RCL,* no. 3 (1977) 198; and no. 3 (1980) 241. For the other publications see *ZhMP,* no. 1 (1979) 79-80; no. 5 (1981) 80; no. 6 (1981) 80; and "Orthodox Prayer Book and Psalter Published," *OC* (August 1981) 2. The latter article mentions a circulation of 150,000.

Pimen's "administration" is such that often one gets the impression that the dioceses exist completely apart from the patriarchate.

There was, however, one case when Pimen did try to apply his authority and power. After the death of the very popular and authoritative abbot Alipy (Voronov) of the Pskov-Caves Monastery, the patriarch at first confirmed the appointment of a certain Archimandrite Gavriil as the new abbot. Gavriil had, prior to the appointment, been the dean of the Pskov cathedral and was known as the chief KGB church informant there. He had always accompanied foreign church delegations to Pskov and to the nearby monastery. After numerous protests by the resident monks, lay believers and the Yakunin Christian Committee for the Defense of Believers' Rights, Pimen at last changed his mind and issued an order removing Gavriil. This was not to the CRA's or KGB's liking. The CRA Vice-Chairman Furov left for the monastery, and on his return the patriarch's order was revoked and Gavriil was reconfirmed as abbot.[70]

But let us return to the *Journal*. The noticeable rise in the frequency of reports on clerical ordinations since approximately 1978 should be mentioned. By 1980 these have certainly surpassed the number of printed clerical obituaries. But only in a minority of cases is a formal theological education of the ordinant mentioned. In some cases this may be just an oversight, due to the brevity of the reports. But, perhaps more often than not, this silence may reflect the significance and frequency of extraseminary ordinations, which result, as has already been mentioned, in a generally more religiously dedicated clergy than the ones produced by the controlled seminaries.

The *Journal* has also begun to publish such educational material, for the layman as well as for the poorer educated clergyman, as explanations of the liturgy—its theological meaning, symbolism and history—as well as other instructive material of a popular-theological and didactic character. Quite often, particularly on the occasion of the six hundredth anniversary of the Battle of Kulikovo, against the Tatars, the national-historical and patriotic role of the Church is emphasized. This displeases the Soviets, who complain in their atheistic publications that the

[70]Yakunin, "O sovremennom polozhenii," 8-16; and oral testimony of Russian clerics.

Church has been trying (allegedly fraudulently) to stress an organic link between Russian culture and the Church.[71] Lately there have also begun to appear photographs of and reports on the tonsuring and veiling of several young monks and nuns. There were also two rather unusual reports on the life of the Leningrad theological schools. The routine reports recount formal ceremonies marking either the beginning or the closing of the academic year (commencement exercises). The two just mentioned tell about the spiritual life of the schools. One, in particular, recounts the monastic tonsuring of a young Siberian physicist who had turned to God at the age of twenty-nine and was now a student in the Leningrad Theological Academy. It also gives a moving account on the preparation of another adult (not a student) for baptism at the seminary chapel. Archbishop Kirill, the rector, gave a sermon related to the occasion, and the whole student body offered special prayers on behalf of the catechumen. Significantly, the name of the catechumen was withheld.[72]

The editor of the *Journal,* however, Archbishop Pitirim (Nechaev) of Volokolamsk, is one of the most conformist hierarchs of the younger generation (born in 1929), and he does not command much respect as an intellectual in church circles.[73] The editor of the other periodical publication of the patriarchate, the annual *Theological Endeavors,* Metropolitan Antony of Leningrad, is also anything but a strong personality,[74] yet his publication has become

[71]See *ZhMP,* no. 12 (1980) 1-27, which contains a clear statement that the memorial church on the battlefield has been converted into a state museum and church delegations had to serve their memorial services in rural churches some miles from the field. Altogether, *ZhMP* has lately begun to publish quite frequently photographs of historical churches that were converted into civic buildings, stressing this fact—as if to imply that it was a temporary irregularity. For the atheist view see *V poiskakh dukhovnykh naslednikov* (Moscow, 1975) 17-20.

[72]See the student S. Pavlov's report on the beginning of the Leningrad theological school year in *ZhMP,* no. 11 (1980) 16-7; and T. Kochetkov, a first-year student, "Pervaya sedmitsa velikogo posta 1981 g. v Leningradskikh dukhovnykh shkolakh," *ZhMP,* no. 6 (1981) 26-7.

[73]The *Journal* itself has been jokingly nicknamed in Russian Orthodox Church circles "Zhalkie Mysli Pitirima," or "The Pitiful Thoughts of Pitirim."

[74]It is said that when Nikodim ran the Leningrad archdiocese no one even knew the name of the local CRA plenipotentiary—all negotiating and settling of problems with the plenipotentiary Nikodim used to take upon himself. In contrast, Antony's response to any question addressed to him is: "Have you asked the plenipotentiary?"

theologically very respectable, by far surpassing the *Journal*. Perhaps the greatest contribution of the *Endeavors* has been the publication of two great twentieth-century Russian theologians: Fr. Pavel Florensky, who died in a Soviet concentration camp; and the late émigré theologian Vladimir Lossky.[75] The expansion of publication activities and the heightening of their quality must reflect the general, though uneven, relaxation of pressure on the Church, or, conversely, such growing pressure on the part of the Church that the civil authorities are forced to let the steam out here and there.

Another illustration of this easing of pressure has been the government decree (no. 1061) changing the category of the tax levy on the incomes of the clergy and of all other personnel paid by the Church or individual parishes as of January 1, 1981 from article 19 to article 18—i.e., from a ceiling of 81 percent to one of 69 percent. This amounts to reclassifying church incomes from the category of commercial, private enterprise to that covering the private earnings of medical doctors, lawyers, educators and other professionals. This, however, does not include the income earned from the production and sale of religious objects, repair contracts, etc., all of which continue to be taxed in accordance with article 19. Thus, the Sofrino patriarchal factory finds itself still in the highest Soviet tax bracket.[76]

Altogether, since the Church is not recognized as a legal social institution, she gets very few supplies, if any, from the official state distribution system. Thus, for instance, much of the printing paper for patriarchal publications comes apparently through unofficial black market channels, and has to be paid for accordingly.[77] Even what the Church obtains from the state she

---

[75] See his theological works in *Bogoslovskie trudy*, nos. 12 and 17. See Lossky's in nos. 14 and 18. Besides a theologian, Florensky was a Moscow University professor of electrophysics, a musicologist and many other things, and had published widely on all these topics.

[76] Sergeeva, 31-2. For the financial legislation source see chapter 10, n. 47.

According to Yakunin, the patriarch, the permanent members of the Synod, officials of the Department of External Ecclesiastical Relations, some theology professors and others whose activity is recognized "as beneficial to the state" have always been taxed as regular Soviet employees—i.e., with a ceiling of 13 percent. "Spravka khristianskomu komitetu . . . o diskriminatsionnom kharaktere gos. nalogov," *Documents of the Christian Committee* 1 (1978) 31-5.

[77] Plekhanov's confidential CRA report of February 1968 on a conversation with Archbishop Aleksii of Tallin mentions a certain Zilberberg who supplies Archbishop

is charged for in accordance with completely different price scales. Thus, while the normal rate for a kilowatt of electricity is four kopeks, the Church is charged twenty-four.[78]

There is ample evidence that the relaxation is indeed very uneven and only in relation to the 1960s. One of the most blatant cases of the opposite trend was a physical attack on the residence of the Ukrainian Exarchate in Kiev in November 1980 by the forces of the KGB and the militia. They surrounded the building and began a massive search of the premises, including brutal body searches of the clergy and officials of the Church. It was only after a vehement protest from Archbishop Makary, the exarchate's foreign relations head, presented personally to the Ukrainian Minister of State Security, that the search and siege of the premises were lifted and, for the first time since the revolution, the Church received an official apology from the republican government.[79] This is the only known case of blatant harassment on such a high level, but on a lower level attacks are frequent and unceasing.

In January 1971, a sixty-eight-year-old mathematics teacher, Boris V. Talantov, died in a Kirov prison hospital while serving a sentence of two years of imprisonment imposed in June 1969. His "crime"? He had signed and cosigned many letters protesting the enforced closure of churches and the expulsion of the most popular priests in the Kirov diocese. Some of these had been addressed to the Moscow Patriarchate, others to the Soviet government, and some to western churchmen, the World Council of Churches and the UN. What was "worse," he had dared to criticize the whole official Soviet church policy and legislation in several letters to Soviet newspapers, and in one, addressed to the Soviet government, he even had proposed how these should be changed.[80]

Young people who join church choirs are harassed by the militia and the KGB and threatened with loss of jobs and educational opportunities if they continue to sing in the churches.

Pitirim with printing paper and is paid 1,000 to 1,500 rubles each time. No receipts are kept.

[78]Sergeeva, 32.

[79]Ibid., 30.

[80]"Konchina Borisa Talantova," *VRSKhD*, no. 98 (1970) 167-9. For Talantov's activities see above in chapter 10.

In some places, it is reported, Soviet officials come to churches during the services, or just before their beginning, and if any young people try to join the choirs, they physically remove them from the churches. A youth church choir founded in Kiev was forcefully disbanded, and the priest of that church lost his registration as punishment and had to take a job as choir director in a small provincial town.[81]

These and similar acts are the regime's "rear-guard actions," aimed at arresting or at least slowing down the movement of the youth toward the Church. It is for this purpose that the militia and its Komsomol auxiliaries cordon off churches at Easter and other major church holy days under the pretext of protecting them from antireligious hooligans and, under the same pretext, prevent young people from entering them. In some cases they let the young people through if they show they are wearing crosses around their necks, but on other occasions even this does not help.[82]

In 1974, simultaneously and independently from each other, two religio-philosophic seminars were organized, one by young intellectuals in Moscow, led by Alexander Ogorodnikov, a former student of cinematography; another, by young intellectuals of Leningrad. The Leningrad seminar has put out a number of unofficial *samizdat* periodicals, the most long-lasting one, still published in 1981 although with irregular intervals, is 37, after the number of the house where the seminar had been meeting, originally in a basement room. The inhabitant of that room, a young philosopher and psychologist, Lev Rudkevich, has since emigrated and now resides in Vienna. Somehow, despite harassment and enforced emigration of a number of its initiators, the seminar survives to the present day. Much more tragic has been the fate of the Moscow seminar, which, by 1978, began to publish its own unofficial journal, *Community* (*Obshchina*). The seminar members had jointly bought a small rural cottage in the Vladimir province, not far from Moscow, where they held their meetings

[81]"Kiev Youth Choir Harassed," *OC*, no. 8 (August 1981) 2; the Christian Committee's appeal to Patriarch Demetrios of Constantinople, in *VRKhD*, no. 126 (1978) 261.

[82]It was, for instance, Andrei Grigorenko, the son of General Peter Grigorenko, who despite showing his cross was physically prevented from entering a church in Moscow on Easter 1975. See *Khronika*, no. 36 (May 31, 1975; Chalidze Publishers reprint) 52-3.

and had room to put up out-of-town visitors overnight. There, Ogorodnikov, who had been expelled from the All-Union Institute of Cinematography for overtly confessing Christianity and trying to preach it among Russian hippies, tried to register as an individual farmer, with the right to live off the attached garden plot and its produce. This was refused, Ogorodnikov was arrested at the end of 1978 and, in 1979, he was sentenced to one year at hard labor for alleged refusal to accept gainful employment ("parasitism"). At the end of the term he was tried again, in the labor camp, and given an additional six years behind bars plus five of internal exile for anti-Soviet propaganda while in the camp. Another of the seminar's founding members, Alexander Argentov, had been arrested as far back as 1976 and kept in a psycho-prison for a year. In the course of 1979-1980 seven other leading members of the seminar received various terms of incarceration, among them Tatyana Shchipkova, a lecturer in Latin and French at the Smolensk Pedagogical Institute, and Vladimir Poresh, a philologist and librarian from Leningrad.[83]

Such harsh treatment meted out to this relatively harmless study group must have been motivated by the following reasons: (1) their attempt to set themselves up as a Christian commune, the last one of which had been suppressed by the Soviets during the forced collectivization of agriculture; and (2) their plans to carry on a wide Christian mission, which was to include even Christian summer camps for children and youth. Although these ideas had only been in the stage of discussion, their missionary activity was already beginning with the coopting of out-of-town members, from Leningrad, Smolensk and Vitebsk (in Belorussia), among other places. The increasing involvement of youth in the Church in Moscow, Leningrad and Kiev is a phenomenon of some years standing, and the authorities have probably given up hope of crushing it. But they would try their best to prevent its

[83]See Shchipkova's article in *VRKhD*, no. 130 (1979) 345-54; on Alexander Argentov, an early casualty of the seminar (he was incarcerated in a psycho-prison for his faith in 1976), see *Russkaya mysl'*, no. 3119 (September 30, 1976) 5; on Shchipkova's trial and sentence of three years of imprisonment see *Russkaya mysl'*, no. 3324 (September 4, 1980). See also "Soviet Crackdown on Religious Movement," *OC*, no. 1 (January 1980) 3; "Soviets Repress Youth Group," *OC*, no. 2 (February 1980) 1; and "Religious Activist Sentenced to 11 Years at Hard Labor," *OC*, no. 11 (November 1980) 3. Also *Khronika*, no. 58 (1980; Chalidze, 1981) 33-4; and *Posev*, no. 3 (1980) 10 and no. 7 (1980) 5.

spread to the provinces as far as they could.[84] Besides, the whole idea of an autonomous and active social organization existing independently from communist organizational initiative and even ideologically antagonistic to it is intolerable to the communist establishment, particularly in the case of as vocal and outward looking a group as the Ogorodnikov seminar hoped to become.

The other important expression of Christian extra-Church activities was the already mentioned Christian Committee for the Defense of Believers' Rights in the USSR. It was inaugurated by Fr. Gleb Yakunin, Viktor Kapitanchuk and the deacon and former political prisoner of the Khrushchev days Varsonofy Khaibulin at the end of 1976, soon after Yakunin's abortive appeal to the patriarch to have him reinstated in full as a priest. The occasion was the tenth anniversary of Yakunin's and Eshliman's interdiction by the patriarch.

The committee began to publicize all known cases of persecutions and administrative suppressions of religious activities in the Soviet Union, irrespective of the denomination in question, by irregularly issuing a typewritten information bulletin, by contacting foreign journalists in Moscow and by sending appeals to the Soviet government and to the patriarch as well as to the World Council of Churches and western church leaders. The committee did not limit itself to church cases alone, but also pleaded for all known cases of persecutions of individuals for their convictions and peaceful expression thereof, believing that this was a moral duty imposed by their Christian conscience. Three years later Yakunin and two of his associates, Lev Regelson and Kapitanchuk, were arrested. The latter two eventually pleaded guilty, were conditionally released and stated that they were ready to suffer for faith but not for human rights. Yakunin stood fast, declaring in court "that his activities were 'my religious duty as a priest.'" In 1980 he was condemned to five years in a strict regime labor camp, to be followed by five years of internal exile. A very pop-

[84]Nikolai Khovansky, "Pis'mo N. Chakovskomu," *VRKhD*, no. 122 (1977) 245-7. The author is writing from Vitebsk to Chakovsky, the editor of the *Literary Gazette*, where on April 13, 1977 a slanderous article appeared on the Ogorodnikov Seminar, among other things, under the title "Freedom of Religion and Slanderers." See also the collection of documents on and excerpts from the *samizdat* publications of both the Leningrad and the Moscow seminars, "Khristianskii seminar," in *VS*, no. 39 (1980).

ular Moscow priest and medical doctor, Fr. Kirill Chernetsky, addressed his flock during the service on the day of Yakunin's trial with the following words: "A righteous man is just now being tried in Moscow, the Priest Gleb. I beg you to join me in a common prayer service for Fr. Gleb's health." Fr. Chernetsky was subsequently removed to one of the more distant parishes in the Moscow diocese.[85]

But the committee's activities were so popular among the Christians that soon after the arrests the committee issued a statement to the effect that some 250 applications had been received from Christians of different confessions to join the committee. In view of the persecutions, the committee decided "to accept ten new members, withholding their names from publication." Just before the arrests the names of two more committee members, however, were made public: V. Shchegolev and, significantly, a young professor of the Moscow Theological Academy, Fr. Vasily Fonchenkov. On Yakunin's arrest, Fr. Nikolai Gainov, an active priest of the Russian Orthodox Church, announced that he was taking Yakunin's place.[86] Although, to the best of our knowledge, the committee has not been active since Fr. Yakunin was sentenced, Fonchenkov disseminated several statements in support of Yakunin and on the warnings and threats he had had from the KGB. One of his statements, published in the West, warned that his position was that of full support for the struggle for human and religious rights in the USSR, and should he be arrested and make statements to the contrary while in prison, these ought to be ignored.[87]

[85]Fr. Chernetsky had for a long time wanted to study theology but the CRA refused to permit his enrolment at the seminary. To circumvent this, the then rector of the seminary Bishop Filaret (now Metropolitan of Minsk) hired him as a physician at the seminary at Trinity-St. Sergius Monastery. Surreptitiously he attended lectures and passed examinations in private. It was over the graduation and ordination of Chernetsky that Filaret lost his post as the seminary and academy rector. (Unofficial Russian church information.) See also Posev, no. 11 (1981) 4; on Kapitanchuk and Regelson see Khronika, no. 58 (1980) 21-32. Both received suspended sentences of five years imprisonment and were released after the trial.

[86]"Zayavlenie khristianskogo komiteta" (Moscow, March 12, 1980), AS 3958; Posev, nos. 1 and 5 (1980) 5 and 7, respectively.

[87]Statement of May 16, 1979, on joining the committee, in VS, no. 35-36 (1979) 123-5; his and Shchegolev's letters warning that should they be arrested any recantations ought to be disregarded are in OC, no. 2 (February 1981) 1, and Posev, no. 1 (1981) 14, respectively.

He must have had in mind Fr. Dimitry Dudko's recantation in June 1980.[88] Dudko was one of the most outspoken Moscow priests, famous for his sermons in the form of dialogues with both believers and unbelievers attending his church, for his human rights and other *samizdat* activities as well as for running unofficial catechetical seminars for youth at his home after Sunday services, and for baptizing thousands of adult converts.[89] He had spent eight years in prisons and camps as a young seminarian in the immediate postwar years, and apparently his resistance broke down at the prospect of repeating the experience in his advanced age. It seems there was also a personal element in his recantation. He was personally emotionally attached to the patriarch. It was Pimen who had him ordained on his return from the prisons, and Pimen had to overcome many obstacles to do so, as the Soviets opposed his ordination. Now, during Lent of 1980, he sent a letter to Pimen from his jail cell (he had been arrested in January of that year) asking him for the traditional Lenten forgiveness and regretting that, through his behavior, he must have caused much discomfort to the patriarch and to the Church. Apparently, the KGB capitalized on this letter, promising both the patriarch and Fr. Dudko the latter's release if he agreed to issue a public recantation for his activities in a similar context. And so, on June 30, Fr. Dimitry, probably pressured by the patriarch as well, appeared on Soviet TV with a long speech recanting his political activities, as he put it, which had harmed the Church and had been contrary to his patriotic duty as a Russian priest. In the same recantation he unjustly attacked by name the western correspondents and travelers who had helped him in his contacts with émigré church circles and in his publication endeavors (he had published several books in the West), and even fraudulently claimed that Archbishop Vasily of Brussels had been involved in his undercover operations, which the archbishop emphatically denied.[90]

[88]See above in chapter 8, n. 44.

[89]See his *O nashem upovanii* (Paris 1975), English ed. *Our Hope* (Crestwood, N.Y.: SVS Press, 1977); "Kreshchenie na Rusi," *VRKhD*, no. 117 (1976) 188-208; "Fr. Dimitri Dudko: an Eye-Witness Account," *RCL*, no. 2 (1976) 21-31.

[90]See his open letter to Pimen of June 5, 1980—when he was still in jail—in *ZhMP*, no. 7 (1980) 40; and his letter in response to Vasily's protest, apologizing "for besmearing your holy name," in *Khronika*, no. 57 (August 1980;

Indeed, in addition to purely ecclesiastical activities—which also included the publishing of a *samizdat* parish bulletin, *In the Light of the Transfiguration,* the only such publication in the contemporary USSR—Fr. Dimitry had involved himself in some unnecessary political declarations and provocative actions from the Soviet point of view. Nevertheless—and this is a promising new phenomenon in the behavior of the church establishment—the patriarchate did try to protect Fr. Dimitry. Metropolitan Yuvenaly of Krutitsy, who had replaced the inept and subservient Serafim in 1978, at first warned Dudko that the Church would defend him as long as his activities remained purely ecclesiastical (presumably, including baptisms, seminars and other missionary activities), but she would not be able to do anything for him if he engaged in political activities. This did not change Dudko's behavior. Still, in the spring of 1979, the metropolitan paid a visit to Fr. Dudko's church, situated about twenty miles from Moscow, concelebrated with him and, in his sermon, praised the holy atmosphere in the church and Fr. Dimitry as a pastor and in particular as a saintly person. After his arrest, hierarchs of the Moscow Patriarchate stated abroad that the patriarchate was making enquiries regarding the priest and would try to help him once he had been officially charged.[91] As soon as he was released he received a new pastoral appointment in the Moscow-Krutitsy diocese, and again Yuvenaly demonstratively came to celebrate a liturgy with him. Moreover, in 1981 Fr. Dimitry renewed the publication of his parish bulletin, this time, most probably, with the approval of the Soviet authorities. If this is so, it could be a precedent, or an attempt to neutralize the effect of suppression of such uncontrolled activities as the Christian Committee, the free religiophilosophic seminars and their truly independent *samizdat* publications by tolerating instead a more controlled, "censored" *samizdat.*[92] Be it as it may, the former

Chalidze, 1981) 43. See also Levitin, "O tekh, kogo nedavno sudili," *Posev,* no. 11 (1980) 47-8.

[91]Our source on Yuvenaly's visit is Dudko's oral information to an OCA cleric, confirmed to this author. See also "Russian Hierarchs Deny Religious Persecution," *OC,* no. 5 (May 1980) 2; and Sergeeva, 30-1.

[92]*Russkaya mysl'* (July 23, 1981) 7 and (September 17, 1981) 4; *OC,* no. 8 (August 1981) 2. Nikita Struve, analyzing Dudko's controversial behavior both prior to and after his arrest, concludes that he fell prey to "the temptation . . .

spiritual children of Fr. Dimitry were so shocked by his repentance on TV that they refused to accept him and have deserted him.[93]

It was probably in order to preclude a KGB game à la Dudko with himself that Fr. Fonchenkov made the precursory announcement cited above. And just as in the Dudko case, the Church did not desert Fonchenkov. Although he was eventually demoted from his teaching post, he still functions as a parish priest in the Moscow provincial diocese (of Krutitsy and Kolomna).

Fonchenkov is a living example of the new cadres entering the Church, which make it harder and harder for the atheistic establishment to represent the Church as an institution housing remnants of the prerevolutionary reactionary and clerical elements and of the most ignorant peasantry. He was born in 1932 into a prominent communist family. A street in Moscow bears the names of his father and uncle, two Civil War Bolshevik heroes. He is a history graduate and used to work as a research associate at the Moscow Museum of the Revolution. Under Khrushchev the museum was charged with directing atheistic propaganda in Moscow. Contact with religion, however, resulted in the conversion of a number of its employees to Christianity; two of them, including Fonchenkov, subsequently became Orthodox priests. His father also returned to the Church shortly before his death. In 1972 Fonchenkov completed his graduate theological studies at the Moscow Academy, joined the Department of External Ecclesiastical Relations and four years later was posted to East Berlin as a priest and editor of the East German Orthodox

of national-Bolshevism"—identifying the state with the nation. "Chto sluchilos' s o. Dimitriem Dudko?" *VRKhD*, no. 132 (1980) 230-2.

A precedent regarding "controlled" *samizdat* was set in the KGB's abortive attempt to control *Veche*, the neo-Slavophile *samizdat* journal. Its failure to manipulate the editor, V. Osipov, resulted in his incarceration in 1975 (eight years at hard labor). See M. Kheifets, "Russkii patrio V. Osipov," *Kontinent*, no. 27 (1981) 159-214; and no. 28 (1981) 134-79. In Russia this is known as *Zubatovshchina*, after S.V. Zubatov's attempts in 1900-3 to set up police-supervised nonpolitical trade unions. See our *Russian Police Trade Unionism*.

[93]Dudko's letter to Struve, *VRKhD*, no. 133 (1981) 293; and a private letter from Moscow (February 1981), which adds that Dudko's spiritual children had consulted individual spiritual elders, and all of them, independently of each other, advised them to abandon Dudko, so that in complete isolation and solitude he would be able "to purge his soul." On the political implications of his recantation see above in chapter 8.

journal *Stimme der Orthodoxie.* Apparently he was not deemed sufficiently politically reliable, because, after one year in Germany, he returned to Moscow to teach Byzantinology and the Soviet Constitution at the seminary.[94]

Even in the case of Yakunin, the Moscow Patriarchate apparently did try to help him. In 1976 he was given the post of reader (psalmist) at a suburban Moscow church; and, according to a normally reliable church source, in late 1978 or early 1979 Metropolitan Yuvenaly offered to restore Yakunin quietly to the priesthood without any gestures of repentance on his part, and to appoint him to a parish.[95] Fr. Yakunin, allegedly, refused the offer. Should this be true, the price he was asked to pay for the restoration was probably the dissolution of his Christian Committee and the suspension of his human rights activities in general. Otherwise, his refusal would be illogical in view of his repeated pleas to the patriarch to restore him to his priestly functions.

Whenever possible, the established Church also dissociates herself from Soviet legal indictments against the clergy. In the case of two archbishops sent to concentration camps under Khrushchev on false charges—Andrei (Sukhenko) of Chernigov, who had been given and served an eight-year sentence (1961-1969), and Iov (Kresovich) of Kazan, imprisoned for six years (1960-1966)—the dissociation was quite emphatic, although by implication only. Soon after their release both bishops were reappointed to head important dioceses.[96] Andrei, for whom this was a second term of long imprisonment, had a mental breakdown not long after his release and never recovered. The Church was forced to retire him to a monastery soon after the 1971 sobor, at which he had shown clear signs of mental disorder.[97] Iov

---

[94]"Avtobiografiya," *VS*, no. 35-36 (1979) 125-8.

[95]An indirect confirmation of this was a statement by Metropolitan Filaret of Minsk that the patriarchate had been in contact with Fr. Yakunin. Characteristically, on Yakunin's activities he only said that they could not be "the path of the whole Church and the church administration." "Russian Orthodox Patriarchal Exarch Visits London," *OC*, no. 3 (March 1981) 7.

[96]The real reason for Andrei's incarceration was his refusal to close down a convent. *Patriarch and Prophets*, 175. On Iov's innocence, see Vasily, "Poslednie vstrechi s m. Nikolaem," 214-5; also, Michael Bourdeaux, "Soviet Archbishop Released from Prison, Reinstated by Church," *Christian Century* (May 27, 1970) 674.

[97]Archbishop Vasily confirms Andrei's behavior at the sobor. "Arkhiepiskop Venyamin," 291-2.

remained a ruling bishop until his death in 1977 at the age of seventy-nine. The implied denial of all state charges against him as a greedy money-hoarder and tax-evader are to be found in his obituary in the *Journal of the Moscow Patriarchate,* which calls him "a man deeply dedicated to the Church, modest and peaceful . . . [who] is remembered everywhere he went as a good and generous pastor, full of zealous devotion to God and of peace toward men." He was given a very solemn funeral service presided over by the Metropolitan of Lvov, and warm messages of condolence were received from all the senior hierarchs of the Russian Church, including the patriarch.[98]

Similarly, the Church apparently decided to stand behind the two monasteries that have had a history of harassment by the state or by local authorities. One of them is the Zhirovitsy Monastery in Belorussia; the other, the Pochaev Lavra, one of the four most revered monasteries in the whole Russian Church, only two of which remain open (the Pochaev and the Holy Trinity-St. Sergius Lavras). In the case of the Zhirovitsy Monastery (as well as the whole Belorussian archdiocese), it seems the worst days are over, at least since the appointment of Metropolitan Filaret (Vakhrameev) as the head of the archdiocese in 1979, particularly since he has also become the head of the Church's Department of External Ecclesiastical Relations in 1981. According to Russian ecclesiastical sources, in Khrushchev's time the government of Belorussia pledged to turn the republic into the first fully "unchurched" one in the USSR, to set an example. To achieve this the Belorussian authorities received the concerted help of all the state atheistic establishments and police forces across the empire. Its only seminary, at the Zhirovitsy Monastery, was closed. All its monasteries, other than the latter, were liquidated, while the remaining nuns were moved into the Zhirovitsy male monastery, violating the whole concept of monastic discipline. The number of functioning churches, in the meantime, was reduced from over 1,200 to fewer than 400, many of them without regular services for lack of priests. The new metropolitan has stabilized the situation. By ordaining several score home-trained priests he has had, by 1981, 383 priests serving 370 parishes, some of which he has expanded under the guise of repairs by adding chapels and

[98]V. Imshennik, "Arkhiepiskop Iov," *ZhMP,* no. 3 (1978) 10-1.

thus making it possible to celebrate several services simultaneously. He often brings foreign guests to his diocese in general and to the Zhirovitsy Monastery in particular, thus probably guaranteeing its survival.[99]

It is in a similar fashion that the patriarchate, apparently, is trying to save the Pochaev Lavra, which has been the subject of intermittent brutal harassment ever since 1961. In 1980 the last garden plot of the monastery was confiscated, thus depriving the monks of the last vestiges of material self-sufficiency. Somewhat earlier the monastery hostel for pilgrims was confiscated and turned into a regional asylum for violent lunatics, whose shouts and shrieks are constantly heard at the monastery cathedral during services. The numerous pilgrims visiting the monastery, literally from all parts of the Soviet Union, are subjected to harassment and brutal police beatings, while women are often violated by the police (militia). After the confiscation of the hostel the monks allowed the pilgrims to stay overnight inside the monastery churches. But now police attack the pilgrims there as well and expel them from the churches, while heavily fining those local residents who let the pilgrims inside their houses for the night. Local hotels likewise are not allowed to offer accommodations to pilgrims. Twenty novices who were being prepared for tonsure at the monastery with the intention of subsequently transferring to Mount Athos in Greece were on one of such occasions rounded up, brutally treated by the police and expelled. Local residents, pilgrims and monks have sent numerous appeals to all instances,

[99]Oral testimony by Russian clerics, and "Russian Orthodox Patriarchal Exarch Visits London." In at least ten issues of *ZhMP* for 1979-1981 there are reports on Filaret's activities, his frequent ordinations and visits to the Zhirovitsy Monastery, which included at least two monastic tonsurings and one veiling there, including the tonsuring of the Leningrad theology student from France, Nikon Yakimov. Foreign visitors to the monastery include clerics and exchange students at the Leningrad Academy. See, in particular, *ZhMP*, no. 4 (1979) 16-7; the illustrations between pp. 24 and 25 in no. 9 (1980); no. 9 (1980) 37-9; no. 3 (1981) 17-8; and no. 6 (1981) 30-2.

There are numerous reports of deanery conferences convoked by Filaret at which he usually delivers a lecture on pastoral themes and discusses parish problems with the clerics, while a CRA plenipotentiary gives a propaganda speech. According to a Russian priest who recently served in Belorussia, there has been considerable real decline in religiosity in eastern Belorussia. Only in western Belorussia (formerly Polish) is there a real shortage of churches, and lately a limited religious revival has begun in Minsk (1982 testimony).

including the UN. They tell about the expulsion from the monastery of Fr. Amvrosy, a highly revered spiritual elder although only forty-four years old. A former father-confessor at the Trinity-St. Sergius Monastery, expelled from there under Soviet pressure, he joined the Pochaev Monastery in 1976 and soon gained fame among the pilgrims as a preacher and confessor. The Soviet authorities have accused him of anti-Soviet sermons and, after finding religious books published in the West in his private library, began arresting and questioning monks suspected of associating with Amvrosy. In the course of the investigations a forty-nine-year-old Archimandrite Olimpy (or Alipy) died during the 1981 Holy Week and another monk, Pitirim, became insane —both apparently as a result of police beatings. The Soviets have clearly renewed their efforts to close the monastery, creating by their harassments an unhealthy atmosphere of extreme fanaticism, intolerance and suspicion on both sides. The inability of the abbot, Fr. Yakov, formerly known as a very pious man, to stop the harassment has led to suspicions of his collaboration with the police, resulting even in an attempt on his life by some fanatical pilgrims.[100]

The Church tried to save the monastery by publishing articles in the *Journal of the Moscow Patriarchate* on its historical importance as a bulwark against Roman Catholic aggression under Polish rule in the past. Other articles reported hierarchical services there by visiting Russian bishops, sometimes with foreign students from the Russian Orthodox theological schools. An American student at the Leningrad Theological Academy was reported tonsured at the monastery, in the apparent hope that establishing an American connection would protect the lavra in the future.[101]

But it is not only the Pochaev pilgrims who are subjected to

[100]*Khronika*, no. 51 (December 1978; Chalidze, 1979) 125-6; *Posev*, no. 4 (1981) 5. According to a *samizdat* report, the persecution of the saintly Amvrosy was carried out in collusion with the monastery abbot. Smolensk Archives, 4300 (December 1979); "Pochaev Pilgrims Direct Appeal to United Nations," *OC*, no. 4 (April 1981) 4; "Believers in USSR Persecuted," *OC*, no. 5 (May 1981) 4. See also *Posev*, no. 11 (1981) 3; and *Russkaya mysl'* (December 3, 1981) 6. Additional information from an inside source in Russia.

[101]*ZhMP*, no. 12 (1979) 9-10; no. 9 (1979) 21-2; no. 1 (1980) 23; no. 4 (1981) 15. The latter article emphasizes the historical importance of the lavra and its popularity among the pilgrims.

harassment and persecutions. It has been already mentioned that Soviet law bans religious group pilgrimages and public processions without express permission in each case, and the permission is usually refused. Many reports have been pouring in telling of brutal harassment of traditional pilgrimages to Russia's many popularly revered holy places. Road blocks are set up; the police beat up pilgrims, arrest them and prosecute and fine local residents for offering hospitality to pilgrims or even for agreeing to ferry them over a river.[102]

As already stated, this merely arouses unnecessary hostility and fanaticism in the believers and agitation among them to the effect that the Soviet system is satanical.[103] Fanatical extremism, however, is useful to atheistic propaganda, which then can depict religious believers as mentally deranged.

The Church and the Outside World

After Khrushchev's demise, as well as after the deaths of Patriarch Aleksii and Metropolitan Nikodim, the activities of the Moscow Patriarchate in the context of Soviet foreign policy remained essentially unchanged.

In July 1969, a World Conference of Religions in Zagorsk was conspicuous by its numerous political speeches praising Soviet peace efforts and condemning American involvement in Vietnam, as well as by the absence of truly religious, let alone theological topics, although the conference contained representatives of all registered confessions of the USSR and forty-four other countries. The latter, however, had no voting rights on the highly political resolutions of the conference.[104]

Soon after his election as patriarch, Pimen, taking the cue from his predecessor, undertook several journeys abroad. Most noteworthy was his journey to the Holy Land in May 1972, during which he met Israel's Minister for Religious Affairs; it was also the first time a Soviet airliner landed in Israel since the 1967

---

[102]See *Posev*, no. 11 (1981) 3; and *Russkaya mysl'* (December 3, 1981) 6.
[103]See above in chapter 11.
[104]"Politics Dominate Conference on Religion," Radio Liberty dispatch, August 19, 1969.

war.[105] The patriarch encountered massive hostile demonstrations of recent emigrants from the USSR reproaching him for concealing religious persecution in the Soviet Union and acting as the Soviet Union's policy spokesman.

In October of the same year he paid visits to Greece, Romania and Yugoslavia. Then, in October 1977, he visited the Ecumenical Patriarch in Constantinople, relations with whom have been strained ever since the Moscow Patriarchate granted autocephaly to the Orthodox Church in America, the legitimacy of which Constantinople has refused to recognize. But to return to the 1972 voyage, while in Greece, the patriarch was received by George Papadopoulos, the Prime Minister in the rightist junta of colonels, although the Moscow Patriarchate had earlier condemned the junta in letters to the Greek Synod. During a press conference in Athens the patriarch was asked to comment on Alexander Solzhenitsyn's "Lenten Message" to him of the same year. In that letter Solzhenitsyn had described the sorry and oppressed state of religion in the Soviet Union and reproached the patriarch for daring, in his previous Christmas message, to call upon the Russian diaspora to take good care for the religious and patriotic education of their children, while, in the Soviet Union, all children were deprived of such education and the patriarch had never shown any concern for this problem.[106] Metropolitan Yuvenaly, then recently appointed head of the Department of External Ecclesiastical Relations in place of the ailing Nikodim (both hierarchs were accompanying the patriarch), acknowledged the receipt of the letter and calmly said that there were "many inaccuracies" in it that reflected Solzhenitsyn's "insufficient acquaintance with the spiritual work of the Russian Church."[107]

A senior cleric of the Russian Church would later elaborate on the same topic in private. He affirmed that Yuvenaly's comment was right: as long as the Church had no legal recognition as an institution, Solzhenitsyn's address was irrelevant—the patri-

---

[105]"Patriarch Pimen's Second Trip Abroad," Radio Liberty dispatch, December 18, 1972; and "Russian Patriarch Visits Constantinople," *OC*, no. 2 (February 1978) 4.

[106]See Pimen's Christmas message in *ZhMP*, no. 12 (1971) 1-2; Solzhenitsyn's message is in *VRSKhD*, no. 103 (1972) 145-9.

[107]"Patriarch Pimen's Second Trip," Radio Liberty.

arch was powerless to do anything, for only the "twenties" had institutional, legal recognition. Thus, Solzhenitsyn should have addressed such a letter either to the Soviet government or to each individual "twenty," or to both. According to *samizdat* sources, on receipt of the letter Pimen said with a sad smile: "If he had only been in my shoes for a couple of days," and then added: "Well, let him write."[108]

At the already mentioned Athens press conference, the tone of Yuvenaly's responses, it should be noted, was remarkably reserved and not hostile. This was probably one of the first signs of the somewhat changing external attitude of the Moscow Patriarchate toward its dissidents ("its" in the sense of their being practicing members of the same Church; "external" because deep down in their hearts many a Russian cleric undoubtedly admires the actions of those heroic individuals who dare to stand up almost singlehandedly against the might of the police in defense of civic and religious rights).[109] Moreover, the flood of dissidents' broadsheets, bulletins and press releases reaching the West have documented too many cases of persecution to be denied, although the late Nikodim once responded to a remark to this effect by a cleric of the Orthodox Church in America: "Let us come to an accord on this question. You publicize these materials in the West, and we shall issue denials."

Two blatant cases of such high-level denials of persecutions that by then looked more pitiful than outrageous were to occur in 1973 and 1975. The first one was in connection with Pimen's official visit to the World Council of Churches headquarters in Geneva in September. For the first time Dr. Philip Potter, the Secretary General of the WCC, welcomed the patriarch and appealed to him to exert himself to extend human rights in the Soviet Union as well as in the rest of the world. In response, Pimen read out a pitifully delusive text prepared by "someone" in advance, which denied any suppression of human and civic rights in the Soviet Union and extolled "the merits of the socialist way of life, which, as we see it, corresponds in great measure to

---

[108]"Kamen davit," *Veche*, no. 5 (May 1972); *VS*, no. 9-10 (Chalidze, 1973) 52.

[109]Our conclusion from encounters with numerous Russian clerics over approximately the last four years.

Christian ideals." He then stated that the difficulties met with by the Christians in the Soviet Union were not antagonistic and that therefore "we ourselves have to work to correct our difficulties and to improve our society."[110] The second part of the statement, despite all its sophistry, is at least an attempt at hinting that there are subjects that he, the Patriarch of Russia, dares not mention. This in itself is an improvement on many earlier public statements by Nikodim and Nikolai (Yarushevich).

The other case was related to the General Assembly of the World Council of Churches at Nairobi (Kenya) in November-December 1975. Fr. Yakunin and Lev Regelson addressed a letter on behalf of persecuted religious believers and prisoners of conscience in general in the Soviet Union to the assembly. The letter briefly recounted the history of Church-state relations since the revolution and the explicit recognition of the persecutions in Patriarch Tikhon's statements. It cited acts and declarations of other religious organizations both in the USSR and abroad in the 1920s on behalf of the persecuted Orthodox Christians and Tikhon's expression of gratitude for them. The letter then speaks about the renewed persecutions under Khrushchev and the WCC's silence on this matter, mentioning such prisoners for their convictions as Vladimir Osipov,[111] as well as a number of others imprisoned for their human rights activities. The authors appeal to the WCC to offer public prayers for the prisoners of conscience and for the persecuted churches of the USSR and to make concerted protests, demanding, for instance, the right to open churches where needed by the believers and to print sufficient quantities of the Holy Scriptures—which are almost impossible to obtain in the country and for the unofficial printing of which a group of Russian Baptists had just been apprehended and incarcerated.

The document was printed in a Kenyan Christian newspaper two days after the assembly had opened, but only thirteen days

[110]"Patriarch Pimen of Moscow and All Russia in Geneva," Radio Liberty dispatch, September 26, 1973. The Rt. Rev. Prof. Alexander Schmemann's appropriate comment was: "The patriarch's . . . statement in . . . Geneva that there are 'neither poor nor rich, neither privileged nor persecuted ones' in the USSR . . . surpasses that measure of untruth after which silence becomes treason. This statement was made at the time when . . . another wave of persecutions has been unleashed [in the Soviet Union] against all dissidents, against all expressions of faith, spirit and freedom." "Mera nepravdy," *VRKhD*, no. 108-110 (1973) 142.

[111]See above.

later, two days prior to the end of the conference, was the document finally included in the official proceedings. Three days after the original publication of the letter, both the Orthodox and the Baptist delegations published their responses in the same paper. It is significant that neither of these responses denied all of Yakunin-Regelson's assertions out of hand. Metropolitan Yuvenaly, the head of the Orthodox delegation, tried to cast doubt on the reliability of the authors by mentioning that Yakunin had difficulties with his own Church, while Regelson was hostile to the whole idea of ecumenism. In the familiar post-1927 line of argument, Yuvenaly claimed that church people have been persecuted for their hostility to the Soviet state, not for their faith, but he admitted that "there have arisen and there do arise problems in the life of the Church, resulting from the infringement upon the laws concerning religious communities, both by local representatives of the state authorities and by members of the church communities." But then he goes on to compliment the CRA for being so "helpful" to the Church, blatantly contradicting the already cited internal CRA reports that make it transparently clear that the very purpose of the CRA is to repress, oppress and suppress the Church whenever and wherever possible.

However, it is pretty clear that, short of a revolution in the Church's external policies, her representatives could not have reacted otherwise to the Yakunin-Regelson letter. And it was an English Baptist delegate, Dr. Ernest Payne, who went out of his way to oblige the CRA more than did the Russian delegation. After the majority had already voted in favor of a resolution that stated that "The WCC is concerned about restrictions of religious liberty, particularly in the USSR. The Assembly respectfully requests the government of the USSR to implement effectively principle number 7 of the Helsinki Agreement," Payne "proposed that the whole matter be sent back to the committee, as the assembly was . . . debating an issue which had not been considered by the committee itself." This was accepted. Under the pressure of the Russian Orthodox delegate the committee watered down the wording to read "alleged infringements of religious liberty," excluding the term "USSR" from the text.[112] It was this relatively harmless amendment that was eventually accepted. Nevertheless,

[112]David Kelly, "Nairobi: A Door Opened," *RCL* 4:1 (1976) 4-17.

for the first time the question of religious persecution in the USSR was openly debated by a WCC assembly, and the subject could not henceforth be wholly ignored.

In March 1976, Yakunin and Regelson addressed a new memorandum to Dr. Potter. This one contained a detailed and critical analysis of the whole Soviet legislation on religion, particularly the amendments of 1975, showing not only its extreme discriminatory character but also the worsening of the status of religion—for the 1975 amendments for the first time gave the Soviet "registering organs" the right to remove from the church organs members elected by the believers. The fact that the amendments do not allow a religious society even to begin to function until approval and registration have been granted by the CRA is tantamount to the transformation of the act of registration of a religious community from a function of *sanctioning,* in accordance with the 1929 legislation, to that of *permitting,* in accordance with the 1975 amendments. Their detailed analysis proved the fact of religious persecution as emanating from a state policy, and thus they appealed to the WCC for decisive condemnatory actions regarding the Soviet treatment of human rights.[113] At the same time, they addressed a letter to Patriarch Pimen reporting on the slander and misrepresentation to which their action had been subjected by a priest in a suburban Moscow parish. They expressed concern lest this become the first act in a comedy produced by the KGB-CRA in which first priests and then the enslaved bishops would play their puppet roles in attacking the authors of the memoranda, misquoting their contents in their sermons to the ignorant believers, etc.[114] Whether this warning did have any effect or whether the times had simply changed and there were not enough clergymen willing to perform such roles, the comedy did not take place. Moreover, as Yakunin and Regelson pointed out in their second memorandum to Potter, even the Soviet press could not completely ignore the reverberations their

[113]*RCL* 4:4 (1976) 9-15; Russian original, AS 2560.

[114]See *VS*, no. 24 (1976) 83-8. The priest in question was Fr. Dimitry Sagan, who, in a weekday service with mostly old people present (February 18, 1976), attacked the letter to Nairobi as allegedly stating that Orthodox believers in general were prevented from frequenting churches in the Soviet Union, then demagogically asked the old women present whether anyone had forbidden them to come to church. The old women responded that this was not true.

first memorandum to the WCC had caused, nor entirely deny its contents, and had to admit that occasionally there had been violations of religious rights by local authorities.[115]

Nevertheless, the WCC waited for another four years before issuing its first direct criticism of Soviet church policies. It was an acting WCC general secretary, Dr. Konrad Raiser, who, while Potter was on leave, addressed a letter to Metropolitan Yuvenaly on October 1, 1980 in which he expressed the WCC's concern at:

> the coincidence of a number of cases involving Christian believers which are presently on trial . . . we are not convinced that the "non-religious" basis on which these trials are said to be conducted will be easily understood, either within or outside the Soviet Union, and we are concerned that the accumulation of these trials and the wide publicity given them in the Soviet media may influence Soviet public opinion against the life of the churches . . . we find the kind of sentences pronounced in the trials already concluded to be disproportionate with the seriousness of the crimes which have allegedly been committed.

Metropolitan Yuvenaly's response was again very reserved, given the circumstances. He said that he had addressed a request to the CRA to provide the exact rationale for the trials and sentences in question. He then dissociated the Church from the state's punitive actions. Then he claimed that he thought that the state had shown leniency by releasing those religious defendants who had pleaded guilty and recanted—e.g., Regelson, who had been released on a five-year probation, and Fr. Dudko, who immediately upon release had received a parish in Yuvenaly's own diocese, although the state criminal investigation had not yet been completed. Thus, once again Yuvenaly implicitly stressed the fact that the Church did not recognize the validity of such criminal charges by the state.[116]

These statements of dissociation from the state's penal policies and signs of attempts at protecting the clergy against them,

[115]*RCL* 4:4 (1976) 10.
[116]"Ecumenical Body Criticizes Soviets for Jailing of Religious Dissidents," and "Metropolitan Juvenaly Responds," *OC*, no. 1 (January 1981) 2.

discussed earlier, are in themselves notable strides forward in the church establishment's reticent self-emancipation, although there still are cases of absurd statements made abroad by some Russian hierarchs amounting to an unquestioning approval of all Soviet policies.[117] These do seem to be on the wane, however. One example of particularly daring behavior was presented by Fr. Vitaly Borovoi, the patriarchate's permanent head representative at the WCC in Geneva. In a public statement made in the US in 1979, he said that the Christians of the Soviet Union would love to see a true Christian society in the noncommunist West, rather than just another form of godless, materialistic secularism. Had western democracies been Christian in their values, aims and social justice, Christians under communism would see them as an alternative to their system.[118]

As to Metropolitan Yuvenaly, a man in rather poor health although only forty-six years old in 1981, he was replaced in that year by Metropolitan Filaret of Minsk in the position of chairman of the Department of External Ecclesiastical Relations. The official reason was health, and Yuvenaly remains the head of the Moscow-Krutitsy archdiocese and a permanent member of the Synod. But there may have been other reasons as well. The late Metropolitan Nikodim's hyperactive participation in external and ecumenical activities and complete toeing of the Soviet foreign policy line was compensated for by the improving and strengthening of the position of the Church at home. Nikodim

[117]For example, while on a visit to Austria in 1980 Metropolitan Aleksii of Tallin once again repeated the cliché, which no one takes seriously anymore, that "In the Soviet Union citizens are never arrested for their religious or ideological convictions." "Russian Hierarchs Deny Religious Persecution," *OC*, no. 5 (May 1980) 2. At the same time, Archbishop Pitirim became a little more evasive in his statements, perhaps at least partly as a consequence of public criticism from a fellow bishop for his earlier absurd assurances that there was no need for church charity because the Soviet government took care of welfare, and no need for religious education of children because, most absurdly, it would be harmful for their upbringing! In his German newspaper interview in 1980, Pitirim simply said that Church-state relations have "stabilized," but then, contrary even to the cited CRA reports, claimed that there was no shortage of clergy in the USSR. See, respectively, ibid., and Archbishop Vasily, "Neskol'ko slov ob interv'yu arkhiepiskopa . . . Pitirima," *VRKhD*, no. 114 (1974) 268-70, which is preceded by Fr. Yakunin's letter to Pitirim protesting the mendacious and antichurch character of the interview (265-7).

[118]The report in *OC* cannot be located by the author.

gained such concessions as the bilateral exchange of theology students, thereby increasing the erudition of young Russian theologians, who would spend two-year periods of study at Roman Catholic seminaries in West Germany (Regensburg), Paris and the Vatican. He invited foreign theologians to lecture at the Leningrad Academy, thus bringing the Russian Church and theology out of the isolation imposed by the regime. Because of Nikodim's stature and international prestige in ecumenical circles, his services to the Soviet state, in the eyes of Soviet officials, appeared to be of such importance that he, his archdiocese and indirectly the whole Church were winning more security inside the country. With Nikodim's death, neither the foreign policy line nor the patriarchate's obligations to the Soviet state changed, but there remained no one in the leadership of the patriarchate of Nikodim's stature and energy, no one to fight for and win concessions from the state for the services. The first effect of this was the partial loss of the exchange program: there have been no Soviet Orthodox theology graduate students in Regensburg since 1979 and no one in the Vatican since 1981. As one Russian cleric has put it, "The external activity of the Russian Orthodox Church . . . has become less effective [under Yuvenaly], which threatens to gradually weaken the Church's internal position as well."

Yuvenaly was Nikodim's disciple, but he lacked many of Nikodim's intellectual and diplomatic qualities. Filaret is a different man. Although six years younger than Yuvenaly, intellectually he is more outstanding. Theologically he is quite erudite as well, having been the rector of the Moscow theological schools prior to his appointment to West Berlin in 1973. He also possesses some foreign-language skills. He has recommended himself as a very dedicated and energetic churchman, who tries as much as possible to avoid uttering statements that lack credibility. He is, moreover, very cautious in his assurances of loyalty to the Soviet state, stopping short, as far as possible, of a blanket approval of its social system and ideology. We have already mentioned the revival of the Belorussian archdiocese in the few years that he has been its head, which parallels the activities of his former deputy, Chrysostom. Given the fact that Filaret is now at the helm of the Moscow Patriarchate's external relations, perhaps it is not too far-fetched to expect some changes from the lines of

Nikodim and Yuvenaly. It is also rumored that Filaret is being groomed for the patriarchate, should the vacancy arise.[119] Nevertheless, he was either unable or unwilling to prevent another dishonorable foreign performance by the patriarch: his trip to New York in June 1982 to read another prepared statement, this time to the UN General Assembly, on disarmament. This time the media of the free world completely ignored his performance, as if through an organized boycott. Indeed, a speech on disarmament by the top churchman from the USSR avoiding any critique of his own government, engaged in a genocidal war against the population of Afghanistan, sounds absurdly ironical, to say the least.

In contrast, in inter-Orthodox relations the Moscow Patriarchate has continued to demonstrate concern for the Orthodox *oikoumene* and a desire to solve the problems of the Orthodox diaspora (although, contrary to the Autocephaly Agreement of 1970, it has prevented the return of some of its North American parishes to the Orthodox Church in America). In connection with the pan-Orthodox council, each of the major local Orthodox churches was asked to prepare draft proposals on this subject. Only the Moscow and the Antiochian Patriarchates proposed a dynamic and ecumenical Orthodox solution, suggesting that new territorial autocephalous churches be created in the new areas of multinational Orthodox concentration and resettlement, in place of the uncanonical multitude of parallel dioceses connected to their national mother churches, which is the prevailing contemporary situation in the Americas, Western Europe and Australia. For America, the Russian Church suggested that the Greek Church grant autocephaly to her American archdiocese, whereupon the newly autocephalous Greek archdiocese and the Orthodox Church in America would merge to form a Patriarchate of the Americas. The Greek Patriarchates of Alexandria and Constantinople con-

---

[119]Filaret's biography in *ZhMP*, no. 1 (1979) 12. Since his appointment there has been a conspicuous rise in the importance of the much more compliant Pitirim, who has become an unofficial chief public relations officer for the patriarchate, constantly traveling abroad. According to unofficial information, Filaret now practically shares foreign relations functions with Pitirim. This seems to be indirect evidence that Filaret's appointment was the choice of the Church, not of the CRA, and was not too much to the latter's liking. If so, then Pimen is not completely passive.

tinued to claim the rights of Constantinople to jurisdiction over all Orthodox churches beyond the borders of the established territorial jurisdictions of other local churches, while the Romanian Patriarchate favored the retention of the uncanonical status quo—i.e., national churches formed originally by emigrants from these countries to retain their subordination to the national churches of origin in perpetuity. This, according to the Orthodox canons, is a minor heresy of phyletism, i.e., nationalism, which contradicts the universality of Christianity.[120]

The Life of the Church and the New Christian Intelligentsia

Reluctantly, and in most cases in a roundabout way, Soviet professional atheists began to concede toward the end of the 1960s and the early 1970s that there has been a rise of religiosity in the country. Whereas in the early to mid-1960s most Soviet surveys on religious believers claimed that of the total urban population they constituted no more than 10 to 15 percent and of the rural population 15 to 25 percent, by the end of that decade and, predominantly, in the 1970s they began to write that "the average proportion of believers in the urban population is 20 percent, plus some 10 percent waverers."[121] The latter category, however, is very ill defined, as some observers admit that, after the surveys had been completed, the "waverers" were found to be attending a church service the following Sunday. Moreover, at least some surveys are carried out by local Komsomol and/or atheist activists, and by personal questioning at that, rather than anonymously.[122] This would discourage many a believer concerned for his or her job and career from giving exact information on the question of faith.

The questionable reliability of Soviet data on the religiosity of the population has already been illustrated in chapter 5 and

[120]"The Problem of the Orthodox Diaspora," *OC*, no. 1 (January 1980) 2.
[121]G.V. Vorontsov, *Leninskaya programma ateisticheskogo vospitaniya v deistvii (1917-1937 gg.)* (Leningrad, 1973) 175; M.A. Morozov and E.M. Lisavtsev, *Aktual'nye zadachi ateisticheskogo vospitaniya* (Moscow, 1970) 8.
[122]See, for example, I.D. Pantskhava, ed., *Konkretno-sotsiologicheskoe izuchenie sostoyaniya religioznosti i opyta ateisticheskogo vospitaniya* (Moscow, 1969) 5; and V.V. Pavlyuk, et al., *Osobennosti sovremennogo religioznogo soznaniya* (Moscow, 1966) 82 and 59.

elsewhere, where it was shown that the assessments varied in the course of the 1920s and 1930s from 10 to 60 percent, while a few years later the reality of massive religious recovery on the German-occupied territories drove German observers to conclude that the number of believers could have been as high as 80 to 90 percent of the population. If the lower Soviet claims of the late 1920s to the 1930s of 10 to 30 percent religious believers are to be accepted, then all the multiple millions spent on antireligious propaganda over these sixty years appear to have been a total waste, the percentage of believers remaining constant. In fact, it may even be rising, because Soviet sources have always claimed that in rural areas the proportion of believers was almost double the urban average. Thus, if the religious believers constitute 20 to 30 percent of the urban population, then they must add up to between 40 and 60 percent of the rural population. As we may remember, the highest Soviet estimate dating from the late 1930s had been 30 percent religious believers in the urban areas and over 60 percent in the rural ones. If, however, the less-partisan German estimates are taken as more accurate, then indeed there must either have been a considerable decline in religiosity since the war, or the contemporary Soviet religious statistics have remained as untrustworthy as the prewar ones. The latter conclusion appears to be closer to the truth, in view of the growing concern

TABLE 12-2
ATTITUDES TOWARD RELIGION AMONG LENINGRAD INDUSTRIAL WORKERS[123]

	1971	1979
Marxist attitudes	27%	10%
vulgar antireligious ("all priests are crooks")	17	4
positive attitudes (religion is good)	11	19
no answer or no opinion	34	49
"waverers"[124]	7.4	8.8

[123]O.V. Leningrad (a *samizdat* pseudonym), in *Posev*, no. 6 (1980) 13. One of the better known atheist authors of the prewar era, A.P. Mariinsky, cites 20 percent as the average proportion of people "embraced by the Church" in the population in 1928. *Protiv popov i sektantov* (Moscow, 1929) 77-81.

[124]Should these be added to the 10 percent "waverers" on the religious side? Does the category likewise conceal secret faith? If so, then the percentage of believers would climb to almost 40 percent of the population.

of the Soviets with the religious situation in the country and, according to Russian church sources, the markedly increased oppression of the Church since 1981. At least as significant, if indirect, indications of the rise of religiosity, or at least of a social climate conducive to it, are unpublished Soviet sociological surveys of atheists (or those who declare themselves as such) and of their attitudes to believers. One such survey was conducted among Leningrad industrial workers in 1971 and repeated in 1979 (see table 12-2).

Of at least as much concern to Soviet atheists since the 1970s is the presence of young people and converts among the religious believers.[125] There are complaints that "school children show a largely positive attitude to religion," that 80 percent of all religious families teach religion to their children, that Komsomol members get married in church.[126] Priests are quoted as preaching to the parents: "If you want to save your children from the fires of hell, implant the truths of Christ's teachings at home in your children, preserve them from satanic atheism."[127] Neither is preaching limited to parents alone. Metropolitan Filaret of Minsk said "that he advises his priests to gather all the children preparing for confession and communion into one group before the liturgy and to hold a discussion with them."[128]

This renewed concern for the religious upbringing of children by the hierarchy, for the absence of which Solzhenitsyn had criticized it in his Lenten letter to the patriarch, is obviously not to the atheists' liking. They also mention the following factors aiding the "survival" of religion: (1) foreign religious broadcasts; (2) illicit infiltration of Russian religious literature from abroad; and (3) the already mentioned efforts by the clergy to activate the religious zeal of parents and to attract the youth, in a large measure by "attempting to adopt the role of the custodian of national spiritual values . . . the patroness of Russian culture and art."[129] We are told that over 50 percent of newborn babies

[125]Confirmed by an inside Russian church source.

[126]RCL, quoting Uchitel'skaya gazeta and Znamya yunosti, in 1:1 (1973) 39; V.K. Arsenkin in Voprosy nauchnogo ateizma, no. 22 (1978) 202.

[127]E.S. Stepanov, O chem propoveduyut s amvonov (Moscow, 1975) 23 et passim.

[128]"Russian Orthodox Patriarchal Exarch Visits London," 7.

[129]Arsenkin, 17-20. In particular he refers to the Belgian Roman Catholic pub-

are now baptized and that in some cases formerly irreligious parents join the Church under the influence of the baptism of their children, especially when they see a sick child recover after baptism.[130] And it is admitted that "young people tend to be drawn to religion at times of trouble,"[131] i.e., it is recognized that the Soviet way of life, sixty-five years after the revolution, still remains an era of trouble (or is the author referring specifically to the current years, and does he by "times of trouble" mean the current ideological vacuum and interregnum?).

Earlier we spoke about the semicryptic physical enlargement of churches that has gathered momentum in particular since the second half of the 1970s, which must reflect an increase in church attendance. Another indication of this was the decree of the Patriarchal Synod of November 28, 1968, permitting the performance of the Presanctified Liturgy in the evenings, no doubt to allow greater numbers to receive communion at this service, which has traditionally been performed only in the mornings.[132]

The rapid increase in the number of priestly ordinations in the course of the 1970s and the early 1980s has already been mentioned. One of the more scholarly Soviet religiologists, V. Kurochkin, noted as early as 1969 or 1970 that small but growing numbers of young members of the Soviet intelligentsia were joining the Church and becoming priests. He foresaw that their influx would have a great impact on the Church and on her status and role in Soviet society.[133] Indeed, one of the achievements of

lishers Life with God, which, among others, publishes in Russian the Moscow Priest A. Men's theological works, which are tremendously popular in the USSR. See also V.A. Zots, "Ateizm i dukhovnaya kul'tura sovetskogo obshchestva," *Voprosy filosofii*, no. 7 (1981) 29-37.

[130]Evgraf Duluman in *Pravda Ukrainy* (March 11, 1973) 3; V.D. Kobetsky, "Obryad kreshcheniya kak proyavlenie religioznosti," in Pantskhava, ed., 162-5. Solzhenitsyn maintains that in his native Ryazan more than 60 percent of all infants were baptized in the early 1970s. Leningrad church circles claim that by the early 1980s the rate of infant baptism had risen in the diocese to 85 percent. The cited secret study of the behavior of atheists (n. 123) shows that only 13 percent of the nonparty member sample and 34 percent of the Party members were against the rite of baptism. But then the report shows an unbelievably low percentage of baptisms in the city: 26 percent of all the newborn in 1976, 19 percent in 1971 and again 26 percent in 1979. Presumably these figures refer to the nonbelieving sample, not to the whole city.

[131]*RCL*, citing *Pravda vostoka*, a Central Asian Soviet daily, in 1:1 (1973) 39.

[132]*RAPV*, no. 5 (May 1969) 78.

[133]*Evolyutsiya sovremennogo russkogo pravoslaviya* (Moscow, 1971) 108-11.

the late Metropolitan Nikodim was that he had managed to break through the unwritten Soviet rule that formerly made it almost impossible for members of the Soviet secular intelligentsia (particularly with completed higher secular education) and even for their children to enrol at the theological schools. Lately, a growing number of such young people have been graduating from the theological schools. Some of them already teach there, acting as a living link between the secular Soviet professional establishment and the Church and breaking the ghetto confines into which the Soviet regime has all these years been trying to push her.[134]

A witness to this process has been borne to us by Fr. Borovoi, who said in his sermon at the London Russian Orthodox cathedral:

a new movement has begun among the educated youth, the coming of the young generation into Church, a generation which has been brought up in atheistic homes as convinced unbelievers. [This generation] gained its conversion to Christ on its own, by way of the most profound reflections and inner trials.

This is not to our credit . . . It is to the credit of our believing people; and the glory and thanks be to God, who spreads his mission through the Holy Spirit among these people who are far away from the Church and, it seems, for whom there is no road to lead them there. And yet they come to the Church by many different ways. . . . this often results in the break-up of families, educational and professional sacrifices, or even in the need to part with a loved one: a bride or a fiancé with whom you

---

[134]According to a recent Russian church source, of the 460 students at the Leningrad theology schools 75 percent are adult converts or reconverts to Orthodoxy, many of whom already held Soviet secular higher education diplomas prior to their theology enrolment. Of the teaching staff of forty-three, nine hold secular academic degrees besides the theological ones and most of them are neophytes. A professor of church archeology is a member of the scholarly staff of the State Museum of Ancient Art at the former St. Andronik Monastery in Moscow. He commutes to the Leningrad academy. At least three other professors are similarly employed by state scholarly institutions. The only stipulation of the seminaries is that they be practicing members of the Orthodox Church. All this illustrates a breakthrough in the artificial state-imposed isolation of the Church.

had to part because she or he took fright of your road or simply lacked your faith.

And we have now hundreds and thousands of such concrete living examples. . . . This is what is new in our Church; it can be slowed down, of course . . . but no one in this world has the power to totally stop it. This movement has begun and it will be accelerating, for behind it is the charisma and power of our Lord Jesus Christ, who has seen the confession of faith by his people; who has put his people to the test in humiliation, difficulties, in such conditions that for a while it appeared that just a little more and the end would come.

The Lord has tested [the faith] . . . of our Russian people. . . . Yes, historically the Russian Church . . . has sinned a lot. But the Lord sees how she has been passing through the crucible of tests; he sees that in these sixty years we have had thousands of times more saints than during the rest of the history of the Russian Church, that today *living* saints walk the face of the earth in Russia. . . . and the time will come when the Russian Church will canonize . . . thousands of new saints. Thus the Lord has seen the faith of his people and now tells it: "Your sins are forgiven, get up and walk!" And the Russian Church rises and goes in the glory of God to preach Christ to the whole world.[135]

As one of the leading officials of the Russian Orthodox Church, Fr. Borovoi modestly denies the Church and her clergy any credit for aiding this process of religious awakening in the Soviet Union. But Soviet propaganda gives them much credit. Fr. Dimitry Dudko and some of his former spiritual children have provided us with some data on the effect of his sermons and missionary activities—illegal in the eyes of Soviet law—prior to his arrest and recantation. In the period from 1961 to 1974, the rate of adult and mature conversions at his parish rose from some ten to over

---

[135]*Russkoe vozrozhdenie*, no. 9 (1980) 38-43. In 1979 there were six students at the Leningrad academy with full secular university degrees. Since then the number has been growing at both academies.

four hundred persons per year, and whereas at first the majority of the neophytes were rather poorly educated people, by the 1970s they were predominantly people with a higher education or its equivalent.[136] There are many Christian neophytes among the recent émigrés from the USSR (many of them of Jewish background), and most of them have stories to tell about their pastors and spiritual fathers (sometimes monks), who helped them find God.[137] Religious *samizdat*, which has grown very remarkably in volume and in quality in the 1970s, is to a great extent the product of those Christian neophytes.[138] These writings contain many interesting confessions of personal conversions and individual roads to God.[139] Since the neophytes are particularly enthusiastic about their newly discovered faith, many are unhappy with the subservience of the church establishment to the godless state and join, and even lead, the criticism of the Moscow Patriarchate and its policies and policy statements. Thus, they often link up with the dissidents in general.[140] In fact, quite a number of the neophytes came to the Church via the general civic and human rights dissent, first rejecting the ideology upon which the oppressive social and political system is based and then, in search for an alternative *Weltanschauung*, discovering Christianity. These, of

[136]Our approximate extrapolations from Dudko's incomplete figures in his "Kreshchenie na Rusi."

[137]In Goricheva's case it was the monastic elder Fr. Tavrion (Batozsky). He died in 1978 at the age of eighty in a skete attached to the Riga convent, after having served a total of twenty-seven years in prisons and camps, among other things for acting as a messenger during the abortive 1926 underground patriarchal elections. He was widely recognized as a holy man who brought many to Christ. See N. Shemetov, "Arkhimandrit Tavrion," *VRKhD*, no. 127 (1978) 253-5; "Pravoslavnye bratstva," *VRKhD*, no. 131 (1980) 169-72; and "Arkhiepiskop Pavlin," *VRKhD*, no. 132 (1980) 157-8. See also the obituary in *ZhMP*, no. 7 (1979) 23-4.

[138]A large volume of it is published regularly in *VRKhD*. There is even a popular-theological *samizdat* periodical, *Nadezhda: Khristianskoe chtenie*, edited by an intellectual Orthodox Christian neophyte, Zoya Krakhmalnikova. It is reprinted by Possev in West Germany and is available by subscription in the West.

[139]See, for example, Valery Levyatov, "Kak ya prishel k Bogu," *Grani*, no. 111-112 (1979) 324-9; Krakhmalnikova, "Vozvrashchenie bludnogo syna," *Nadezhda*, no. 2 (1979) 383-436; "Desyat' obrashchenii," *VRKhD*, no. 132 (1980) 212-29, and no. 133 (1981) 221-34.

[140]Some examples are Evgeny Barabanov, Vladimir Osipov, Goricheva, Yu. Voznesenskaya and Solzhenitsyn. See Nikolai Gerasimov, "Vkhozhdenie v tserkov' i ispovedanie Tserkvi v tserkvi," *VRKhD*, no. 128 (1979) 41-96.

course, as a rule, do not break with their earlier human rights activities and carry them over onto a new platform of Christian ethics.

Solzhenitsyn is a good example. We have already mentioned his 1972 "Lenten Message" to Pimen. The letter caused considerable reverberations in dissident circles within the Russian Church. A pseudonymous writer in *Veche* defended the patriarch, but so did a most outspoken priest, Fr. Sergii Zheludkov, who was active in *samizdat* and the human rights movement and was deprived of his clerical registration. He argued that Solzhenitsyn could accord himself more freedom than the patriarch, owing to the world opinion on whose support he could count as a world famous writer. In response, Solzhenitsyn maintained that there was no excuse for the lack of personal courage and readiness for personal sacrifice among the ranks of the higher clergy. The patriarch is not a lonely, defenseless figure, he argued, but commands the support of scores of millions of believers. "What did you know about me nine years ago? Nothing. In other words, there is a way." A lay *samizdat* activist likewise criticized Zheludkov's position. But he saw Solzhenitsyn's overpessimistic picture of the Church as belonging to "yesterday." Today, "the fields have become green"—i.e., there is a church revival.[141]

Searching and finding in the Church pastors and bishops whose moral profile better corresponds to their ideas of a Church relatively free from control and interference by CRA agents, some of them argue that the Church should break up again into practically autocephalous dioceses, in accordance with Metropolitan Agafangel's 1922 instruction. They maintain that the patriarchal center is so powerless in the current conditions that it cannot properly direct and protect individual dioceses, let alone parishes and priests, against the militantly antireligious state. If the Church decentralized, much would depend on the personality of the local bishop, on his relations with the local Soviet authorities and on his clergy and laity. Thus, in their view, the situation of the Church would vary from diocese to diocese, while her status now is universally intolerable and local bishops' prerogatives are too narrowly circumscribed, both by the centralized patriarchate and by the CRA, to achieve much on the local level. Moreover, owing

---

[141]See above, and *VRSKhD*, no. 103 (1972) 145-72.

to the hierarchical centralization, whenever a local bishop becomes too independent, the CRA forces the patriarchate to remove him from his diocese and to move him about so that he does not take root anywhere.[142] This tension within the Church has been noted by the atheists as well—for instance, by Kurochkin: "the evolution of contemporary . . . Orthodoxy is a complex and controversial process concealing in itself a possibility of alienation of the institution of the Church from the believers, of a church schism in fact."[143] What Kurochkin is here speaking about is the frequent justification of the Soviet social system in the official pronouncements of church leaders. However, he draws a fine but accurate distinction between this external adaptation of the Orthodox Church to the Soviet regime and its theoretical societal aims, on the one hand, and the "left Christianity" of the West, on the other. He stresses that even as the western leftist Christianity confuses and merges Christianity and Marxism, the Russian Orthodox Church, in contrast, declares "that the philosophical and *weltanschauungliche* foundations of communism and Christianity are incompatible with each other."[144]

We have already mentioned a sermon of Archbishop Chrysostom along these lines that got him into trouble. But there are quite a few priests in the USSR who also dare discuss existential and apologetic questions in their sermons, submitting Marxism and atheism to a scathing philosophical scrutiny, arguing that neither is very scientific and both are morally deficient.[145] It is perhaps this fundamental, self-imposed alienation of the Church from Marxism and the behavior of such more daring and independent clergymen that keeps the most outspoken critics of the patriarchate from breaking away from it, from proposing another schism. The lesson of the 1920s, most probably, has been learned not in vain, either. Indeed, there are other dissidents who argue

[142]Yakunin, "O sovremennom polozhenii," 11 and 66-78; Gerasimov, 71-3.

[143]"Evolyutsiya religii i tserkvi v sotsialisticheskom obshchestve," *Voprosy nauchnogo ateizma*, no. 21 (1977) 19-36.

[144]Ibid., 28-33.

[145]See, for instance, Fr. Dudko's sermons in *Our Hope.* Hieromonk Savva (Kolchugin) was deprived of a parish in 1979 and thrown into a psycho-prison a year later for sermons in which, among other things, he stressed the incompatibility of communism and Christianity and the impermissibility of a Christian joining the Komsomol. *VRKhD,* no. 132 (1980) 211.

strongly against such general critiques of the existing Church. They maintain that the priests should be pitied and prayed for, rather than severely criticized for their external subservience to the state. They maintain that many of the clerics are sacrificing themselves by these morally burdensome compromises to buy the right to serve as true shepherds to their flocks the rest of the time; that the flocks appreciate this and are grateful to them for this sacrifice as long as they remain personally clean, truly stand up for the flock and preach and practice the word of God.[146]

And many priests do this with much zeal and self-dedication. At the time when Fr. Dudko pioneered the question-and-answer form of the sermon, he had trouble over it, and the late Metropolitan Serafim banned this form of preaching. But now, we hear, the young Archbishop Kirill, the rector of the Leningrad theological schools, engages in similar sessions at the seminary church. Here is how a young, Paris-born student at the seminary describes church life in the Soviet Union in general and in the seminary in particular:

> I was amazed by the religious fervor of the people surrounding me. Although one generally hears that the churchgoers consist of "grannies," I soon discovered that among these "grannies," some 30 percent are young people below twenty-five years of age. . . . A characteristic of Russian church life not encountered in the West is the questions with which the faithful approach the priest after the service. . . .

> The other form of service at the seminary church, which at the same time serves as a regular parish church, is the Akathist to the Holy Mother of God and the sermons that follow. The people come to them with . . . questions written down in advance. Archbishop Kirill, the rector . . . responds to these questions. . . . The whole Akathist is sung by the whole people, and the service together with the question-and-answer session lasts over three hours. From 30 to 40 percent of the flock at these Akathists are young people. The typical sight in the entrance hall of

[146]For example, Goricheva and most contributors to the now-defunct *Veche*.

the seminary, in the adjacent street and at the main door is always groups of young Soviet people engaged in lively conversations with the seminarians. I participate in such conversations very often. Almost every day someone approaches me and asks questions relating to religion. In no case has it ever been empty curiosity, but genuine interest preceded by much thinking and probing about the Church.

. . . I was tonsured at the Zhirovitsy Monastery by Metropolitan Filaret. . . . In this monastery I have had direct contacts with the believing flocks who come to the monastery on pilgrimages from places two or three thousand kilometers distant with the sole purpose of enriching their spiritual world.

Then I served for a while at the Holy Trinity Cathedral in Leningrad. . . . I have always been impressed by the masses of people at weekday services, and almost always some of the flock would be made up of young people . . . especially during the school examination weeks.

. . . in these few years in Russia . . . against all logic of history, it seems, I have encountered the living Church.[147]

A recently received *samizdat* document, however, gives us a vivid illustration of the efforts and struggle at the price of which this *living* Church is maintained. Owing to its authorship, it is probably the most significant one since the Eshliman-Yakunin memorandum of 1965. It is a letter of thirty-six typed pages dated 1977 by Bishop Feodosy of Poltava to Leonid Brezhnev, the late CPSU Central Committee General Secretary. Its further significance lies in the fact that it is the first full confirmation by a ruling Russian bishop of Fr. Yakunin's writings (particularly his letters to the Nairobi WCC assembly and to Dr. Potter) regarding the arbitary tyranny of the CRA over the Church.

Bishop Feodosy points to 1958 as the year when the CRA's (CROCA at the time) arbitrariness began. Up until then, he

---

[147]Hieromonk Nikon, "Vpechatleniya ochevidtsa," *VRKhD*, no. 132 (1980) 206-8.

writes, the CROCA plenipotentiaries were simply liaison officials between the believers and the nonbelievers, between the Church and the state. From that year on they became the oppressors, causing "the destruction of churches . . . historical monuments, deprivation of many priests of the right to serve by means of newspaper slander campaigns." In his diocese alone the number of functioning churches was reduced from 340 in 1958 to 52 in 1964. The improvement after Khrushchev's fall did not last very long, "because the aim of the plenipotentiaries as representatives of atheism has remained actually the same, although implemented in a more gentle way [than under Khrushchev]."

The report is a detailed account, with concrete examples of how "gentle" these methods are. It cites examples of rural prayer houses not larger than 30 square yards and serving twenty-two villages which the plenipotentiary forbids not only to be enlarged but even to be repaired. It takes up to three years to gain permission to repair a leaking roof on a prayer house, to install heating in a church or to elevate the roof so that the hundreds of believers crammed into a tiny prayer house would not suffocate. Nechytailo, the plenipotentiary, refuses to grant registration to a rural religious association on the grounds that the warden is semiliterate and the believers can walk (sic) to the nearest urban church, seven to twelve miles away from the rural communities served by the prayer house with suspended services. But when the parishioners of that prayer house come to the bishop for advice and he translates their petition to the CRA head office into literary Russian, the plenipotentiary attacks him for allegedly breaking the law.

Every year six to seven priests retire or die in the Poltava diocese, but the plenipotentiary does not allow the bishop to ordain new priests. At first he forbade him to ordain candidates from outside the diocese or to invite priests from other parts of the Soviet Union. Then he permitted the bishop to ordain only those nonseminarians who had served as readers in the Poltava diocese for at least ten years. Finally, he forbade him to ordain any candidates but graduates of the seminaries who came from the Poltava diocese, which would mean less than one ordination per year. The latest limitations were in retaliation for the bishop's refusal to present to the plenipotentiary lists of seminary applicants from his diocese in advance. The bishop remarks that he would never agree to this because the plenipotentiary then would make life miserable for these young men, organize their harassment at their place of work or study, prevent their enrolment at the seminary as much as he could, etc.

The same Nechytailo tries to stifle parishes by forcing them to increase their "voluntary" contributions to the Peace Fund and to the Fund for the Renovation and Upkeep of Historical Monuments, to which the Church had agreed to contribute regular *voluntary* donations since 1968. In fact, the bishop writes, the parishes used to give 5 percent of their incomes to the above funds, gradually raising their contribution to 10, 15 and now to 20 percent of their total income. In money terms this has expressed itself in a rise in the sum total of the diocesan contributions from 36,210 rubles in 1968 to 161,328 in 1976—the latter sum being 36,402 rubles more than their total contribution to the diocesan administration. Needless to say, all these "voluntary" contributions are in addition to the exorbitant taxes we have discussed earlier. Yet, Nechytailo demands that the donations be raised to 30 percent of a parish's income. This would render many parishes insolvent in one year.[148] But this is precisely what the plenipotentiary wants: he had asked the bishop to cooperate with him in further reducing the number of functioning churches, and when the bishop refused, Nechytailo asked how would he react if the CRA began closing the churches without his permission. The bishop replied: "Every church is more valuable than my life, and I shall defend it more zealously than my own life, I will defend it to my last breath."

Feodosy does not stop at merely reciting his conflicts with Nechytailo. He protests against the whole false status of the Church—her humiliating subordination to the CRA, which, he

[148]As illustration he cites the budget of a prayer house in the village of Polivyanoe, which Nechytailo is trying to close for insufficient donations. If it were to donate 30 percent of its income to the funds, the budget would be allocated in the following way: (1) annual salary to the priest and the reader—1,500 rubles; (2) annual salary to the parish executive organ—370 rubles; (3) annual wages to the lay church workers (cleaners, etc.)—376 rubles; (4) repairs and upkeep—200 rubles; (5) would-be donations to the Peace and Preservation Funds—1,050 rubles. No money would be left to pay the land tax or state insurance contributions, to purchase goods necessary for church services or to make contributions to the clergy pension fund.

points out, contradicts the constitutional separation of Church and state. Similarly to Yakunin's and other *samizdat* documents, he drafts a program of how to realize in practice this separation:

(a) Put an end to the humiliating and illegitimate system of registration of all private church rites;

(b) Let the bishops ordain as many priests as are needed . . .

(c) No obstacles to the repair and upkeep of churches;

(d) Let the plenipotentiaries . . . perform only the functions of liaison officers, neutral in church questions, as required by the law;

(e) No closure of churches by force;

(f) Allow the increase of religious publications, of which there is an acute shortage . . .

(g) No obstacles to the clerics' choice of place of work and residence;

(h) Let there be no such attacks against religion in the press that would promote atheists' hate for the believers . . .

(i) It is absolutely necessary to emancipate the Church from the oppressive control by the plenipotentiaries; bishops should have more powers in matters of faith.

And he warns that by slandering the believers as reactionaries the Soviet press is writing off "as reactionaries a good half of the Soviet population." This estimate of believers, of course, is far above all the others discussed in this chapter, except those by the Germans in World War II. Yet, the letter is very reserved in tone, based on facts and figures, and the bishop clearly takes a great responsibility in addressing himself to Brezhnev. Hence, the estimate could not have been drawn "from the air." In full appreciation of the risks, he prophesies in the letter that for such conflicts with the plenipotentiary he is facing the prospect of, at best, removal to a small and distant diocese. This is precisely what would happen to him: in 1979 he would be moved to the seventeen-parish diocese of Vologda, and in 1980, on his petition that the northern climate did not agree with his health, to the north Caspian diocese of Astrakhan. Prior to his removal from the Ukraine, however, his title was raised to that of archbishop. Thereby the church administration obviously wanted to make it clear to Feodosy and to all those "who have eyes to see" that it was not the Church that was punishing him for his defense of Christianity.[149]

---

[149]Perhaps this is the reason why the document found its way to *samizdat*. The document, dated October 26, 1977 from Poltava, is in AS 4456. For data on Feodosy's subsequent shifts and reappointments, see *ZhMP*, no. 1 (1979) 12; and no. 2 (1980) 2.

Conclusion

Our final analysis of the above-cited CRA internal documents (the CRA's secret reports to the CPSU Central Committee), juxtaposed with Archbishop Feodosy's letter to Brezhnev, leads us to the conclusion that the Soviet government, while forced to live with the Church, would like to limit her activities and scope to fulfilling three functions.

First of all, the Church would serve to convince a Billy Graham or a Dr. Potter of the WCC that there is religious freedom in the Soviet Union, thus bringing in more tourist money and improving the international image of the Soviet government. This would be accomplished by retaining in cities frequented by foreign tourists a minimum necessary number of churches, functioning as oriental, mystical "theaters" of sorts, with the utmost splendor in rites and ceremonies, beautiful vestments, impressive choirs, etc.

Secondly, the Church would satisfy the religious thirsts of the old, semi-literate masses. To avoid any relevance to the realities of social life in general, however, the services would be performed in Church Slavonic—a language imcomprehensible to the average Soviet Russian—and sermons would be limited to routine, moral-didactic topics, with no real relevance to daily life. The splendid but incomprehensible rituals would also serve the esthetic inclinations of a few intellectual snobs who frequent churches out of fashion and as a way of demonstrating their alienation from official values in a safer form. True, it is unpleasant for the regime to tolerate even this much religious activity; but it is less harmful than a dynamic and active priesthood, serving in the living language and delivering topical and spiritually elevating sermons.

The third and the most positive purpose of the Church from the point of view of the Soviet government is the political propaganda activities of her representatives in the World Council of Churches, at various peace conferences, etc., mainly abroad, in promoting Soviet foreign policy interests. In these forums the churchmen are to refer to God, Church and theology as rarely and as abstractly as possible. They are to condemn the noncommunist West, appeal to international agencies to support "local wars of liberation" and promote the so-called theology of liberation. Even Patriarch Pimen, as we have seen, gets a reprimand from the CRA for criticizing the overemphasis of the WCC on social Christianity. It is only social Christianity, in the eyes of the Soviets, that the Moscow Patriarchate should be speaking of in international forums—but God forbid it should be practiced inside the USSR! And the term is to be interpreted as aid to terrorists and guerrillas across the globe (in the guise of charity to victims of wars).

As we have seen, the reality of the Church and her life in the USSR far from satisfies the Soviet needs. The price that the Soviet government has to pay for the foreign policy contribution of the Church leaders is the toleration of an internal role and function of the Church that often goes far beyond the limits set for her by the state.

Unfortunately for the Church, however, it is her patriarch who, instead of being a symbol and reference point for the behavior of the rest of her pastors and laymen, most zealously performs the role of a Soviet propaganda puppet. The year 1982 ends after two particularly depressing illustrations of Pimen's sycophancy. The first was his pitiful performance at the United Nations General Assembly on June 24, when he singled out Leonid Brezhnev as a peacemaker at the very time that Soviet armed forces were carrying out genocide in Afghanistan.[1] But he surpassed even himself in his funeral oration for Brezhnev at the requiem he served at the Moscow patriarchal cathedral on November 14. Pimen called Brezhnev "an outstanding statesman . . . to whom we are paying our religious due as to a man so close to our hearts . . ." Again he called him a great peacemaker whose era was marked by "a period of fruitful peacemaking activity" of the Soviet Union. How cynical this sounds while Soviet bac

[1]See *ZhMP*, no. 7 (July 1982).

teriological weapons are destroying millions of lives in Afghanistan and forcing other millions to flee their homeland.

He goes on to say that to Brezhnev "belongs the lofty and noble thought that man's first right is the right to live."[2] This is a rather strange utterance from a churchman who should have associated the priority of this idea with the Lord and the Scriptures. All this was being said about a man during whose reign the use of drugs to mentally mutilate opponents of the regime— including many priests, monks, nuns and lay religious believers in Soviet forensic institutions—has been expanding without precedent. This was being said when his own priest, Fr. Gleb Yakunin, was serving a prison sentence for daring to record religious persecutions in the Soviet Union; when Nechytailos,[3] presiding over CRA directorates, were continuing to persecute the Church and while bishops like Feodosy were being removed from their dioceses for defending the Church.

It is to be hoped that this study presents sufficient material to demonstrate that the Church in the USSR is a genuine, living and vibrant Church (almost miraculously so) and that the patriarch, at least the current one, has nothing to do with her spiritual achievements. She lives and gains spiritual victories not because of her patriarch but in spite of him—by the will of God, who tolerates the sins and lies of her leading hierarchs because of the redeeming faith and sacrifices of her flock and of her better pastors. It is these living saints, in the words of Fr. Vitaly Borovoi, who warrant her existence and bring about her resurrection.

---

[2]*ZhMP*, no. 1 (January 1983).
[3]The name is itself a symptomatic pun: *nechytailo* is derived from a Ukrainian term meaning someone who cannot read, an uncouth illiterate.

Appendix 1

Excerpts from Bishop Leonty of Chile's "Political Controls over the Orthodox Church in the Soviet Union"

[The following excerpts, relating to the formation and actions of the Ukrainian Autocephalist Church, are taken from the memoirs of a former Kievan monk and bishop of the Ukrainian Autonomous Church under the German occupation. While the manuscript represents a very subjective and personal account by a clear antagonist of Ukrainian nationalism in general, and in particular in church affairs, it is a valuable testimony because (1) it is an eyewitness account from a man totally devoted to the Church, who was ordained under the Soviets and was persecuted and imprisoned for his faith several times; and (2) it is not a "Muscovite" attack on Ukrainian church separatism—it is by an ethnic Ukrainian, and thus is characteristic of the split between separatism and antiseparatism among the genuine ethnic population of the Ukraine.

The material below is taken from pp. 23-7 of the manuscript, which is located in the Bakhmeteff Archives.]

... In the Ukraine the Soviet government decided to deal blows to the Orthodox Church ... with the help of the so-called "Autocephalous Ukrainian Orthodox Church," i.e., to blow up the Orthodox Church from within by means of Ukrainian revolutionaries in cassocks ...

In the spring of 1919 ... a chauvinistic Ukrainian group of priests—Vasyl Lypkivsky, Nestor Sharaevsky and Petro Tarnavsky—enjoying the full sympathy and support of the Soviet government for this action, unilaterally declared itself the "All-Ukrainian Orthodox Council," with a certain [layman] Mykhailo Moroz as its chairman, who would later renounce his faith and God. He assumed the de facto rights of the metropolitan of the Ukraine. By his efforts the Soviets confiscated the St. Nicholas ... the St. Andrew ... and the St. Sophia Cathedrals from the Orthodox by force, and handed them over to this group ...

When Denikin's army occupied Kiev for a short time and Metropolitan Antony [Khrapovitsky], appointed to the Kiev see [by Patriarch Tikhon], returned, ... he gave back the churches to the Orthodox and interdicted the instigators . . . For those willing to have church services in Ukrainian he provided the St. Makarios house chapel and appointed a Ukrainian priest for services there. But in those days there were not many enthusiasts for Ukrainian services . . . this relatively small church was rarely filled. . . . On their return the Bolsheviks again gave the above churches to the rebels. The All-Ukrainian Council (*Rada*) began to function again with full Soviet backing . . . Its statute was approved and registered by the Soviet authorities.

[Leonty describes how the Orthodox community resisted the taking over of the main St. Sofia Cathedral by the nationalists despite threats by the Soviet authorities. Then an armed militia was sent with Moroz at its head and the cathedral was confiscated by force.

The nationalists' main concern was to find a canonical bishop, but none agreed to cooperate. Bishop Nazary, administering the diocese in place of Antony—who had evacuated with the Whites—at first tried patiently to talk the rebels out of their extremist positions. When all efforts failed he issued an official encyclical in 1920 interdicting them.]

The Ukrainian *rada*, in its session of May 5, 1920, reached the following decisions: (1) in the name of the renaissance of the Ukrainian Church, the Orthodox bishops and Nazary's bans should be ignored, and services should continue as before; (2) all Orthodox bishops on the territory of the Ukraine are enemies of the Ukrainian people because they are in alliance with the Moscow Patriarchate and its head, Patriarch Tikhon; and (3) therefore, the Ukrainian *rada* declares itself *autocephalous*, independent of any other Church . . .

. . . This was the first time ever in the whole history of the Orthodox Church that a group of banned priests headed by a layman, without the participation of a single bishop, declared autocephaly.

. . . At their conference in the St. Sophia Cathedral in June they congratulated themselves with having gotten rid of the bishops. But at the same time they were perplexed as to where to find bishops . . . in order to continue to be considered Orthodox. But in this they failed completely . . . Even the Renovationist Bishop Antonin (Granovsky) [a Ukrainian], who had nearly agreed at first, refused eventually . . .

In the meanwhile the communists became fully established in the Ukraine, which helped the Autocephalists in their struggle against the Orthodox Church; the latter, being repressed by the Bolsheviks, was unable to paralyze the Autocephalist movement . . . This was not a religious movement, which would have had masses behind it, but simply a new political adventure receiving all sorts of aid from the Soviets—for instance, in the form of physical confiscation of churches from the Orthodox. . . . The following was the typical procedure. First, the so-called "missionaries," i.e., agitators, would arrive in a town or even village and present their credentials to the local Soviet authorities ... and the statute approved by the communists, which gave them the right to expand across the whole of the Ukraine. The local government would receive beforehand secret directives from the GPU to aid the Autocephalists, but in such a way as not to raise any suspicions in the population that the Soviet government was behind them. ... It was usually reckless youths who centered around the agitator. They knew next to nothing about questions of ecclesiology, and Komsomol members formed quite a high proportion of their ranks. The agitator would make a speech on how in the past the tsarist government and the Orthodox Church with the bishops at its head had suppressed the Ukrainian culture, deprived the Ukrainians of the right to pray in their own language, and then would praise the Soviet power, which has brought freedom to everyone, including religious freedom, allowing them to free themselves from the old church chains and to become independent. This freedom they ought to bring into reality immediately if they want to have a free Ukrainian Church. The mob then, headed by the agitator, rushes with songs and threatening shouts toward the local church. If the local peasants were smart enough, rang the tocsin on time, gathered a force to attack the pogromists with stones and fists, the church was saved and the "autocephalists" dispersed. In other places parishioners were met unawares; then the "autocephalist" mob would storm the priest's house, force the priest to hand over the keys, and the church would physically pass into their hands. ... If the priest refused to recognize the new "jurisdiction" he would be forced to leave the parish house and the town immediately. ... His belongings would be thrown out of the house. ... Where was the priest to go, particularly if this occurred in the middle of the winter? The local peasant is afraid to offer the evicted priest and his family hospitality, for he will likely be harassed for this by the GPU. And off the poor priest goes, with only as many belongings as he can carry in a packsack, with his wife, children and often old parents dragging themselves behind him ...

This is no exaggeration, but the cruel, bitter truth. Take, for instance, ... the case of the seizure of the Ascension Church in Pereyaslav. The whole band [with the agitator] burst into the church while the liturgy was on, threw the priests serving at the altar out and began serving on their own. During the German occupation ... our Orthodox Exarch of the Ukraine, Metropolitan Aleksii (Gromadsky), and I were imprisoned, not without the hand of the Autocephalists. [In prison] I met two veterans of the Autocephalist movement who with pride remembered those days, when they stormed Orthodox churches, including the one in Pereyaslav.

After this wide campaign of storming and confiscating churches the Autocephalists held their first sobor in Kiev in October 1921. Of some 400 delegates, about 60 were veteran priests. Exactly one-half of them quit the sobor and the Autocephalists when they realized what was going on.... The most incendiary speeches, which had little to do with ecclesiology, were those of Professors A. Krymsky, V. Danylevych, V. Chekhivsky and of the banned clerics V. Lypkivsky and N. Sharaevsky.

[The rest of his account either parallels the story contained in the main part of the book or is too personal to be reproduced here. However, his account of the biography of Lypkivsky and the profiles of the latter priest as well as of his chief aides, although subjective, are of interest.]

[The priest V. Lypkivsky] was born in the area of Kiev in 1864. He graduated from the Kiev Theological Academy, always held leftist radical views and was in constant contact with the Galician Ukrainians. He wrote for leftist newspapers and helped to organize the All-Ukrainian Church *Rada*, in which participated also Ukrainian Uniates, former prisoners of war [from the Austrian army] set free by the revolution. This [cooperation with non-Soviet Ukrainians] the Bolsheviks would later use against him. Apparently, when he became the ruling metropolitan of the... Autocephalous Church, the GPU shadowed every step of his so closely that he began to hate the Soviet government, and remained its hater until death.

His aide, the Priest N. Sharaevsky, later the so-called archbishop, was a man with full higher theological education, but even according to Lypkivsky was of very limited intelligence, without initiative and generally a weak personality. Down in his heart his attitude to the Soviet power must have been similar to that of Lypkivsky. Of the leading lay members must be mentioned Volodymyr Chekhivsky, a man of undoubtedly outstanding intelligence, obscured, however, by fanatical chauvinism. He also held an advanced degree in theology... At their sobor he was their canonist and author of their resolutions. He was not sincerely devoted to the Soviets, but acted as their convenient tool. The other leaders of the Autocephalists... were mostly dodgy opportunists,... provocateurs, transparent Bolshevik agents inserted into the organization as watchdogs and for the purpose of destroying it from within. Others were petty operators who had joined the movement not for Christ's name but for bread and "fame." Lypkivsky himself would say that in a moral sense their lives were below all criticism. There were very few among them who could be credited with some genuine ideals.

Appendix 2

Excerpts from A. A. Valentinov's *The Black Book*

[*The Black Book* is a collection of documents on the persecution of religion in the USSR in the early years of Soviet power. It was published in English and German in 1924, although the Russian date and place of publication is not given.
The consequences of the Soviet enactment of the decree of January 23, 1918 on the separation of Church and state is described in the following illustrations.]

In Kharkov no baptisms, church marriages or burials could take place without prior approval from Comrades Kagan and Rutheiter, who were in charge of the appropriate departments of the Kharkov Executive Committee. Transgression of this regulation was punishable by the Military-Revolutionary Tribunal . . . children were dying without baptism; corpses disintegrated before the permission for a Christian burial could be obtained. And this did not happen in Kharkov alone.

[At the same time the civil authorities ordered priests to perform Christian marriages for persons who were divorced by the civil authorities without church authorization. Noncompliant priests were prosecuted.
A detailed description follows of the general confiscation of all home chapels and institutional churches and chapels and their transformation into dancing halls, theaters, clubs and workshops. Frescoes were invariably painted over with Bolshevik slogans, and sanctuaries were turned into stages or orchestra platforms. In many areas the Red Army used churches for artillery target practice.]

Eighteen cannon shots were fired at the church in the Meshchersky farmstead. . . . in the town of Kamensk such shooting went on while there was a service at the church. Consequently, six persons were killed, twenty wounded. [24-31]

[There are numerous descriptions of tortures and murders of the clergy, especially monks and bishops. Here are some illustrations.]

The separation of Church and state . . . has become an excuse to ban the preaching of religion—to which the martyr's death of Bishop Nikodim in Belgorod is a witness.

The bishop kept aloof from all politics, but in his sermons ... called on his flock to follow the teaching of Christ, stressing that the laws of God are above those of man ... At Christmas time, 1918, the notoriously cruel Commandant Saenko ... arrested the bishop and took him to the *Cheka*. But the protest of the people against the arrest of their beloved bishop took such proportions that Saenko was forced to release him. But after another sermon, the same evening, in which he condemned the violence and killings, he was rearrested. Saenko shouted that the revolution failed [sic!] because of the clergy. When a local priest's wife went to plead with Saenko for the bishop, he shot her with his own hands. Then he had the bishop killed the same night. Fearing repercussions among the people, he wrapped the naked body in a military greatcoat and threw it into a mass grave ...

In Kharkov an eighty-year-old monk, Amvrosy, was severely beaten with rifle butts and then shot. A priest, Dimitry, was taken to a cemetery and stripped naked. When he raised his hand to cross himself the murderer cut his right hand off. They did not allow his body to be buried, but threw it to the dogs. When another priest tried to speak up in defense of a peasant condemned to death, the priest was beaten to death with ramrods and cut up with sabers ...

In the Monastery of Our Savior the sailor Dybenko arrested the seventy-five-year-old abbot ... during the very first night Fr. Rodion was killed: ... first his skull skin and hair were scalped off, then his neck was chopped up with sabers ...

A priest in the Kherson province was crucified. ...

Archpriest Vostorgov, condemned to death along with some other people, refused to be blindfolded and asked to be shot after all the others, so he could comfort them before the execution and help them depart for the other life ...

Fr. Mikhail Lisitsyn, a priest in Ust-Labinsk, was first led around the town by a rope tied around his neck. At the same time he was being beaten so severely that he knelt and begged to be shot. After the execution his wife had to pay 610 rubles for the right to have the body returned to her and buried. ...

The forty-nine-year-old Fr. Ivan Prigorovsky of Nelomaevsk was a notorious extreme-left sympathizer. [Yet] on Holy Saturday he was led out of his church, attacked by Red Army soldiers with curses and beatings, and his face was disfigured; bleeding and half-dead he was dragged out of town and killed ...

[The catalogue of murders and tortures of priests, bishops and monks takes up twelve pages (36-48). Some of the clerics were executed for actively criticizing the Reds, advising local people to support the Whites or elevating prayers for the Whites; other victims appear to have been completely apolitical or even sympathizers of the revolutionary movement. The cases we have included in this survey have been chosen from the latter two categories.

There then follows a protocol of the questioning by a French officer of a Siberian *Cheka* functionary, Pavel Naumov, who was taken prisoner by the Kolchak forces, dated February 10, 1919. Before the revolution Naumov was a local policeman, then fought the Germans in World War I. On returning home to Perm he worked for a while in a factory. When the factory closed down he joined the *Cheka*.]

The *Cheka* enjoyed the fulness of power ... and could have arrested all the chief commissars if it wanted. The head of the Perm *Cheka* was a twenty-five-year-old factory worker, Pavel Malkov, who could hardly sign his own name. The man in charge of the Department to Combat Counterrevolution was the almost completely illiterate twenty-year-old factory worker Grigory Vorobtsov.

... Executions were conducted arbitrarily, without any resolutions. If a commissar wanted to shoot someone, he sent a paper to this effect to two other commissars who, without studying the case and without even ever having seen the victim, confirmed the decision. This was enough to kill a man.

During the eight months of the [Perm] *Cheka's* existence only ten executions were recorded in the files, while in fact 150 took place in the city of Perm alone, and another 400 in the suburban country....

Hostages, in compliance with Sverdlov's orders, were taken from the ranks of the Constitutional Democrats and Mensheviks, as well as the clergy. There were very many of them under arrest ... and very few survived.

[The report continues with the shooting of the local diocesan bishop Andronik, while the report to Patriarch Tikhon from the Perm *Cheka* said he was exiled to Arkhangelsk, which by then was under British occupation. Simultaneously with the above report the Bishop of Perm published a list of forty-two Perm diocesan priests tortured and killed by the Bolsheviks in the eight months preceding the coming of the White forces to the city (49-51).

Later on in the book (254-7) we find the following letter from the priest G. Loshako, describing to the world the persecutions faced by the believers.]

An Appeal by the Church of Ekaterinodar to the Christian Churches of the Whole World, April 5, 1919

Brothers! Our sufferings have overfilled the cup of trials. A cruel persecution has fallen upon the Orthodox Church in Russia. . . . Many temples have either been desecrated and ruined by the Red Army or sealed by the Soviet authorities—or converted by them into fun houses, jails or even refuse dumps. Fourteen bishops and hundreds of priests—especially preachers of the word of God—were shot by firing squads, hanged, drowned or burned alive. Executions of clergy are often accompanied by the cruelest of tortures. For instance, they gorged out the eyes of Andronik, Bishop of Perm, cut out his cheeks, and then he was led around the town bleeding while they mocked him. In the Kherson province a priest was crucified on a cross. Such things are common occurrences in every diocese. We can cite such cases in our own Kuban province . . . in Nezamamevsk, during the night of Easter eve, Fr. Ioann Prigorovsky was savagely murdered just before the reading of the Acts. Right in the middle of the church they gorged out his eyes, cut off his ears and nose and mashed his skull. In Ust-Labinsk the priest Fr. Mikhail Lisitsyn was tortured for three days, from Friday to Sunday. He was killed on February 22, 1918. His body, when it was found, had more than ten gashes, and his head was axed into pieces. The body of Fr. Alexander Fleginsky of Georgie-Afipsk was found shredded into pieces. Fr. Georgy Boiko of Plastunovsk was killed by torture. There was an ugly gash in his throat; apparently it had been ripped as a torture. In Korenovsk Fr. Nazarenko was murdered, while the church was desecrated and the altar turned into a lavatory, the holy vessels having been used as night pots. In the city of Ekaterinodar several cases of desecration of icons were recorded . . . on a St. Nicholas icon eyes were knifed out, whereafter the icon itself was thrown onto a dunghill.

School prayers have been banned. Holy icons have been removed from all public buildings in spite of the protests of the population, while those in private houses have been taxed. . . .

. . . What fills us with trepidation is the moral savagery which is the result of the Bolshevik fratricide and unprecedented violence. Violating everything that has been dear to the people in the sphere of beliefs and veneration, the Bolsheviks are trying to incite in the nation the instincts of hatred and plunder. The main attraction for the darkest masses is the letting loose of animal passions and lust. The Bolsheviks are building up their power on the combination of this with terror. A glaring example is the publication of local decrees [by the Bolsheviks] on the socialization of women that reduce their status to that of simple sex objects to be used by any lewd debaucher. . . . the power usurpers, Russian tyrants with Ulyanov-Lenin and Bronstein-Trotsky at their head . . . are trying to convince the outside world that their cruel experiments on the body of the suffering nation have been performed by the will of the people. In actual fact, however, the main executors of their fierce decrees and perpetrators of tortures and murders ... are Chinese and Latvian traitors. The whole [Russian] nation, except for the criminal elements and a few degenerates, hates the bloody tyranny, but being defenseless, unarmed and overwhelmed by the murders and executions, it remains silent against its will, it suffers inhumanly and appeals to the Lord in hope and expectation of a merciful Samaritan who would deliver it from the new gangsters....

Beloved brothers! We pray unto God that the misfortunes which have befallen us do not reach you, but we cannot abstain from warning you that the evil may overflow to your homes as well. The anti-Christian Bolshevism is a terrible threat to the whole Christian world. The temptations it carries are too great for the dark masses, for all the unfortunate and the unhappy, of whom there are always plenty under all social conditions. They become easy prey to any promises of paradise on earth, which are generously disseminated by the Bolsheviks. It is in this that the danger threatening Christianity and all world civilization is hidden. [The sense of this danger] should unify Christians of all churches. This is why we appeal to you in the name of the Lord Jesus Christ, the God of love, truth and peace, in the name of love for mankind, in the name of salvation of the whole mankind from Bolshevism, to rise in defense of Christianity against its modern persecutors, and thus to become the merciful Samaritan for the Russian people and the timely defender of the rest of humanity against Bolshevism—the cruelest enemy of our Savior Jesus Christ and of all Christianity.

(Signed) Priest G. Loshako
Chairman of the Kuban Diocesan Council

April 5, 1919
Ekaterinodar

Appendix 3

Letter to the Priest P.F.

[Below follows an abbreviated version of a November 4, 1927 letter, allegedly by Archbishop Illarion (Troitsky) of Vereya to a certain P. F. (probably Pavel Florensky, the famous mathematician, Moscow University professor of electricity, musicologist, theologian and Orthodox priest who would end his days in the 1940s in a concentration camp). Archbishop Illarion was one of the most outstanding theologians in Patriarch Tikhon's entourage, his learned secretary and policy adviser, who urged a moderate course toward the Soviet government but an intolerant one toward the Renovationists. He was arrested in 1924 and died in prison in 1929. At the sobor in 1917 Illarion's speech was among those that swayed the assembly in favor of the patriarchate. However, he was not an inflexible person. According to the Karlovcian church historian Fr. Mikhail Polsky, in 1922 Illarion favored Patriarch Tikhon's retirement, and in 1925 he was temporarily moved from the Solovki concentration camps to a prison in Yaroslavl where he was "royally" treated: he was receiving literature, was allowed to engage in theological writings, his manuscripts were passed on from jail to believers (proto-*samizdat*) and he was visited by Tuchkov, who tried to convince him to join the Grigorians in order to add at least one bishop with prestige and charisma to that schism. According to the same source it was Illarion who had suggested to Tuchkov that he should stake his hopes on the Patriarchal Church rather than on the Renovationists, who were doomed because of lack of mass support. He promised that in return for such recognition the Church would give full loyalty to the Soviets. (*Novye mucheniki rossiiskie*, 1 [Jordanville, N.Y.: Holy Trinity Monastery, 1949] 130-3)

In a public discussion in Moscow in August 1923, Archbishop Illarion stated: "The October Revolution frightened Russian society and the Church along with it. The external *terrifying façade* of the revolution was mistaken for the *very essence of the revolution*. Now Russian society has mastered the course of political literacy.... A *change of landmarks* is taking place. The Church is also changing the landmarks. She has definitely cut herself away from the counterrevolution and welcomes the new forms of the Soviet construction." A few days later he co-signed with the patriarch and two other bishops a declaration along the same lines as the above statement, which also said: "The Church recognizes and supports the Soviet government, for there is no other *power than that from God*. The Church elevates prayers for the Russian land and for the Soviet power. The state system of the Russian Republic must form the basis for the construction

483

of church life." (M. Agursky, *Ideologiya natsional-bol'shevizma* [Paris, 1980] 111-2, citing Soviet newspapers of the time)

The above, reflecting the typical hopes of the NEP era that the Soviets had given up on the communist utopia and were reconstructing a strong Russian national state, logically prepared the ground for Metropolitan Sergii's 1927 declaration. It is no wonder, therefore, that Illarion, as indicated by Polsky and other sources, supported Sergii while in the Solovki concentration camp, although Regelson quotes Illarion's letter to Sergii calling on him for restraint and a more independent policy. According to all evidence, Illarion was not a Machiavellian politician but a man of strong principles who in tsarist times was not afraid to publicly call Peter the Great satanic. (S. A. Volkov, "Arkhiepiskop Illarion," *VRKhD*, no. 134 [1981] 227-34)

In view of this, the text below stands in remarkable contrast to all Illarion's other known statements. Either the material belongs to another author, or it reflects his total disillusionment as a result of his imprisonment. Whoever the author, the document reflects the views and fears in church circles regarding Sergii's declaration, and contains prophetic thoughts.

The author begins by quoting some of his notes of March 3/16, 1924.]

Perhaps in a short while we shall find ourselves a tiny island in an ocean of profanity . . . The scenario of church relations can undergo a change like in a kaleidoscope. The Renovationists may rise as the ruling "Church Party" in Russia and face very limited opposition if the overt Renovationists and covert traitors will find a modus vivendi with each other and jointly disguise themselves under the cover of canonicity.

[The next paragraph, he writes, is from his notes of January 14/27, 1925.]

The difficulty of our time for an Orthodox is . . . that the contemporary life of the Church demands of him a high spiritual self-discipline in personal life. He cannot rely on guidance from the official pastors (bishops and presbyters). The church canons cannot be formally applied to problems arising in church life. Altogether, a juridical attitude is insufficient; it is necessary to have a spiritual intuition to show the way of Christ among the multitude of paths made by wolves in sheeps' clothing. Life has posed questions that can be solved in a truly churchly manner only by bypassing mores, forms, regulations and being led by senses trained to recognize virtue from evil. Otherwise it is easy to defile the sacredness of one's soul and to allow one's conscience to disintegrate through a legalistically regulated reconciliation with fraud and profanity, brought into the Church by the bishops themselves. By means of laws it is possible to reconcile oneself even with the devil.

[This is followed by his comments of November 4, 1927.]

Aren't the latest events a confirmation of the above premonitions?

Hasn't the horror that the soul sensed already two to three years ago come so close to us after Metropolitan Sergii's return to administer the Church [i.e., after his release from prison in May and the June declaration]? Hasn't Sergii's declaration, which has caused varied and fully justified negative reactions, thrown the church organization, headed by him, into the loathsome, adulterous embraces of the atheistic, blasphemous and Christomachistic power, and hasn't it introduced a frightening prophanity into the bosom of our Church? Please note that this declaration appeared not from the hands of the schismatic Renovationists... [it came] from a canonical, lawful, apparently Orthodox hierarch. The main assertions of the declaration are based on scriptural texts (although, occasionally, with the help of their misinterpretation...) and on the historical experience of the ancient Church, as if it were similar to the current one. On the other hand, the declaration hopes to quench the essential thirst of believers exhausted by persecutions, for it promises them peace and quiet. And hence multitudes, especially from the clerical ranks, are sympathetically responding to the declaration of Metropolitan Sergii and his Synod.

This symphony between the theomachistic power and the regular Orthodox hierarchy has already produced some "blessings": some bishops (although not the best ones and not the most "guilty" ones) are returning from exile (not from a very distant one, however) and are being appointed to dioceses (not to the same ones from which they had been deported, however); ... Metropolitan Sergii has a Synod (which is more like the office of the overprocurator) which consists of regular hierarchs (alas, with questionable reputations owing to their longtime and solid cooperation with the godless GPU...); Metropolitan Sergii's name is being elevated as that of the captain of the Church, but, alas, this name is but a forgery, because the real master of the destiny of the Russian Church and her bishops, both those in positions as well as the persecuted ones... is the current "Overprocurator" of the Russian Orthodox Church, Evgeny A. Tuchkov.

Everybody with ears to hear and eyes to see knows that contrary to the decree on the separation of Church and state, the Orthodox Church has entered into a close alliance with the state. And what state?... a state whose government aims at the destruction of any religion on the face of the earth, and the Orthodox Church before all the others, because it justly sees in her a basic world foundation of religious faith and a first-class fortress in the struggle against materialism, atheism, theomachism and satanism (practiced, according to hearsay, by some members of the contemporary powers that be)....

[Quotations from Revelation (17:3, 5, 6; 12:6; 18:2) are cited and followed by a comparison of the current church situation with the apocalyptic scenario of the whore sitting on a red beast. The situation is particularly tragic, he says, because:]

it is not a lawless, schismatic woman who saddles a beast with profane names, but a faithful woman having an image of genuine piety. In this is the chief frightening aspect of that which has been occurring before our eyes, which affects the most profound spiritual interests of the church flock. The consequences are impossible to assess even approximately; but their significance is of a global character ... for now the forces of Hades are attacking [the Church] with unprecedented power ... How should we behave in these terrible moments of the new threat, advancing by Satan's counsel upon our mother, the holy Orthodox Church?

[He quotes Revelation 18:1-2 and 4, on the coming of an angel, whereupon Babylon and the great whore fell down. But he warns the recipient of the letter that he is not mechanically asserting that the present reality is the fulfilment of these apocalyptic prophecies.]

I only trace a dotted line between the apocalypse and the contemporary church developments, which involuntarily direct our thoughts toward these prophetic images. Even in the Old Testament one can see how in some cases prophecies at first were fulfilled on a small scale only to be later expressed in a loftier and final fulfilment. ... Neither scholarship of the broadest possible scope, nor the deepest natural intelligence, nor the finest powers of mysticism can satisfactorily grasp God's secrets. [In the present Russian church developments] we come into contact with the final secret of the terrestrial existence of the Church and of mankind. ...

... in the words of Bishop Ignaty Bryanchaninov ... Whoever does not obtain the kingdom of God within oneself will not recognize the Antichrist, and will inevitably ... become his follower; he will not recognize the coming of the end of the world. ... Obscured by its terrestrial reasoning mankind will refuse to believe in the second coming of Christ altogether. ...

There is no doubt whatsoever that the "dark power" dominating today thinks, argues and acts in the style of such blasphemers ... But isn't it possible that the contemporary *churchmen* ... having entered into a relationship with the blasphemers of this world, ... will treat the thoughts of my soul as nothing but "madness, worthy of contempt"?

Recently a bishop supporting Sergii's orientation threatened ... that Sergii's opponents would become such a small minority as to be eventually reduced to one of a multitude of small sects. How pitiful is such an

argument in defense of the newly born "Soviet Orthodox Church"!...
Has the bishop forgotten the multitude of apostolic prophecies on the
reduction of faith and the dissemination of all sorts of false teachings
in the latter days?...

Pluralities and majorities are necessary for parliaments and parties
but not for God's Church, which is the pillar and foundation of faith,
independently of the above categories and even in contradiction of
them....

... Some two or three weeks ago ... a blessed woman, when asked
about Metropolitan Sergii and reminded that he was not a heretic, said:
"So what?... He is worse than a heretic. He has bowed to the Antichrist, and, if he does not repent, his destiny is in hell together with the
satanists."

All this ... forces the living faithful souls to be on the alert and
to watch the picture of the woman saddling the beast with great attention. These people sense a new and unprecedented danger for Christ's
Church and, naturally, ring the alarm bell. Most of them are in no
hurry to make a final break with the church "adulterers" in the hope
that their conscience has not entirely burned out ... God grant that it
be so, but in the depth of my soul I have deep doubts, and yet avoid
dotting the i's. Let ... the Lord do this. And let Him also protect us
from superficial haste as well as from a criminally indifferent sluggish-
ness in this *terrifyingly* responsible situation into which we have been
placed by the will of God's providence.

Appendix 4

The Administration of the Metropolia
(Decisions of the 1937 New York Sobor)

[The following excerpts from this document, taken from *Russko-amerikanskii pravoslavnyi vestnik*, no. 11 (1937) 156-7 and 160, show that, contrary to the opinion of the so-called "Professors' Letter" to the Cleveland Sobor of 1946 (see above, chapter 8, n. 65), the Metropolia was an autonomous associate member of the Karlovci Synod after the 1937 Sobor, not its subordinate. Note also the preference in the document for the vague term "Diaspora" (*Zarubezh'e*) Church Administration in place of the official title of the Karlovci Synod. The obvious connotation of this is that the Metropolia reserved for herself the right to fraternally cooperate with any Orthodox church formations outside Russia, not just with the one in Karlovci. This provoked the objections of the Karlovci-imposed bishops in America (Tikhon, Vitaly, Ioasaf and Ieronim), who participated in the 1937 Sobor but refused to endorse its statements, arguing that they did not accord with some points of the statutes of the Karlovci organization.]

A.   While acting in cooperation with all the churches of the diaspora in affairs which relate to the preservation of the faith and to supervision over church life, in administrative matters our Orthodox Church in America remains temporarily autonomous.

B.   The head of the administration is the sobor-elected Metropolitan, who also presides over the Council of Bishops and the Metropolitan Council.

[The next four paragraphs enumerate the Metropolitan's independent functions of convoking sobors, bishops' councils, etc., with no reference to the émigré Synod. Only point 5 reads:]

5.   On behalf of the Metropolia he enters into contact with the superior organs of the Diaspora Church Administration, as well as with the representatives of [other] churches, institutions and organizations.

[Again independently he takes care of episcopal vacancies, etc.]

8. He fraternally advises other bishops [of the Metropolia] ... in extremely important cases, with the agreement of the other bishops of the Metropolia, he refers matters to the supreme organs of the Diaspora Church Administration.

[Points 9-12 enumerate such functions as the reception and appointment of clergy, etc. Some functions the Metropolitan performs on his own, others in conjunction with the council of *his* bishops.]

C. The Council of Bishops with the Metropolitan at its head is the highest administrative authority of the Orthodox Church in America. . . .

[The rest of the document lists the functions and responsibilities of the Council of Bishops, which reveal its complete independence from the Karlovci establishment. The latter is not mentioned even once in connection with any limitations on the powers and prerogatives of the council. Only points 3 and 6 mention the émigré church body, in the following terms:]

3. [The Council of Bishops] elects its representatives to the sessions of the Synod and the Council of Bishops of the diaspora Church . . .

6. [It] elects from among its members representatives for participation in the work of the Synod and Council of Bishops of the diaspora.

Appendix 5

Address of Thanks to Adolph Hitler, Leader of the German People, from Metropolitan Anastasy of the Karlovci Synod

[The text below was written in 1939 on the occasion of the consecration of the new Orthodox church in Berlin. The text below is an English translation of the address, found by this author in the Bakhmeteff Archives, E. Sablin collection, box 51, file: "Russian Orthodox Church in Exile." Let readers judge for themselves whether the later claim of the Synodal hierarchy that the letter was merely an act of polite gratitude for building the Berlin Orthodox church is valid in view of the tone, sweep and vocabulary of the message. Anastasy and his Synod were then in neutral Yugoslavia, and hence there is no parallel between his situation and that of Russian bishops and patriarchs inside the Soviet Union. Neither is the comparison valid between this message and the one sent to Hitler by Fr. John (Shakhovskoi), a priest in Berlin and the future Bishop of San Francisco in the Orthodox Church in America, in 1941 on the occasion of the German attack against the USSR. The illusion that the war would liberate Russia from communism was shared by millions of Russians on both sides of the front; and Fr. John was an ordinary priest and his errors were only his own, while Metropolitan Anastasy was speaking in the name of his entire church organization.]

As we witness this, the consecration of our Berlin Cathedral, which has been erected through the generosity of your Government, and after you had accorded to our Holy Church full legal recognition, our thoughts turn first of all with sincere and warm gratitude to you as its real creator.

We see the special hand of providence in the fact that just at this time, when Churches and National Shrines are being trampled down and destroyed in our Fatherland your constructive policy includes the building of this Church.

As one of many omens, the creation of this Church strengthens the hope that our longsuffering Fatherland has not reached the end of its History, and that He who governs the destiny of all will, in the same way as He sent you to the German people, send to us a leader who,

491

having resurrected our Fatherland, will restore to it its National greatness.

In addition to the usual prayers which are offered up for the Heads of the State at the end of each divine service the following prayer is included: "God Almighty, sanctify those who love the splendour of Thine House and glorify them by your Heavenly Strength." Today especially it is our deep conviction that you also are included in this prayer. Prayers for you will be offered, not only in this newly erected Church and throughout Germany, but also in all Orthodox Churches in Russia.

Not only will the German people with a warmth of love and devotion pray for you before the Throne of the Almighty, but also the devout people of all nations desiring peace and justice, seeing in you a leader in a world struggle for peace and truth.

We have learned from most reliable sources that the faithful in Russia, groaning under the yoke of serfdom, await their deliverer and pray God unceasingly that He will preserve you, guide you and grant you His all-powerful help. Your great achievements on behalf of the German people and towards the greatness of the German Empire have made you an example worthy of imitation, a model of devotion to one's own people and one's Fatherland, and of how one must stand up for one's national and spiritual values. These values also find their consecration and immortalisation in our Church. National values are the honour and glory of every nation, and, for this reason they find a place also in the everlasting kingdom of God. We shall never forget the words of the Holy Scriptures that the Kings of this earth will bring to the Kingdom of Heaven their own glory and the honour and glory of their people. Thus the erection of this Church strengthens our belief in your historical mission. You have erected a House to the Heavenly Lord. May He bless your national building labours—the creation of your Empire. May God succour you and the German people in your fight against those hostile powers, who seek also the destruction of our people. May He grant you, your country, your government and your army health, prosperity and progress for many years to come.

In the name of the Bishop's Synod of the Russian Orthodox Church abroad.

(Signed) Metropolitan Anastasius

Appendix 6

The 1975 Amendments to the 1929 Legislation on Religious Associations

[Following is a comparison of the amendments to the laws on religious associations, decreed by the Presidium of the Supreme Soviet of the RSFSR on June 23, 1975, and the original articles that were affected from the legislation of April 8, 1929 (amended in 1932, but changing only the names of the authorities). The text of the 1929 laws is taken from William B. Stroyen's *Communist Russia and the Russian Orthodox Church, 1943-1962* (Washington, D. C.: Catholic University of America Press, 1967) 121-7. The amendments have been translated by this author from *Vedomosti verkhovnogo soveta RSFSR*, no. 27 [873] (June 1975) 487-91.

Although these laws are for the RSFSR, almost identical changes and amendments were subsequently introduced into the laws of all the other constituent republics of the USSR. The reader is advised to consult Stroyen's book for the complete text of the 1929 legislation.]

Laws of 1929	*Amendments of 1975*
[4] A religious society or group of believers may start its activities only after the registration of the society or group by the committee on religious matters at the proper city or district (raion) soviet.	[4] A religious society or a group of believers may begin to function only after the Council for Religious Affairs . . . has made a decision regarding the registration of the society or group.
	The decision on the registration of a religious society or a group of believers and on the establishment of a prayer house is made by the Council . . . on the recommendations of the Councils of Ministers of autonomous republics or the executive committees of regional, provincial or city (Moscow and Leningrad) soviets of workers' deputies.

493

Laws of 1929

Amendments of 1975

[5] In order to register a religious society at least 20 initiators must submit to the agencies mentioned in the previous Article an application in accordance with the form determined by the Permanent Committee for Religious Matters at the [Council of Ministers].

[5] In order to register a religious society its founders, consisting of at least twenty persons, address a petition to the executive committee of the district or city soviet . . . requesting the registration of the society and the opening of a prayer house . . .

[The soviet] . . . addresses the received petition of the believers with its resolution to the Council of Ministers of the autonomous republic, [or] the executive committee of the regional, provincial, city (Moscow and Leningrad) soviet . . .

[6] In order to register a group of believers, the representative of the group (Art. 13) must submit an application to the agencies mentioned in Article 4 of the city or district where the group is located in accordance with the form determined by the Permanent Committee for Religious Matters at the [Council of Ministers].

[6] In order to effect the registration of the group, the petition signed by all the believers of the given group is submitted to the executive committee of the district or urban soviet . . . which forwards this petition with its resolution attached to the Council of Ministers of an autonomous republic, to the executive committee of a regional, provincial or ([in the cases of] Moscow and Leningrad) city soviet . . .

[7] The registration agencies shall register the society or group within one month, or inform the initiators of the denial of the registration.

[7] The Council of Ministers of an autonomous republic, or the executive committee of a regional, provincial or city (Moscow and Leningrad [only]) soviet . . . having received the materials regarding the registration of a society or group of believers, is to complete their scrutiny within one month and then to forward them with its representation to the Council for Religious Affairs of the USSR Council of Ministers for authorization.

The Council for Religious Affairs . . . studies the materials . . .

Laws of 1929   *Amendments of 1975*

and makes the decision [no time
limit given] whether to register or
to refuse to register the ... group,
and informs the latter on its decision.

[8] The registration agencies shall
be informed on the composition of
the society, as well as on their
executive and accounting bodies
and on the clergy, within the period
and in accordance with the forms
determined by the Permanent Committee for Religious Matters at
the [Council of Ministers].

[8] The Council for Religious Affairs keeps a register of all religious associations, houses of
prayer and [other church] buildings ... [and] establishes the order of submission of data on
religious societies or groups of believers, their executive and auditing organs and the clergy.

[10] For the satisfaction of their
religious needs, the believers who
have formed a religious society
may receive from the district or
city soviet, under a contract, free
of charge, special prayer buildings
and objects intended exclusively
for the cult.

Besides that the believers who
have formed a religious society or
group of believers may use for
prayer meetings other premises left
to them by private persons or local
soviets on lease. Such premises shall
be subject to all regulations provided for in the present Law relating to prayer buildings; the
contracts for the use of such premises shall be concluded by individual believers on their personal responsibility. Such premises shall be
subject to technical and sanitary
regulations.

A religious society or group of
believers may use only one prayer
building or [complex of] premises.

[10] For the satisfaction of religious needs the believers making
up a religious society may, on the
decision of the Council for Religious Affairs ... receive a special
building for prayer, free of charge,
on the conditions ... stipulated in
the agreement concluded between
the religious society and a legitimate representative of the executive committee of the district or
urban soviet.

In addition, believers comprising a religious society or a group
of believers may use for their com-
munal prayer other structures on
lease-holding conditions placed at
their disposal by individual persons
or executive committees of district
or urban soviets. ... These structures are subject to all regulations
of the legislation in force regarding houses of prayer. ... Moreover,
these structures must correspond to
the regular building and sanitary
safety regulations.

A religious society or group of
believers may use only one house
of prayer.

Laws of 1929

[12] For each general assembly of a religious society or group of believers, permission shall be obtained: in cities from committees for religious matters of the city soviets, and in rural areas from the executive committees of the district.

[18] Teaching of any kind of the religious cult in schools, boarding schools, or preschool establishments maintained by the State, public institutions or private persons is prohibited. Such teaching may be given exclusively in religious courses created by the citizens of the U.S.S.R. with the special permission of the Permanent Committee for Religious Matters at the [Council of Ministers].

[20] The religious societies and groups of believers may organize local, All-Russian or All-Union religious conventions or conferences by special permission issued separately for each case by:

(a) the Permanent Committee for Religious Matters of the [Council of Ministers] if an All-Russian or All-Union convention or congress on the territory of the RSFSR is supposed to be convoked.

(b) the local Committee for Religious Matters, if a local convention is supposed to be convoked.

The permission for convocation of republican conventions and con-

Amendments of 1975

[12] General meetings (other than prayer meetings) of religious societies and groups of believers may take place [only] on the permission of the executive committee of the district or urban soviet. . . .

[18] No religious doctrines whatsoever may be taught in educational institutions. The teaching of religion is permitted in theological schools only, which may be established in accordance with the existing regulations.

[20] Religious societies and groups of believers may convoke religious congresses and conferences only with the express permission of the Council for Religious Affairs in each particular case.

Religious centers, spiritual administrations and other religious organizations elected at such congresses and conferences have administrative jurisdiction only over the religious (canonical) activities of religious associations. They are supported by the contributions of religious associations collected exclusively by means of voluntary donations.

Religious centers and diocesan administrations have the right to produce church-plate and [other] objects of the religious cult, and to sell the same to societies of believers. [They also have the right]

Laws of 1929	*Amendments of 1975*
ferences shall be granted by the Committee for Religious Matters of the appropriate republic.	to obtain means of transportation, to rent, build and purchase buildings for their own needs in accordance with the legally established order.
[27] Prayer buildings and religious objects shall be leased to believers forming religious associations for use by the Committee for Religious Matters at the city or district soviet.	[27] Houses of prayer and religious belongings are transferred to the believers comprising a religious society for use on conditions and in the order established in the agreement concluded between the religious society and a plenipotentiary representative of the executive committee of a district or urban soviet. ...
[33] Prayer buildings shall be subject to compulsory fire insurance for the benefit of the appropriate local government at the expense of the persons who signed the contract. In case of fire, the insurance payment may be used for the reconstruction of the prayer building destroyed by fire, or upon decision of the appropriate local government for social and cultural needs of a given locality in full accordance with the Decree of August 24, 1925 on the Utilization of Insurance Payments Acquired for Prayer Buildings Destroyed by Fire.	[33] Houses of religion must be insured at the cost of the persons signing the agreement [on behalf of the religious society] [but] in favor of the executive committee of that district or urban soviet, ... on whose territory the structure is situated. The insurance payments for prayer houses destroyed by fire are used, in accordance with the decision of the Council of Ministers of an autonomous republic or the executive committee of a regional, provincial or city (Moscow and Leningrad [alone] soviet, ... coordinated with the Council for Religious Affairs, for the reconstruction of the ruined buildings or for cultural needs of the district or town in which the ruined prayer house was situated.
[34] If there are no persons who wish to use a prayer building for the satisfaction of religious needs under the conditions provided for in Articles 27-33, the city or dis-	[34] If the believers do not submit a petition to lease to them for religious purposes a building and its belongings necessary for the religious cult, ... the Council of

Laws of 1929

Amendments of 1975

trict soviet puts up a notice of this fact on the doors of the prayer building.

Ministers of an autonomous republic or the executive committee of a regional, provincial or city (Moscow and Leningrad [alone]) soviet . . . decides on the subsequent use of the prayer house and all its belongings in accordance with articles 40 and 41 of this enactment.

[36] The transfer of a prayer building leased for the use of believers for other purposes (liquidation of the prayer building) may take place only according to a decision of the [Council of Ministers] of the autonomous republic or oblast which must be supported by reasons, in a case where the building is needed for government or public purposes. The believers who formed the religious society shall be informed regarding such decision.

[36] A cult building used by believers may be reassigned for other needs [i.e., a prayer house may be simply closed down] exclusively by a decision of the Council for Religious Affairs . . . after a request from the Council of Ministers of an autonomous republic or from the executive committee of a regional, provincial or city (Moscow and Leningrad) soviet, . . . if this building is necessary for state or public needs. Believers comprising the given religious society are to be informed of the decision.

[41] Prayer buildings and wayside shrines subject to liquidation, which are registered in special local agencies for State funds, may be transferred for use free of charge to proper executive committees or city soviets under the condition that they will be continuously considered as nationalized property and their use for other purposes than stipulated may not take place without the consent of the Minister of Finance.

[41] Prayer houses subject to closure which are not under state protection as cultural monuments may be . . . rebuilt for other uses or demolished only by decision of the Council for Religious Affairs . . . on the representation from the Council of Ministers of an autonomous republic [etc.] . . .

[43] When the religious association does not observe the terms of the contract or orders of the Committee for Religious Matters (on re-registration, repair, etc.), the

[43] Religious associations may be deprived of registration if they transgress the legislation on cults.

Deregistration of religious associations is enacted by the Coun-

Laws of 1929

Amendments of 1975

contract may be annulled.

The contract may also be annulled upon the presentation of lower executive committees by the [Council of Ministers] of the autonomous republic, oblast, etc.

cil for Religious Affairs ... on the representation from the Council of Ministers of an autonomous republic [etc.] ...

[44] When the decision of the authorities mentioned in Article 43 is appealed to the [Council of Ministers] within two weeks, the prayer buildings and property may actually be taken from the believers only after the final decision of [the Council].

[44] In case of nonobservance by the religious association of the agreement on the use of the prayer house or cult belongings the Council for Religious Affairs ... has the right to annul the agreement on a representation from the Council of Ministers of an autonomous republic [etc.] ...

[45] The construction of new prayer buildings may take place upon request of religious societies under the observance of the general regulations pertaining to construction and technical rules as well as the special conditions stipulated by the Permanent Committee for Religious Matters at the [Council of Ministers].

[45] On the request of religious societies and with the permission of the Council for Religious Affairs ... on the representation from the Council of Ministers of an autonomous republic [etc.] ... believers may be permitted in individual cases to build new prayer houses out of their own resources.

[54] The members of the groups of believers and religious societies may pool money in the prayer building or premises and outside it by voluntary collections and donations, but only among the members of the given religious association and only for the purpose of covering the expenses for the maintenance of prayer building or premises and religious property, and for the salary of the clergy and activities of the executive bodies.

[54] Religious societies and members of groups of believers may voluntarily pool their resources together and solicit voluntary collections inside the prayer house among members of the given religious association for purposes connected with the maintenance of the building, [the purchase and upkeep] of the cult belongings, the hiring of the clergy, and support of the executive organs.

[59] A special permission [granted] for each case separately by the Committee for Religious Matters

[59] Religious processions, the performance of religious ceremonies in the open air, as well as in

Laws of 1929

is required for the performance of religious processions as well as the performance of religious rites in the open air. An application for such permission must be submitted at least two weeks prior to the ceremony. Such permission is not required for religious services connected with funerals.

[63] The registration agencies of religious associations (Art. 6) submit data to the Committee for Religious Matters at the city and district soviets in accordance with the forms and within the period established by the Permanent Committee for Religious Matters at the [Council of Ministers].

Amendments of 1975

apartments and houses of believers, may take place only by the express permission in each individual case from the executive committee of the regional or urban soviet. . . . Petitions for permissions [for the above ceremonies] . . . must be submitted at least two weeks prior to the date [of the desired action] . . .

Religious ceremonies in private residences requested by dying or very seriously ill believers may be performed without the [above] permission or request [of the same]. . . .

[63] The Council of Ministers of an autonomous republic [etc.] . . . reports all information on religious associations to the CRA . . . in accordance with the established order.

Bibliography

Documents and Other Primary Sources includes official documents, statements, reports, laws, collections of any of the above, and major unpublished *samizdat* works relevant to this work located in archival collections. Articles and memoirs are included under the general heading of *Books and Articles,* unless they represent an official statement or a major document. Only major articles are included under their separate titles; others are found in the relevant periodicals as indicated in the footnotes.

An invaluable aid in the research for this work has been the oral testimony of various persons intimately connected to church life in the USSR, given in interviews with the author. Among the persons interviewed were Metropolitan Anthony (Bloom) of Surozh (London, December 1978); Valentina Lass, a recent émigré (Boston, July 1980); Yury Olshansky, a recent émigré and adult convert to the Orthodox faith while in the USSR, of a Jewish background (New York, May 1981); Sergei Soldatov, a practicing Orthodox Christian who recently emigrated after a prolonged period of political imprisonment (Munich, July 1981); Fr. Konstantin Tivetsky, former Moscow archpriest and recent émigré (San Francisco, June 1980); and Larisa Volokhonsky, a Soviet adult convert of a Jewish background who recently emigrated and became a student at St. Vladimir's Seminary (Crestwood, N.Y., May 1980). In addition, multiple interviews were conducted with recent arrivals from the USSR in Vienna in January 1979, and with numerous Soviet Russian churchmen who prefer to remain anonymous.

Archives

Archives of the Orthodox Church in America. Syosset, N.Y.

The Bakhmeteff Russian Emigré Archives. The Butler Library, Rare Books and Manuscripts Library. Columbia University, New York.

German Military Documents, "Abteilung Fremde Heere Ost." National Archives and Records Service, Washington, D.C.

Dr. Lieb Archiv. Oeffentliche Bibliothek der Universitaet Basel, Basel, Switzerland.

Samizdat Archives. Radio Liberty, Munich.

Samizdat Religious Archives. Keston College, Keston, Kent, England.

Smolensk Archives. Widener Library. Harvard University, Cambridge, Mass.

The Trotsky Archives. Hampton Library. Harvard University, Cambridge, Mass.

The Yiddish (YIVO) Institute, "German World War II Documents." New York.

Documents and Other Primary Sources

Alexeev, Wassilij. "Russian Orthodox Bishops in the Soviet Union, 1944-1953." Research Program on the USSR, Mimeographed Series, 61. New York, 1954.

Aleksii (Shimansky), Patriarch. *Slova, rechi, poslaniya, obrashcheniya, doklady, stat'i*, vols. 1, 2, 3. Moscow, 1948, 1954, 1958.

The Anglo-Russian Theological Conference. London: Faith Press, 1956. Proceedings of the conference that took place in Moscow, July 1956.

Arkhiereiskii Sobor Russkoi Pravoslavnoi Tserkvi. "Deyaniya." *ZhMP*, no. 8 (August 1961). A *samizdat* description of the same is "Opisanie Arkhiereiskogo Sobora 1961 g." AS 701.

Autocephaly. Crestwood, N.Y.: SVS Press, 1971. Documents relating to the autocephaly of the Orthodox Church in America.

Bogolepov, A.A. *The Statutes of the Russian Orthodox Church of 1945.* New York, 1959.

Bourdeaux, Michael. *Patriarch and Prophets: Persecution of the Russian Orthodox Church Today.* London: Macmillan, 1969. A collection of major *samizdat* documents on the subject.

————. *Religious Ferment in Russia: Protestant Opposition to Soviet Religious Policy.* London: Macmillan, 1968.

Christian Committee for the Defense of Believers' Rights in the USSR, documents of, vols. 1-12. Moscow, 1978-1979 (*samizdat*); reprinted in San Francisco by the Washington Research Center, February 1978-January 1980.

Council for Religious Affairs, internal reports. See Sovet po delam religii.

Czesniak, Boleslaw, ed. *The Russian Revolution and Religion.* Notre Dame, Ind.: University Press, 1959. Documents on the communist persecution of religion from 1917-1925.

Deyaniya russkogo vsezagranichnogo tserkovnogo sobora. Sremski Karlovci, 1922.

Deyaniya soveshchaniya glav i predstavitelei avtokefal'nykh pravoslavnykh tserkvei v svyazi s prazdnovaniem 500-letiya avtokefalii russkoi pravoslavnoi tserkvi, 8-18 iyulya, 1948 g., 2 vols. Moscow, 1948-1949.

Deyaniya vtorogo vsezarubezhnogo sobora russkoi pravoslavnoi tserkvi zagranitsei. Belgrade, 1939.

Elevfery, Metropolitan. *Moi otvet Mitr. Antoniyu.* Paris, 1935.

Gidulyanov, P.V. *Otdelenie tserkvi ot gosudarstva v SSSR.* Moscow, 1926.

――――. *Tserkov' i gosudarstvo po zakonodatel'stvu RSFSR.* Moscow, 1923.

Gruppa peterburgskikh svyashchennikov. *K tserkovnomu soboru: Sbornik.* St. Petersburg, 1906. The first Renovationist program of reforms.

Yakunin, Gleb. "O sovremennom polozhenii russkoi pravoslavnoi tserkvi i perspektivakh religioznogo vozrozhdeniya v Rossii." *Vol'noe slovo,* no. 35 (1979). A report to the Christian Committee for the Defense of Believers' Rights by its chairman, together with other documents of the committee.

Yavdas, Mytrofan. *Ukrains'ka avtokefal'na pravoslavna tserkva: Dokumenty.* Munich, 1956.

Kanonicheskoe polozhenie pravoslavnoi russkoi tserkvi zagranitsei. Paris, 1927.

"Khristianskii seminar," documents of. In *Vol'noe slovo,* no. 39 (1980).

Kurdyumov, M., and P. Poltoratsky, eds. *Dni primireniya: Mitropolit Nikolai v Parizhe (24 avgusta–5 sentyabrya 1945 g.). Sbornik materialov.* Paris, 1946.

Leonty, Bishop of Chile. "Political Controls over the Orthodox Church in the Soviet Union." A manuscript for the Research Program on the USSR located in the Bakhmeteff Archives, containing the memoirs of a former Kievan monk and wartime bishop of the Autonomous Orthodox Church in the German-occupied Ukraine.

Leonty (Turkevich), Metropolitan. Papers located in the archives of the Orthodox Church in America, Syosset, N.Y. Includes letters by the Renovationist "bishop" Solovei from Berlin, a private letter by the Karlovcian Bishop Serafim from the Jordanville monastery (January 22, 1947), other letters from Karlovcian bishops, and numerous clippings and pieces of court correspondence in connection with Renovationist activities in the US in the 1920s.

Manuil (Lemeshevsky), Metropolitan. *Russkie pravoslavnye ierarkhi . . . s 1893 po 1965 gody,* part 1. Kuibyshev, 1966 (*samizdat*). Reprinted as *Die russischen orthodoxen Bischoefe von 1893 bis 1965* in Erlangen in 1979.

"New Instructions to Soviet Local Officials on How to Treat Orthodox Christians." BBC, Central Research Unit, Background Note no. 4/67. London, February 24, 1967.

Orleansky, N. *Zakon o religioznykh ob'edineniyakh RSFSR.* Moscow, 1930.

Otzyvy eparkhial'nykh arkhiereev po voprosu o tserkovnoi reforme. 4 vols. St. Petersburg, 1906.

Pervyi vserossiiskii sobor Khristian-Pomortsev, priemlyushchikh brak. *Deyaniya.* Moscow, 1909.

Polnoe sobranie zakonov rossiiskoi imperii, vol. 6. St. Petersburg, 1830. Contains the state laws on religions and Church-state relations.

Pomestnyi sobor russkoi pravoslavnoi tserkvi, 30.5-2.6, 1971 g. Moscow, 1972. In particular, the report of Metropolitan Pimen (soon to be the patriarch) on the life and activities of the Russian Church, pp. 29-136.

Polsky, Mikhail. *Novye mucheniki rossiiskie.* 2 vols. Jordanville, N.Y.: Holy Trinity Monastery, 1949-1957. An incomplete and not error-free catalogue of Russian Orthodox bishops and clergymen martyred by the Soviets for their faith, with details on their lives and deaths when available.

Protokoly 7-go vseamerikanskogo tserkovnogo sobora, sostoyavshegosya v Sv.-Feodosievskom sobore. A record of the council held in Cleveland, Ohio, November 26-29, 1946.

Raz'yasnenie dlya priezzhayushchikh v Ameriku DiPi. New York, 1950. An instruction issued by the Synodal Church to Orthodox displaced persons arriving in the US, explaining why they should not join the Metropolia.

Russkaya pravoslavnaya tserkov' i velikaya otechestvennaya voina: Sbornik tserkovnykh dokumentov. Moscow, 1943.

Russkaya pravoslavnaya tserkov': Ustroistvo, polozhenie, deyatel'nost'. Moscow, 1958.

Russkaya pravoslavnaya tserkov' zagranitsei, 1918-1968. New York, 1968.

Sbornik materialov po antireligioznoi propagande. Leningrad, 1938.

Shafarevich, Igor. *Zakonodatel'stvo o religii v SSSR.* Paris: YMCA Press, 1973. A report to the Moscow Human Rights Committee.

Sistematicheskoe sobranie zakonov RSFSR, ukazov prezidiuma Verkhovnogo Soveta RSFSR i reshenii Pravitel'stva RSFSR, vol. 2. Moscow, 1968.

Solzhenitsyn, Alexander I. "Pis'mo Vserossiiskomu Patriarkhu Pimenu." *VRSKhD,* no. 103 (1972). Solzhenitsyn's famous "Lenten Letter." The same issue also contains other related *samizdat* documents.

Sovet po delam religii pri Sovete Ministrov SSSR. Confidential internal reports of the CRA on various aspects of the Church. Of particular interest are two signed by Deputy Chairman V. Furov: "Iz otcheta . . . chlenam TsK KPSS . . ." *VRKhD,* no. 130 (1979); and "Iz otcheta . . . za 1970 g. . . . Monastyri," *VRKhD,* no. 131 (1980).

Other CRA internal reports for 1967-1970 can be found in the Keston College Archives.

The Statute of the Orthodox Church in America. New York: Chancery of the OCA, 1974.

Svyashchennyi Sobor Pravoslavnoi Rossiiskoi Tserkvi. *Deyaniya,* vols. 1-10. Moscow-Petrograd, 1918.

————. *Polozhenie o vysshem i eparkhial'nom upravlenii pravoslavnoi tserkvi.* Warsaw, 1922.

————. *Prikhodskii ustav pravoslavnoi tserkvi.* Warsaw, 1922.

————. *Sobranie opredelenii i postanovlenii: Prilozheniya k Deyaniyam.* 4 vols. Moscow, 1918.

Tarasar, Constance J., et al., eds. *Orthodox America, 1794-1976.* Syosset, N.Y.: OCA, Department of History and Archives, 1975.

Tretii sobor "Zarubezhnoi Russkoi Tserkvi." "Pis'mo A. Solzhenitsyna Tret'emu Soboru." *VRKhD,* nos. 112-113 (1974).

————. "Obrashcheniya III vsezarubezhnogo sobora . . ." and other related documents. *VRKhD,* nos. 114 (1974) and 115 (1975). Other sobor documents are found in *Pravoslavnaya Rus'* (1974).

"Ukaz Prezidiuma Verkhovnogo Soveta RSFSR ot 23 iyunya, 1975 g." *Vedomosti Verkhovnogo Soveta RSFSR,* no. 27 (873) (June 1975).

Valentinov, A., comp. *The Assault of Heaven: The Black Book.* London: Boswell, 1925.

Zakonodatel'stvo o religioznykh kul'takh: Sbornik materialov i dokumentov dlya sluzhebnogo pol'zovaniya. Moscow, 1971; reprint New York: Chalidze Publications, 1981.

Zhurnaly i protokoly zasedanii vysochaishe utverzhdennogo Predsobornogo Prisutstviya. 4 vols. St. Petersburg, 1906-1907.

Serial Publications

Amerikanskii pravoslavnyi vestnik. Appeared first as *Pravoslavnyi amerikanskii vestnik* in 1896 as the official, bilingual journal of the Russian Orthodox Missionary Archdiocese of America. Later its name was changed to *Russko-amerikanskii pravoslavnyi vestnik.* Ceased publication in the mid-1970s, having been superseded by the English-language *The Orthodox Church.* At various times was published in Cleveland and New York.

Bogoslovskie trudy. An irregular serial volume of theological works by the faculties of the Russian Orthodox seminaries. Published since the early 1960s, once to twice annually.

A Chronicle of Current Events. The English translation of *Khronika,* the main *samizdat* human rights information journal, issued three to six times per year since 1968. The English edition is produced by Amnesty International in London.

Ezhegodnik muzeya istorii religii i ateizma. USSR Academy of Sciences annual of atheistic "religiology," issued from 1957 to 1962.

Grani. A Russian émigré publicistic and literary quarterly, published since 1946 by Possev in Frankfurt am Main.

Khristianin. An irregular journal of the Educational Committee of the Renovationist Church, edited by Metropolitan Evdokim (Meshchersky). First published in 1924 in Moscow.

Kontinent. A literary, sociopolitical and religious quarterly published in Paris since 1974 by Christian intellectuals of the most recent Russian emigration. Edited by the former Soviet writer Vladimir Maximov.

Nauka i religiya. An official Soviet atheistic monthly, directed toward a broad readership. Published by the Znanie society since 1959.

Nadezhda: Khristianskoe chtenie. A *samizdat* periodical devoted to Orthodox Christianity. Issued since 1977 in Moscow, reprinted by Possev in Frankfurt am Main.

Novoe russkoe slovo. The oldest Russian-language daily, published in New York since 1910.

One Church. The organ of the Moscow Patriarchal parishes in North America. Issued from New York.

The Orthodox Church. The official monthly of the Orthodox Church in America. Published since 1965 under the editorship of the Very Rev. Professor John Meyendorff in Syosset, N.Y.

Posev. A journal of politics and Russian affairs, published by the NTS (National Alliance of Russian Solidarists). Began in 1945 as a weekly, issued since January 1968 as a monthly. Printed at the Possev-Verlag Publishing House in Frankfurt am Main.

Pravoslavnaya mysl'. An irregular theological periodical published by the faculty of the St. Sergius Institute in Paris.

Pravoslavnaya Rus'. A semi-official, bimonthly organ of the Synodal Church. Published since 1947 at the Holy Trinity Monastery in Jordanville, N.Y.

Put'. A journal of religious thought, philosophy and Christian culture, edited by Nicholas Berdyaev in Paris. A total of sixty-one issues appeared between 1925 and 1940, when it ceased publication.

Religion in Communist Lands. A now triannual journal published since 1973 by Keston College (formerly Centre for the Study of Religion and Communism), Keston, Kent, England.

Russkaya mysl' (*Pensée russe*). A Russian weekly from Paris since 1947, at first as a thrice-weekly newspaper.

St. Vladimir's Theological Quarterly. Published by the faculty of St. Vladimir's Orthodox Theological Seminary in Crestwood, N.Y. Began in 1957 under the title *St. Vladimir's Seminary Quarterly*. Currently edited by Very Rev. Professor John Meyendorff and Dr. John Erickson.

Soviet Jewish Affairs. Published since 1968 by the London Institute of Jewish Affairs, at first twice yearly, now quarterly.

Tserkovnye vedomosti. A theoretically bimonthly, but in practice monthly, organ of the Karlovci Synod. Issued from 1922 until the early 1930s.

Veche. A *samizdat* journal devoted to religion, Christian culture, Russian history and Russian nationalism. Founded in the village of Rozhdestvo (Vladimir province) in 1971 by Vladimir Osipov, who edited nine issues until the spring of 1974. A tenth issue was put out by antagonists of Osipov in 1974 after he had closed the journal. Since spring 1981, an independent Russian almanac under the same name, edited by Evgeny Vagin and Oleg Krasovsky, has been published in Munich.

Vestnik russkogo studencheskogo khristianskogo dvizheniya. Published since 1926 in Paris, then Germany, then Paris again, variously as a monthly, six times annually, and now as a quarterly. Presently edited by Nikita A. Struve. Since no. 112-113 (1974), the adjective *studencheskii* has been dropped from the title. Maintains good contacts with the Christian intelligentsia inside the USSR, and lately more than half of its material has been authored within the USSR.

Vestnik Svyashchennogo Sinoda pravoslavnoi rossiiskoi tserkvi. The official organ of the Renovationists. Appeared irregularly prior to 1925 under variants of the above title, and for several years after 1925 on a monthly basis.

Vol'noe slovo. Formerly *Posev, spetsial'nyi vypusk*. A four to six times annually publication of selections of *samizdat*, issued as a supplement to *Posev*.

Voprosy istorii religii i ateizma. An irregular official publication of Soviet "religiology." Appeared under this title as an organ of the Academy of Sciences of the USSR until 1964, when its publication was transferred to the Academy of Social Sciences attached to the Central Committee of the CPSU and the title was changed to *Voprosy nauchnogo ateizma*. This transfer signifies the particular ideological importance attached to the struggle against religion by the Soviet communist leadership.

Voprosy nauchnogo ateizma. See previous entry.

Vozrozhdenie. A Paris Russian daily issued between the two world wars.

Zemlya. A *samizdat* journal of a tolerant Christian-patriotic orientation, founded by Vladimir Osipov after his discontinuation of *Veche*. Osipov was arrested after the appearance of the first issue, and the second and last issue appeared when Osipov was already in prison for his publication activities.

Zhurnal Moskovskoi Patriarkhii. The official monthly organ of the Moscow Patriarchate. Published irregularly between 1931 and 1935, renewed on a regular basis since September 1943.

Books and Articles

Abramov, I. *V kul'turnom skitu: Ob odnoi protsvetayushchei kommunisticheskoi obshchine.* St. Petersburg, 1914. Concerning Nepluev's Christian commune.

Agursky, M. *Ideologiya natsional-bol'shevizma.* Paris: YMCA Press, 1980.

Aivazov, I.G. *Obnovlentsy i starotserkovniki.* Moscow, 1909. Thoughts on church reform by an early Renovationist.

————. *Pravoslavnaya tserkov' i vysshie gosudarstvennye upravleniya v Rossii.* Moscow, 1912.

Akademiya obshchestvennykh nauk pri TsK KPSS. *Konkretnye issledovaniya sovremennykh religioznykh verovanii.* Moscow, 1967.

Aksakov, N.P. "Chto govoryat kanony o sostave sobora?" *Tserkovnyi golos.* St. Petersburg, 1906.

Alekseev, N. "Khristianstvo i sotsializm." *Put'*, no. 28 (June 1931).

Aleksii (Dorodnitsyn), Bishop. *Polnoe sobranie sochinenii.* Saratov, 1913-1914.

Alexeev, W., and T. Stavrou. *The Great Revival.* Minneapolis: Burgess Publishing Co., 1976.

Amosov, N. *Antireligioznaya rabota na poroge vtoroi pyatiletki.* Moscow, 1932.

————. *Oktyabr'skaya revolyutsiya i tserkov'.* Moscow, 1937.

Anastasy, Metropolitan, ed. *Tserkovnaya letopis'.* Lausanne, 1945.

Andreev, Ivan. *Blagodatna li sovetskaya tserkov'?* Jordanville, N.Y.: Holy Trinity Monastery, 1948.

Andryanov, N.P. *Evolyutsiya religioznogo soznaniya.* Leningrad, 1974.

Antony (Khrapovitsky), Metropolitan. *Sbornik izbrannykh sochinenii.* Belgrade, 1935.

Antonov, N.P. *Russkie svetskie bogoslovy i ikh religiozno-obshchestvennoe mirosozertsanie.* St. Petersburg, 1912.

Armstrong, John. *Ukrainian Nationalism.* New York: Columbia University Press, 1963.

B., Aleksei. "Az iesm' khleb zhivoi." *Put'*, no. 42 (January-March 1934). A sermon and notes on the sacraments by a Moscow priest who was exiled to Solovki in 1930.

Babushkin, S.D. *Tserkovno-prikhodskaya obshchina i zemskii sobor.* Kazan, 1905.

Balevits, Z. *Pravoslavnaya tserkov' v Latvii pod sen'yu svastiki.* Riga, 1967.

Berdyaev, N.A. *Russkaya religioznaya psikhologiya i kommunisticheskii ateizm.* Paris, 1931.

Bilinets, S. *T'ma i ee slugi.* Kiev, 1960.

Blackwell, W. *The Beginnings of Russian Industrialization, 1800-1860.* Princeton, N.J.: University Press, 1968.

Bociurkiw, Bohdan. "The Catacomb Church: Ukrainian Greek Catholics in the USSR." *RCL* 5:1 (1977).

————. "Religious Situation in Soviet Ukraine." In *Ukraine in a Changing World.* New York: Ukrainian Congress Committee of America, 1977.

————. "The Renovationist Church in the Soviet Ukraine, 1922-1939." *Annals of the Ukrainian Academy of Arts and Sciences in the U.S.* 9:1-2 (1961).

————, and J. Strong, eds. *Religion and Atheism in the USSR and Eastern Europe.* Toronto: University Press, 1975.

Bogolepov, Alexander A. *Church Reforms in Russia, 1905-1918.* Bridgeport, Conn.: Committee of the Metropolitan Council of the Russian Orthodox Church of America, 1966.

————. *Tserkov' pod vlast'yu kommunizma.* Munich, 1958.

Bolshakoff, Serge. *Russian Nonconformity: The Story of "Unofficial" Religion in Russia.* Philadelphia, 1950.

Bourdeaux, Michael. *Faith on Trial in Russia.* London: Hodder & Stoughton, 1971.

Bulgakov, Sergius. *Avtobiograficheskie zapiski.* Paris, 1946.

Bullock, Alen. *Hitler: A Study in Tyranny.* London: Penguin, 1975.

Casey, Robert Pierce. *Religion in Russia.* New York: Harper & Brothers, 1946. More sympathetic toward the Church and her sufferings than Professor Curtiss' book.

Chrysostomus, J. *Kirchengeschichte Russlands der neusten Zeit.* 3 vols. Munich-Salzburg, 1965-1968.

Conquest, Robert. *Religion in the USSR.* New York: Praeger, 1968.

Crummey, Robert. *The Old Believers and the World of Antichrist.* Madison: University of Wisconsin Press, 1970.

Cunningham, James W. *A Vanquished Hope: The Movement for Church Renewal in Russia, 1905-1906.* Crestwood, N.Y.: SVS Press, 1982.

Curtiss, John S. *Church and State in Russia, 1900-1917.* New York: Octagon Books, 1940.

————. *The Russian Church and the Soviet State, 1917-1950.* Boston: Little, Brown, 1953. The author tends to blame the victim rather than the executioner.

Dallin, Alexander. *German Rule in Russia, 1941-1945.* London: Macmillan, 1957.

Demyanov, A.I. *Istinno-phavoslavnoe khristianstvo.* Voronezh, 1977.

d'Erbini'i (d'Herbigny), M. *Tserkovnaya zhizn' v Moskve.* Paris, 1926.

————. *Les evêques russes en exil.* Paris, 1931.

Drujski, A. *Religious Life in Belorussia: The Orthodox Church.* Chicago, 1976.

Dublyansky, A. *Ternystym shlakhom.* London: The Ukrainian Autocephalous Church Publications, 1962.

Dudko, Dmitry, Protoierei. "Kreshchenie na Rusi." *VRKhD,* no. 117 (1976).

————. *Our Hope.* Crestwood, N.Y.: SVS Press, 1977.

E.L. *Episkopy ispovedniki.* San Francisco, 1971.

Elevfery, Metropolitan. *Nedelya v Patriarkhii.* Paris, 1933.

Elfimov, V.F. *O. prichinakh i usloviyakh sushchestvovaniya religioznykh perezhitkov v SSSR.* Vologda, 1971.

Ellis, Jane, tr. and ed. *An Early Soviet Saint: The Life of Fr. Zachariah.* London: Mowbrays, 1976.

Emelyakh, L. "Sekretnye doneseniya episkopov pravoslavnoi tserkvi ob antiklerikalizme i ateizme krest'yan v period pervoi russkoi revolyutsii." *EMIRA* 6 (1962).

Evlogy (Georgievsky), Metropolitan. *Put' moei zhizni.* Paris: YMCA Press, 1947.

Fedorova, S.G. *Russkoe naselenie na Alyaske i v Kalifornii.* Moscow, 1971.

Fireside, H. *Icon and Swastika.* Cambridge, Mass.: Harvard University Press, 1971.

Fletcher, William. *Nikolai.* London: Collier-Macmillan, 1968.

————. *The Russian Orthodox Church Underground, 1917-1970.* Oxford: University Press, 1971.

————. *Religion and Soviet Foreign Policy, 1945-1970.* London: Oxford University Press, 1973.

————. *A Study in Survival.* New York: Macmillan, 1965.

Florovsky, G. *Puti russkogo bogosloviya.* Paris: YMCA Press, 1937.

Fotiev, K.V. *Popytki ukrainskoi tserkovnoi avtokefalii v XX veke.* Munich, n.d.

Gagarin, Yu.V. *Religioznye perezhitki v Komi ASSR.* Syktyvkar, 1971.

Georgy, Hegumen. "Dukhovnye uchebnye zavedeniya v SSSR." In *Russkaya pravoslavnaya tserkov' v SSSR.* Munich, 1962.

Gilyarov-Platonov, N.P. *Voprosy very i tserkvi.* Moscow, 1905.

Gordienko, N.S. *Kritika novykh tendentsii sovremennogo pravoslaviya.* Leningrad, 1974.

————, V.I. Nosovich and L.R. Kharakhorkin. *Sovremennoe pravoslavie i ego ideologiya.* Moscow, 1963.

Grabbe, Georgy. *Pravda o russkoi tserkvi na rodine i za rubezhom.* Jordanville, N.Y.: Holy Trinity Monastery, 1961.

————. *The Canonical and Legal Position of the Moscow Patriarchate.* Jerusalem: The Russian Ecclesiastical Mission, 1971.

Grekulov, E.F. *Pravoslavnaya tserkov'—vrag prosveshcheniya.* Moscow, 1962.

Grunwald, Constantin de. *The Churches and the Soviet Union.* New York: Macmillan, 1962. The author is an émigré Soviet patriot, who buys the official line of the friendly coexistence of Church and state in Russia.

Hecker, Julius F. *Religion and Communism.* New York: John Wiley & Sons, 1934. The author is an American Methodist fellow traveler who went to teach at the Renovationist theological academy and eventually perished in the purges. A biased pro-Soviet book.

Heyer, Friedrich. *Die orthodoxe Kirche in der Ukraine von 1917 bis 1945.* Cologne, 1953.

Hutten, Kurt. *Iron Curtain Christians.* Minneapolis: Augsburg Publishing House, 1967.

Ioann (Shakhovskoi), Archbishop. *Utverzhdenie pomestnoi tserkvi.* New York: Waldon Press, 1972.

Kandidov, B.P. *Tserkovnyi front v gody mirovoi voiny.* Moscow, 1927.

Kartashev, A. "Tserkov' i natsional'nost'." *Put',* no. 44 (July- September 1934).

————. "Revolyutsiya i sobor 1917-1918." *Bogoslovskaya mysl'* (1942).

Kartsov, V.G. *Religioznyi raskol kak forma antifeodal'nogo protesta v istorii Rossii.* Kalinin, 1971.

Kharlampovich, K.V. *Malorossiiskoe vliyanie na velikorusskuyu tserkovnuyu zhizn',* vol. 1. The Hague: Mouton Reprints, 1968.

Khudyakov, S.N. *O preodolenii religioznykh perezhitkov v SSSR.* Moscow, 1958.

Kischkowsky, A. *Die sowjetische Religionspolitik und die Russische Orthodoxe Kirche.* Munich, 1960.

Klibanov, A.I. *Konkretnye issledovaniya sovremennykh religioznykh verovanii.* Moscow, 1967.

Kline, George. *Religions and Anti-Religious Thought in Russia.* Chicago: University Press, 1968.

Kobetsky, V.D. "Issledovanie dinamiki religioznosti naseleniya SSSR." In *Ateizm, religiya, sovremennost'.* Leningrad, 1973.

Konstantinov, Dmitry. *Pravoslavnaya molodezh v bor'be za tserkov' v SSSR.* Munich, 1956.

Komsomol i antireligioznaya propaganda: Sbornik statei i ocherkov. Moscow, 1937.

Krasnov, Anatoly E. See Levitin-Krasnov.

Kupranec, Orest, OSBM. *The Orthodox Church in Poland, 1918-1939.*
Analecta OSBM, 2. Rome, 1974.

Kurbatov, G.L. "Klassovaya sushchnost' ucheniya Ioanna Zlatousta."
EMIRA 2 (1958).

Kuroedov, V.A. *Sovetskoe gosudarstvo i tserkov'.* Moscow, 1976.

Kuznetsov, N.D. *Po voprosam tserkovnykh preobrazovanii.* Moscow,
1907.

Levitin-Krasnov, A. *Vospominaniya.* 4 vols.: *Likhie gody,* Paris, 1977;
Ruk tvoikh zhar, Tel Aviv, 1979; *V poiskakh novogo grada,* Tel
Aviv, 1980; *Rodnoi prostor,* Frankfurt am Main, 1981.

———. *Zashchita very v SSSR.* Paris, 1966.

———, and Vadim Shavrov. *Ocherki po istorii russkoi tserkovnoi smuty.*
3 vols. in 1. Kuesnacht, Switzerland, 1978.

Lisavtsev, E.I. *Kritika burzhuaznoi fal'sifikatsii polozheniya religii v
SSSR.* Moscow, 1971.

Lomako, G. *Tserkovno-kanonicheskoe polozhenie russkogo rasseyaniya.*
New York: Russian Orthodox Metropolia of America, 1950.

Lot-Borodina, M. "Kritika 'Russkogo khristianstva.' " *Put',* no. 52 (November 1936-March 1937). A critique of A. Kartashev's religious
nationalism.

Luka (Voino-Yasenetsky), Archbishop. *Dukh, dusha, telo.* Brussels, 1978.

Lunacharsky, A.V. *Khristianstvo ili kommunizm: Disput s mitr. A. Vve-
denskim.* Leningrad, 1926.

Lypkivsky, Metropolitan Vasyl'. *Vidrodzhennya tserkvy v Ukraini.* Toronto, 1959.

Lzhe-pravoslavie na pod'eme. Jordanville, N.Y.: Holy Trinity Monastery,
1954.

Mandelshtam, Nadezhda. *Vtoraya kniga.* Paris: YMCA Press, 1972.

Marshall, Richard, Jr., ed. *Aspects of Religion in the Soviet Union, 1917-
1967.* Chicago: University Press, 1971.

Martynenko, N.I. *Kritika pravoslavnogo ucheniya o nravstvennosti.* Voronezh, 1973.

Meyendorff, John. *Living Tradition.* Crestwood, N.Y.: SVS Press, 1978.

Mikhail (Semenov). *Kak ya stal narodnym sotsialistom.* A brochure without date or place of publication, located in the Lieb Archive. The
author was at first a monk-priest and professor at the St. Petersburg
Theological Academy, and after 1907 an Old Believer bishop.

———. *Pochemu nam ne veryat? K tserkovnoi reforme.* St. Petersburg,
1906.

———. *Khristos v vek mashin.* St. Petersburg, 1907.

My porvali s religiei. Moscow, 1963.

Nepluev, N.N. *Trudovye bratstva.* Leipzig, 1893.

Nichols, Robert, and Theofanis G. Stavrou, eds. *Russian Orthodoxy under the Old Regime*. Minneapolis: University of Minnesota Press, 1978.

Oleshchuk, F.N. *Kto stroit tserkvi v SSSR?* Moscow-Leningrad, n.d., but probably 1929 or 1930.

————. *O zadachakh antireligioznoi propagandy*. Moscow, 1937.

Olsufiev, Count D. *Mysli soboryanina o nashei tserkovnoi smute*. With a foreword by Metropolitan Antony. Paris, 1928.

Ostraya Luka. A samizdat novel in the Keston College Archives.

Pantskhava, I.P. *Konkretno-sotsiologicheskoe izuchenie sostoyaniya religioznosti i opyta ateisticheskogo vospitaniya*. Moscow, 1969.

Pascal, Pierre. *The Religion of the Russian People*. Crestwood, N.Y.: SVS Press, 1976.

Patriarkh Sergii i ego dukhovnoe nasledstvo. Moscow, 1947.

Pavlyuk, V.V. *Psikhologiya sovremennykh veruyushchikh i ateisticheskoe vospitanie*. Lvov, 1976.

Platonov, N.F. "Pravoslavnaya tserkov' v 1917-1935 gg." *EMIRA* 5 (1961). The author is a former Leningrad "metropolitan" of the Renovationists.

Polsky, Mikhail. *Kanonicheskoe polozhenie vysshei tserkovnoi vlasti v SSSR i zagranitsei*. Jordanville, N.Y.: Holy Trinity Monastery, 1948.

————. *Polozhenie tserkvi v sovetskoi Rossii: Ocherk bezhavshego iz Rossii svyashchennika*. Jerusalem, 1931.

Popovsky, Mark. *Zhizn' i zhitie Voino-Yasenetskogo, arkhiepiskop i khirurga*. Paris: YMCA Press, 1979.

Pospielovsky, D. *Russian Police Trade Unionism*. London: Weidenfeld & Nicolson, 1971.

Pravda o religii v Rossii. Moscow, 1942.

Preobrazhensky, I.V., ed. *Tserkovnaya reforma*. St. Petersburg, 1905. A collection of articles from the church and secular press.

Prokhanov, Ivan. *In the Cauldron of Russia, 1869-1933*. New York, 1933.

Prugavin, A.S. *Raskol-sektantstvo: Materialy dlya izucheniya religioznobytovykh dvizhenii russkogo naroda. Bibliografiya staroobryadchestva*. Moscow, 1887.

Putintsev, F.M. *Vybory v sovety i razoblachenie popovshchiny*. Moscow, 1937.

Putnam, George F. *Russian Alternatives to Marxism*. Knoxville: University of Tennessee Press, 1977.

Rahr, Gleb. *Plenennaya tserkov'*. Frankfurt am Main, 1954.

Razumovsky, G. *Ekumenicheskoe dvizhenie i russkaya pravoslavnaya tserkov'*. Moscow, 1948.

Regelson, Lev. *Tragediya russkoi tserkvi, 1917-1945*. Paris: YMCA Press, 1977.

Rodzyanko, Mikhail. *Pravda o zarubezhnoi tserkvi*. Munich, 1954.

Rogger, Hans. "Was There a Russian Fascism? The Union of Russian People." In Henry A. Turner, Jr., ed., *Reappraisal of Fascism.* New York: New Viewpoints, 1975.

Russkaya pravoslavnaya tserkov' v SSSR: Sbornik. Munich, 1962.

Sakharov, A.M., ed. *Religiya i tserkov' v istorii Rossii.* Moscow, 1975.

Samoilovich, Yu. *Tserkov' ukrainskogo sotsial-fashizma.* Moscow, 1932.

Sazonova, Yu. "Religioznye iskaniya v otrazhenii sovetskoi literatury." *Put',* no. 21 (April 1930).

Scheffbusch, Winrich. *Christians under the Hammer and Sickle.* Grand Rapids, Mich.: Zondervan Publishing House, 1974.

Sergeenko, Andrei. *O polozhenii tserkvi v Rossii: Doklad chlena tserkov-noi delegatsii pobyvavshei v Rossii.* Paris, 1947.

Shavelsky, G.I. *Vospominaniya poslednego protopresvitera russkoi armii i flota.* New York: Chekhov Publishing House, 1954.

Sheinman, M.M. *Khristianskii sotsializm.* Moscow, 1969.

Shishkin, A.A. *Sushchnost' i kriticheskaya otsenka obnovlencheskogo raskola v russkoi pravoslavnoi tserkvi.* Kazan, 1970.

Simon, Gerhard. "Church, State and Society." In G. Katkov, et al., *Russia Enters the 20th Century.* London: Temple Smith, 1971.

————. *Church, State and Opposition in the USSR.* London: 1974.

Sokolov, N.M. *Russkie svyatie i russkaya intelligentsiya* and *Ob ideyakh i idealakh russkoi intelligentsii.* St. Petersburg, 1904.

Solzhenitsyn, Alexander, et al., eds. *From under the Rubble.* New York: Bantam Books, 1976.

Spinka, Matthew. *The Church and the Russian Revolution.* New York: Macmillan, 1927.

————. *The Church in Soviet Russia.* New York: Oxford University Press, 1956.

Stratonov, Irinarkh. "Iskhodnyi moment russkoi tserkovnoi smuty poslednego vremeni." *Put',* no. 12 (August 1928) 76-100.

————. *Russkaya tserkovnaya smuta, 1921-1931.* Berlin, 1932.

Stroyen, William B. *Communist Russia and the Russian Orthodox Church, 1943-1962.* Washington, D.C.: Catholic University Press, 1967.

Struve, Nikita. *Christians in Contemporary Russia.* London: Harvill Press, 1967.

Struve, Petr B., ed. *Iz glubiny: Sbornik statei o russkoi revolyutsii.* Paris: YMCA Press, 1967. This work was originally published illegally in Moscow in 1921. The Paris edition is a reprint.

Svetov, Feliks. *Otverzi mi dveri.* Paris: YMCA Press, 1978.

Svitich, Alexander. *Pravoslavnaya tserkov' v Pol'she i ee avtokefaliya.* Buenos Aires, 1959.

Talberg, N.D. *Tserkovnyi raskol.* Paris, 1927.

Timasheff, N.S. *Religion in Soviet Russia.* London, 1943.

Titlinov, B.V. *Novaya tserkov'*. Petrograd-Moscow, 1923. The author was a leading Renovationist theologian.

Tokarev, S.A. "O religii kak sotsial'nom yavlenii." *Sovetskaya etnografiya*, no. 3 (May-June 1979).

Troitsky, S.V. *Chto takoe zhivaya tserkov'?* Warsaw, 1928.

————. *O nepravde karlovatskogo raskola: Razbor knigi protoiereya Pol'skogo*. Paris, 1960.

————. *Razmezhevanie ili raskol?* Paris, 1932.

Trubetskoi, Prince Grigory N. *Krasnaya Rossiya i svyataya Rus'*. Paris, 1931.

Trubnikova, Alla Ya. *Komandirovka v 13-i vek*. Moscow, 1965.

Tschizewskij, Dmitrij. *Russian Intellectual History*. Ann Arbor: Ardis, 1978.

Valentinov, A. *Religiya i tserkov' v SSSR*. Moscow, 1960.

Vasilevskaya, V.Ya. "Katakomby XX veka." A samizdat document located in the Keston College Archives.

Vitaly, Archbishop. *Motivy moei zhizni*. 2d ed. Jordanville, N.Y.: Holy Trinity Monastery, 1955.

Vvedensky, A.I. *Revolyutsiya i tserkov'*. Petrograd, 1922. The author was the leading Renovationist orator and the last ruling metropolitan of the schism.

————. *Tserkov' i gosudarstvo*. Moscow, 1923.

————. *Tserkov' Patriarkha Tikhona*. Moscow, 1923.

Yaroslavsky, E. *Protiv religii i tserkvi: Sobranie sochinenii v 5 tomakh*. Moscow, 1935.

————. *Religion in the USSR*. London: Modern Books Ltd., 1932.

Zapiski religiozno-filosofskikh sobranii. St. Petersburg, 1906.

Zatko, James. *Descent into Hell: The Destruction of the Roman Catholic Church in Russia, 1917-1923*. Notre Dame, Ind.: University Press, 1965.

Zenkovsky, V.V., ed. *Pravoslavie i kul'tura: Sbornik religiozno-filosofskikh statei*. Berlin, 1923.

Zheludkov, Sergii O. *Pochemu i ya khristianin*. Frankfurt am Main, 1973.

Zots, V.A. *Nesostoyatel'nye pretenzii: Kriticheskie ocherki pravoslavno-bogoslovskoi interpretatsii problem dukhovnoi kul'tury*. Moscow, 1976.

Zybkovets, *Natsionalizatsiya monastyrskikh imushchestv v Sovetskoi Rossii (1917-1921 gg.)*. Moscow, 1975.

Dissertations

Grigorieff, Dmitry F. "The Russian Orthodox Church in America." Diploma thesis, St. Vladimir's Orthodox Theological Seminary, n.d.

Johnson, Michael. "Archbishop Evdokim and the Orthodox Church in America, 1914-1917." Master of Divinity thesis, St. Vladimir's Orthodox Theological Seminary, 1976.

Matusiak, John. "The Orthodox Church in America, 1917-1922, Following the Russian Revolution." Master of Divinity thesis, St. Vladimir's Orthodox Theological Seminary, 1975.

Rojkov, Vladimir. "Tserkovnye voprosy v gosudarstvennoi dume." Dissertation of an exchange student from the USSR at the Gregorian University, Rome, 1975.

Weiant, E.T. "Sources of Mass Atheism in Russia." Doctor of Philosophy dissertation, University of Basel, 1950.

Index

Adam (Filippovsky), Bishop 287

Afanasy (Sakharov), Bishop—break with Sergii 161, 162; imprisoned for loyalty to Sergii 108; recognition of Aleksii and return to Patriarchal Church 149, 161, 180, 189, 203-4, 370, 383

Afonsky, Fr. Nikolai 417

Agafangel (Preobrazhensky), Metropolitan of Yaroslavl—breaks with Sergii 150, 162, 186; declares temporary autocephaly in his diocese 120, 368; designated locum tenens by Tikhon 56, 107, 108; makes peace with Sergii 156

agricultural collectivization and the Church 171

Agursky, Mikhail 88

Aksakov, N. 23

Alaska—Orthodox Church in 279-80; school and education in 279, 280

Aleksii, Bishop of Kuban 412

Aleksii (Bui), Bishop 152, 158, 168, 180, 368

Aleksii (Dorodnitsyn), Bishop 24

Aleksii (Gromadsky), Metropolitan 238-40, 244, 245, 475

Aleksii (Ridiger), Archbishop of Tallin 390-1, 392-3, 410, 431, 451

Aleksii (Simansky), Bishop, Metropolitan, Patriarch—admiration for "catacombs" 377-8; and church administration 213-4, 399, 428; death of 379, 387, 444; and diaspora 270, 275, 295, 297-8; and ecumenical see 309-10; elected patriarch 149, 189, 209-10; Middle East pilgrimage 219, 303, 309; opposition to, from believers 158, 160; patriotic role in WWII 199, 207, 216, 231; refuses to flee revolution 114; and Renovationists 155; see also next entry

Aleksii (Simansky), Patriarch, relations with Soviets—implicit support for Soviet propaganda 341; letters to Khrushchev 335-6; relations with Stalin 147, 201-2, 207-8, 218, 318-9; resists government pressure 359, 388; succumbs to pressure 155, 191, 315; see also next entry

Aleksii (Simansky), Patriarch, sermons, speeches, writings—address to Council of Bishops 338-40; address to émigré Synod 267; at consecration of bishops 319; message to Uniates 308; on spiritual renewal 320; on priestly vocations 353; speech at Kremlin Conference of the Soviet Public for Disarmament 333-5, 420

Alexander I 205

Alexander II 45

Alexander, Metropolitan of Latvia 228, 229

Alexander (Inozemtsev), Metropolitan 257

Alexander (Nemolovsky), Archbishop of North America (Synodal) 283

---

*I should like to express my deep gratitude to my wife, Mirjana, and my son, Andrew for their help in compiling this index.

Alexander Nevsky, St. 197, 199
Alexeev, Wassilij 175, 221, 227, 232, 238, 244, 245, 246
Alipy, or Olimpy (Voronov), Abbot 429, 443
All-Russian Central Executive Committee Presidium's Permanent Commission on Religious Cults, instruction of 216
All-Russian Preparatory Conference of Clergy and Laity 26-7
All-Russian Sobor, 1917-1918 26-9, 33, 210-11; election of patriarch 29-30; organization of 26-9; see also next entry
All-Russian Sobor, 1917-1918, church structure and Statute—conciliar system 37-8; diocesan conferences 34; Higher Church Council 33, 211; metropolitan districts 33; parish statute 33; prerogatives of patriarch 34, 36; Synod of Bishops 33; see also next entry
All-Russian Sobor, 1917-1918, declarations and resolutions—on excommunication of communists 38; on monasticism 35-6; on Old Believers 35; on patriarchal powers 33, 34, 36; on preaching 34-5; on women 35-6; response to Soviet attacks 36-7
All-Russian Sobor, 1943—elects Sergii patriarch 207
All-Russian Sobor, 1945 209-15
All-Russian Sobor, 1971—and Karlovcians 396; anti-Zionism 389; election of delegates 398; election of patriarch and Soviet influence on 391-4; lifts bans on Old Believers 396; and 1961 Statute 388, 395
Amvrosy, Fr. 443
Anastasy (Gribanovsky), Metropolitan—head of post-Karlovci Synod 142, 255; and Nazis 223, 491; and Orthodox America 294-6; and Patriarchal Church 267, 271; reforms Synod in Munich 257; and Tikhon 258; and 1935 reconciliation council 261
Andrei (Sukhenko), Archbishop of Chernigov 339, 440
Andrei (Ukhtomsky) 27
Anthony (Bloom), Metropolitan of England 274, 396, 418
antireligious propaganda 196, 301, 331, 340-1; attacks on church charity 354; attacks on church income 348-9; in schools 330-2; press attacks 316, 329-30, 356; recognition of errors in 358-9
antireligious "scholarship"—houses and museums of scientific atheism 317, 439; institutes of scientific atheism 331; professional atheists 454; publications 317, 330, 356-7; see also "believers, proportion and numbers" and "Soviet studies on religion"
Antonin (Granovsky), Metropolitan—criticizes Renovationists 54, 55, 83; in prerevolutionary period 53, 81; as Renovationist leader 55, 56, 58, 60, 474; as Renovationist theologian 65, 80-3, 358
Antonov, peasant rebel leader 96, 367
Antony, Metropolitan of Leningrad 430
Antony (Khrapovitsky), Metropolitan of Kiev—attempt at reconciliation with Evlogy 259-61; appointed Metropolitan of Kiev 73, 473; biography 128-31; death of 265; and founding of Karlovci Synod 115, 120, 130; as head of Synod 116, 135, 137-8, 186; leaves diocese 114, 123, 133; in prerevolutionary period 49, 128, 213, 286; and Renovationists 53, 65; stature as theologian 130, 184, 186; and Tikhon 121, 123, 124, 131; and 1917-1918 All-Russian Sobor 31, 88, 125, 129; and 1921 émigré sobor 119, 131
Antony (Vadkovsky), Metropolitan of Petrograd 22, 23, 24, 47
Apolinary, Archbishop of North America (Synodal) 289
Argentov, Alexander 434
Armstrong, John 221, 241

Askochensky, V.I. 45
Athanasius, St. 23
Athenagoras, Patriarch of Constantinople 142, 299
Avgustin, Metropolitan of Estonia 228, 229

Bakaev, *Cheka* official 98
Bandera partisans, and terror—see "Ukrainian Autocephalous Church"
Barabanov, Evgeny 460
Beilis, Jewish worker—trial of 98
believers, life of 379-80; appeals to UN 443; deprivation of parental rights 342; pensioners in church life 355; role in church activities 355; and Soviet authorities 422; young believers, harassment of 432-3, 456
believers, proportion and numbers 170-1; among army recruits 172; children 172, 456; at Leningrad cathedral 325; surveys of 172, 454
Belkov, Renovationist priest 97
Bellyustin, I.S. 45
Belorussia, Orthodox Church in—postwar persecution of 441; revival under Metropolitan Filaret 452; see also "Orthodox Church, in German-occupied Belorussia"
Berdyaev, Nicholas 47, 51
Beria, Lavrenty 320
Berlin, Russian cathedral in 491-2
bishops—consecrations of 44-5, 317, 319; and CROCA/CRA 400-1, 411-2, 415-8, 465-70; distrust of 380; election of 26, 34; as legal nonpersons 400; new generation of 328-9, 390, 409; persecutions, arrests, murder of 67, 339-40, 478-80; relations with parish clergy 418; resistance to government 359, 465-70; selected biographies and endeavors 412-4; see also "Council for Religious Affairs, reports of"
Biskupsky, General 223
Bjerring, Nicholas 280
Black Book 477-81
Black Hundreds, Union of Russian People and Union of Archangel Michael 54
Bogolep, Bishop of Kirov 400, 412
Bogolepov, Alexander 213, 214, 217
Boris (Vik), Metropolitan 324
Bormann, Martin 225
Borovoi, Fr. Vitaly 340, 380, 389, 451, 458, 459, 471
Bourdeaux, Michael 341, 346
Boyarsky, Renovationist priest 88, 97
Brest union 306; see also "Uniate Church"
Brezhnev, Leonid 333, 397, 464, 467, 469, 470, 471
Brown, Leopold 111
Bulgakov, Sergius 27, 28, 30, 47-9, 50-1, 132

calendar—Gregorian 47; Julian 272
canons—of Fourth Ecumenical Council 168; on emigration of bishops 114
Carpathian Ukraine (Ruthenia) 303-4, 307; emigrants in US 281; Orthodox Church of 303; Uniate Church of 303, 307
Carrol, Wallace 176
"catacomb" Church and clergy 177, 179-82, 276, 358, 370-1, 374-5, 377-8, 379,

381, 382, 383, 385; and autocephalies 368-9; and Moscow Patriarchate 371, 377; Noncommemorators 179-80; secret "sobor" of 370-1; wandering priests 376; see also "True Orthodox" and "Old Believers"

"catacomb" sects—Buevshchina 368-9; Fedorovtsy 180, 367-8; Imyaslavtsy 180; Ioannity 366-7; Iosifites 164, 172; Molchalniki 180, 372; Sedmintsy 371

Catherine the Great 19, 44

Chakovsky, N. 435

Chang, Fr. S. 264

Cheka 478-9

Chekhivsky, Volodymyr 476

Cheltsov, Mikhail 168

Chepurin, Nikolai 168

Chernetsky, Kirill 436

Chernov, Alexander 373-5, 378, 384, 385

Chertkov, priest 332

Christian Committee for the Defense of Believers' Rights 434-6; appeals to WCC 447-9; criticism of Soviet laws on religion 449; and human rights 440; persecution of 438, 440, 447-9

Chrysostom, Archbishop of Kursk and Belgorod 408, 410-1, 462

Church and state 382, 483-4, 485; friction, admitted by cleric 410; separation of 47, 467, 477; submission to secularism 381

church construction, reconstruction, reopenings 327, 410; lack of 323; in Far East 405, 406; restoration and enlargement 406, 457

church life and practices in Soviet conditions—baptisms (adult) 402, 425; baptisms (infant) 357, 457; charity work 354, 419-20; liturgical innovations 358; reform and modernization 357-8, 457; services in absentia 357, sociocultural activities 164, 433-5

church properties—limited rights regained 399; nationalization of 31-2, 173

church revival, World War II 68; in German-occupied areas 225-46; in Romanian-occupied areas 247-8

church self-defense statements—and legal rights 333-5; premonitions of Khrushchev's attacks 353-4; role of Church in Russian history 333-5; and Russian culture 333-5, 457; and Russian national consciousness 333

church statistics 172, 173-5, 179, 229; in annexed territories 174, 193-4, 230, 234-5, 240, 242-4, 247-8; lack of reliable figures 401-3; WWII reopenings 206; 1936-1939 liquidation 168, 173-8

churches, closure, confiscation, destruction 173, 324, 332, 341-2, 346-9, 397-8, 404, 410, 477, 480; Holy Trinity (Leningrad) 404; Poltava diocese 465-6; Riga Orthodox cathedral 388

clergy—compromise with regime 463; canonical and administrative discipline 167, 353-4; defections of 332; Jewish converts 402; liberals 353, 406; liquidation of 168, 170, 174-7; new generations of 354-5, 390, 402, 408, 439, 458; ordinations 176, 323, 408, 429, 465; parish clergy 328, 418-21; shortage of 320; Soviet pressures on 332, 347-8, 354-5, 418-20, 422; torture and murder of 477-81; trials and persecutions of 346, 347, 349, 353, 418

Communist Party—and church splits 62; Central Committee resolutions on antireligious propaganda (1944) 301, (July 1954) 329-31, (November 1954) 331, (1960) 332-3, (1964) 358-9

Conquest, Robert 325

Constitution (1936) 168, 182-3

continuous work week 194

Council for Religious Affairs (CRA) 388, 390, 393, 464; assessment of bishops

400, 415-7; centralization and power of (1975) 399, 493-8; control over clergy and seminaries 407-8; control over parish life 467; control over patriarchate and bishops 392, 397, 408-9, 411-2; opening and closing of churches 397-408; relations with bishops 401; reports of 392, 394, 400-12, 415-21; Statute of 343, 397-8

Council for Russian Orthodox Church Affairs (CROCA) 26, 57-64, 202-3, 214, 337, 339, 347; change in role of 343, 465; and closure of parishes 342

Council of Florence (1439) 310

Curtiss, John 143

Dallin, Alexander 221
Danylevych, V. 476
Darmansky, Pavel 332
Demyanov 374
Denikin 115, 134, 473
Deryabin 314
d'Herbigny 81
Diakonov, Renovationist priest 54
Dimitrije, Serbian Patriarch 130
Dimitrios, Ecumenical Patriarch 142
Dimitry, Bishop of Gdovsk 154, 155
Dimitry, Archbishop of Hailar 256, 261
Dimitry Donskoi 199-200
Dionisy, Polish Metropolitan 236-8, 239-40, 241, 304-5
displaced persons 271; and Synodal churches in North America 271
Dorotheos, Metropolitan 129
Dostoevsky, Fedor 85, 89
Dublyansky 239, 241, 243
Dudko, Dimitry 418, 450, 460; confession on Soviet television 278, 437, 439; publications of 438; sermons of 437, 459, 462-3; and Synodal Church 278-9
Dukhobors—see "sects and sectarians"
Duluman, Evgraf 332

eastern patriarchates 311; Antiochian 453; Bulgarian 304; Romanian 454; Serbian 263-4, 303
Ecumenical Patriarchate 258-62, 270, 309, 454; and North America 299, 453; and Prosynod 259; and Renovationists 258-9; and Synodal administration 114-5; and Tikhon 60; and West European (Evlogian) archdiocese 142, 257-61, 270
Ehrenburg, Ilya 312
Ekzemplyarsky, Vasily 49
Elevfery, Metropolitan and Baltic exarch 111, 120, 141, 227, 262-3; death of 193, 227; meeting with Sergii 109, 127, 140; response to Karlovcian accusations 265
émigré Synod—attacks on Moscow patriarchate 114, 267-70; and Belorussian bishops 234; canonization of Nicholas II 272-3; and Solzhenitsyn 275, 276-7; Third Sobor 269, 273-8; and Western Christians 273; see also "Karlovci Synod," "Russian Orthodox Church Abroad" and next entry
émigré Synod, history—Karlovci phase 255-67; Munich phase 267-71, 297; US phase 271-9; see also "Karlovci Synod" and "Russian Orthodox Church Abroad"
Ermogen, Archbishop of Tashkent and Central Asia 327, 393-4, 421, 422
Ern, V. 46

Eshliman, Nikolai 346, 389, 421, 422, 435, 464
Evdokim (Meshchersky) 53, 60, 61, 63, 65, 282
Evgeny, Bishpop 164
Evlogy (Georgievsky), Metropolitan—appointed head of West European diocese
    by Tikhon 117-9, 130, 134, 284, 288; biography 128, 133-4; and Declaration
    of Loyalty of Sergii 135, 139-40, 263; deposed by Sergii 141, 166, 227, 263;
    disobeys Tikhon's order and favors Antony 120, 131, 135, 141; enters jurisdic-
    tion of Ecumenical Patriarch 129, 142, 167-8, 258-9; opposition from Karlov-
    cians 121, 129, 132, 137-8, 222, 257-9, 262, 266, 285, 289; at reconciliation
    council with Karlovcians 159-62; rejoins Moscow Patriarchate 270; at 1921
    Karlovci sobor 117
excommunications—of church defectors 332; of Soviet leaders 38, 332

Faddei (Uspensky), Archbishop 153
Fedor (Pozdeevsky) 156
Fedoseev, P. 178
Fedotov, G.P. 291
Feodosy, Archbishop of Poltava 464-8, 469, 471
Feofan, Archbishop 286
Feofil (Buldovsky) 78-9, 241, 246
Filaret (Vakhrameev), Metropolitan of Minsk—biography 452-3; head of Belo-
    russian archdiocese 491-2, 456, 464; head of Department of External Ecclesias-
    tical Relations 441, 451, 452; rector of Moscow seminary 436; support of
    Yakunin 440
Filatov, Soviet Academician 175
Filipp (Gumilevsky), Archbishop 155
Filofei (Narko), Archbishop 233
Fireside, Harvey 221, 224, 225
Fletcher, William 156, 194, 206, 208, 214, 309, 312, 314, 318, 377
Florensky, Pavel 431, 483
Florovsky, Georges 19, 45, 46, 85
Fonchenkov, Vasily 436, 439
Frank, Semen 21
Fund for the Upkeep of Historical Monuments (All-Russian Society for the Pro-
    tection of Monuments of History and Culture) 466
Furov, V., deputy chairman of CRA 407, 429; church statistics of 349; reports on
    bishops 400, 408, 412, 415-7, 419

Gainov, Nikolai 389, 436
Galkin 107
Gapon, Georgy 184
Gavriil, Bishop 68
Gavriil, Archimandrite 429
Georgian Orthodox Church 204; and nationalism 424; revival of 424
Georgieva, Lydia 406
German, Finnish archbishop 304
Gerodnik, priest 332
Gilyarov-Platonov, N.P. 23
Golomstock, Igor 350
Golubinsky, E.E. 46

Goricheva, Tatyana 182, 315, 346, 376, 385, 460, 463
GPU—and Grigorians 72; infiltration in Church 63-4, 293; and Orthodox diaspora 286-7; and Renovationists 61
Grabbe, Georgy 120, 222, 260, 275
Graham, Billy 469
Grigorenko, General Peter and son Andrei 433
Grigorians 66, 70, 72; attack on Sergii 67; Provisional Supreme (Higher) Church Council (VVTsS) 71
Grigorios VII, Ecumenical Patriarch 64, 258-9
Grigory (Chukov), Metropolitan of Leningrad 98, 168, 297-8, 303-4
Grigory (Lisovsky), Bishop of Lubny 78
Grigory (Yakovetsky), Archbishop of Ekaterinburg 66, 70-2, 111
Grossman, Vasily 350
Gurovich, defense counsel of Metropolitan Venyamin 55, 98

Hegel 90
Hermogen, Synodal bishop in Croatia 256
Heyer, Friedrich 78, 221, 239, 240, 242, 243, 244
Higher Monarchist Council 116; Bad Reichenhal Congress 116, 222; and Karlovcians 116; and Tikhon 266; and Nazis 221-2
Hitler, Adolph 54, 111, 161, 196; church policies of, in Germany 222-3, 262, 491; church policies of, in occupied Soviet territory 206, 224-5; and émigré monarchists 221-3, 270, 491; 1939 pact with Stalin 195

Ieronim, Synodal bishop in US 256, 489
Ignaty (Bryanchaninov), Bishop 486
Iliodor, Renovationist cleric 54
Illarion (Ohienko), Archbishop of Holm 239
Illarion (Troitsky) 28, 30, 72, 146, 160, 483-4
Ilya, Patriarch of Georgia 424
Innocent (Venyaminov), and Alaskan mission 279-80
intelligentsia, and Church 46-7; see also "neophytes"
Ioann, West European bishop 270
Ioann (Maximovich), Archbishop of Shanghai 256
Ioann (Sokolov), Metropolitan of Kiev 322-3, 377
Ioasaf, Synodal bishop in US 489
Ioasaf, Archbishop of Rostov 416
Iona, Bishop of Stavropol 416
Iosif (Chernov), Metropolitan of Alma-Ata and Kazakhstan 390-1, 410, 412
Iosif (Petrovykh), Metropolitan 71, 108, 152-4, 156, 158, 162, 168, 368
Iosyf (Slipy), Metropolitan of Galicia 306
Iov (Kresovich), Archbishop of Kazan 339, 440
IPKh—see "True Orthodox Christians"
IPTs—see "True Orthodox Church"
Ireney, Metropolitan of North America 277

John Chrysostom 85
John of Kronstadt 272, 366-7
John (Mitropolsky), Bishop of Alaska 280

John (Ioann Shakhovskoi), Archbishop of San Francisco 256, 491
Joseph of Volokolamsk 147
Journal of the Moscow Patriarchate (ZhMP) 166-7, 173; and CRA 421; defense
    of peace section 317; profile of 209
Justin (Popovich), Archimandrite 129

Kachur, Paul 17
Kalinovsky, Renovationist priest 54, 55, 90, 97
Kapitanchuk, Viktor 389, 435
Karelin, Felix 389
Karlovci Synod 113-5, 255-6; and Breslau Orthodox Theological Faculty 223; and
    Ecumenical Patriarchate 260-2; and Evlogy 257-64; in Germany 257, 262;
    message to Hitler 223, 491-2; and Nazis 221-4, 262, 266; and Serbian Church
    263-5; and Sergii 262-5; and Stalin 256; and Temporary Statute 261, 262; and
    Tikhon 118-9, 122-3; Vienna session 231; and Vlasov army 224; and WWII
    255-6; see also "émigré Synod" and "Russian Orthodox Church Abroad"
Karpov, Georgy 203, 214, 217, 332, 399
Kartashev, A.V. 125
Kashevarov, Alexander 279
Katyn, mass execution at 197
Kazem-Bek 222
Kedrovsky 285, 286, 289
Kerensky 27
KGB 314, 432; and clergy 407, 437; and election of patriarch 391; and monastic
    administration 429
Khrushchev, Nikita—and antireligious campaign 160, 181, 208, 302, 316-7, 322-3,
    329-32, 340-1, 348-9, 356-7, 372, 402-3, 440, 444; and antireligious propa-
    ganda 439; and Leninism 351; and peaceful coexistence 361; relapses to
    Khrushchevism 387, 404, 465; and "socialist legality" 341; Soviet critical
    analyses of 350, 358-9; see also "antireligious propaganda," "persecutions,"
    "churches, closure and destruction"
Kirill, Archbishop and rector of Moscow theological schools 403, 430, 463
Kirill (Smirnov), Metropolitan of Kazan—appointed deputy locum tenens by
    Tikhon 107-8, 151, 189, 274; breaks with Sergii and heads Noncommemorators
    150-2, 156, 161, 162, 179, 383; clandestine patriarchal election of 105; rejects
    Tuchkov offer 105-6, 213
Kirill Vladimirovich, Grand Duke 222
Klibanov, A.I. 158, 176, 365
Klimov, E.N. 374
Koch, Erich 225-6, 239
Kolesnikov, peasant rebel leader 367
Komsomol, secret believers among 456
Kornily (Sobolev) 153
Korobeinikov, Alexander 418
Kostelnyk, Havrylo 307, 308
Kosygin, Aleksei 333, 416
Krasikov 107
Krasnitsky, Vladimir 97, 98, 155; conspires to retire Antonin Granovsky 60; as
    head of Living Church 58, 82-3; prerevolutionary right-wing activities 54; sets
    up Renovationist Supreme Church Administration 55-6
Krymsky, A. 476

Kurochkin, V. 457, 462
Kuroedov, CROCA official 340, 395, 425

Las, Valentina 218
League of Militant Godless (LMG) 171-2, 178-9, 197
legislation on religious association—see "religious associations," "Soviet decrees"
Lenin 31, 36, 37, 39, 51, 53, 56-7, 94-6, 341, 350
Leonid, Metropolitan of Riga 396
Leonty, Bishop of Chile 190-1, 223, 305, 473, 474
Leonty, bishop in Crimea 410
Leonty (Turkevich), Metropolitan of North America 271, 272, 288, 294, 297
Levitin-Krasnov, Anatoly 55, 80, 84, 89, 155, 168, 170, 174, 177, 183, 201, 202-3,
    307, 335, 340, 354, 392, 421
Living Church—see "Renovationist schism"
local soviets and churches—closure of churches 347, 349; implementation of legis-
    lation on cults 337; registration of congregations 165
Lohse 225-6
Lossky, Vladimir 184, 205, 431
Ludendorff, German field marshal 198
Luka (Voino-Yasenetsky), Archbishop 183, 200, 203, 206, 208-10, 216
Lvov, Vladimir 26, 67, 186
Lypkivsky, Vasyl, and Self-consecrators 74-8, 237-40, 473, 476
Lyubimov, D.N. 132

Makartsev 395
Makary, Metropolitan of Moscow 24
Makary (Oksiyuk), Metropolitan of Lvov 305
Makharoblidze 120, 186, 222
Maksimov, Vladimir 383
Manuil (Lemeshevsky), Bishop 58, 111
Manuil (Tarnavsky), Bishop of Vladimir-Volynsk 244
Mariinsky, A.P. 455
martyrs, under Soviets—betrayal of by patriarchate 341, 380; as "living saints" 459
Marxism-Leninism—decline of 351; and religion 52-3, 462; and society 350-2
Meliton, Bishop of Tikhvin 410
Melnykites 306
Men, Alexander 161, 179, 456
Meyendorff, John 262, 361
Michael, Grand Duke 25
Mikhail (Chub), Archbishop 325, 327, 396
Mikhail (Ermakov), Ukrainian exarch 108
Mikhail (Mudyugin), Archbishop of Astrakhan 395, 413-4
Mikhail (Semenov) 23, 47, 51, 69, 90
Mikhailovsky 49
Mikoyan 333
Molokans—see "sects and sectarians"
Molotov 201, 218, 301
monasteries—and KGB 429; persecution and closure of 353, 429, 441-3; revital-
    ization of 353; role in Russian life 346
monasticism 343-5, 353; "learned" 43-5; Soviet persecution of 343-5, 353; taxation
    of 343, 345; tonsurings 344-5

Moroz, Mykhailo 473, 474
Moscow Patriarchate—and "catacombs" 371, 377, 384-5; clergy of 438, 440; duplicity of 359, 381-3; and monasteries 441-3; and persecutions 359, 381-3, 440, 446, 450; press for legal person status 399; publications of 427, 430; and Renovationists 167; and Uniates 308-9; see also next entry
Moscow Patriarchate, international activities—with Anglicans 219, 310, 311; anniversary celebrations 309-11; and eastern patriarchates 311; and Ecumenical Patriarchate 259, 262, 310, 445; and émigré Synod 267, 273-5; and Orthodox Church in Poland 305; and Orthodox *oikoumene* 270, 273, 309, 311, 453; and Roman Catholics 308-10, 361-2; and Russian diaspora 303-6, 444-5; and Serbian Church 363-4; and 1948 conference 310-1; and 1969 world conference (Zagorsk) 444; see also "Russian Orthodox Church, Department of External Ecclesiastical Relations" and "World Council of Churches"
Moslems—and Soviet government 40; revitalization of 352
Mstislav, Bishop of Kirov 400
Mstyslav (Skrypnyk), Bishop 239-41

Nazary, Bishop 474
Nazi church policies—in Baltic republics 228-9; "divide and rule" 225, 228, 232-46; and Karlovci Synod 223-4, 231; and Moscow Patriarchate 228, 231-4, 237-8; and nationalism 228-9, 232-46; in occupied Soviet territory 198, 224-7, 228-31; Tolerance Edict 225
Nechytailo 465, 466, 471
neophytes (adult converts) 425, 457-60; from Jewish background 402
NEP era 89, 169, 484
Nepluev, N. 48
Nestor, Bishop of Kamchatka 37
Nicholas I 19
Nicholas II 23, 25, 168, 267, 272-3, 278
Nietzsche 85, 89
Nikanor (Abramovich), Archbishop of Kiev 244, 245
Nikodim (Rotov), Metropolitan of Leningrad 215, 302, 314, 329, 337, 340, 382, 446, 453; as administrator of Leningrad archdiocese 383, 390, 399-400, 413-5, 420-1, 428, 430, 451-2, 458; attack on Karlovcians 396; biography 360; and entry into WCC 361; establishes close ties with Vatican 361-2, 452; as head of Department of External Ecclesiastical Relations 359-63; Soviet foreign policy activities 361, 363, 415, 445, 447, 451; theological opposition from believers 389
Nikolai, Metropolitan of Lvov 412
Nikolai (Yarushevich), Metropolitan of Krutitsy 147, 155, 193, 339, 362; attack on Vatican 219, 315; concelebrates with Evlogy 270; conflict of political and pastoral activities 318, 355, 359, 360, 412-13; dismissal and forced retirement (1960) 332, 335, 359-60; and émigrés 274, 303; meets with Stalin (1943) 201, 203; meets with Stalin (1945) 218-9, 301-2; role in WWII 196, 208, 232, 237; as Soviet foreign policy spokesman 196-7, 207, 302, 312-5, 447; visits Great Britain 219
Nikolsky, N.M. 172
Nikon, West European bishop 270
Nikon (Rklitsky), Bishop 131, 222
Nil Sorsky 147
NKVD 307, 309

Ogorodnikov, Alexander 433-4, 435
Old Believers 69; catacomb branch 366; lifting of bans on (1971) 396; and Renovationists 31, 69
Oleshchuk 179, 325
Olsufiev, Count 124, 286
Orthodox Church, in America—Albanians 282; Arabs/Syrians 280-1; Carpatho-Russians 281, 287, 295; Greeks 282-3, 299; Serbians 281-3; Ukrainians 283; see also "Orthodox Church in America (OCA)"
Orthodox Church, in Baltic republics—Estonia 228-9, 303; Latvia 224, 227-9, 232, 303; Lithuania 227
Orthodox Church, in China 304-6
Orthodox Church, in Czechoslovakia 303-5; autocephaly of 305
Orthodox Church, in Finland 304
Orthodox Church, in German-occupied Belorussia 232-6; and autocephaly movement 233-4; devastation and revival of 234-6; failure of German policy toward 232-4; failure of national movement among 233-4
Orthodox Church, in Hungary 303
Orthodox Church, in occupied Russia—Pskov mission 227-32; religious revival and strength 227, 230, 241, 245, 248
Orthodox Church, in occupied Ukraine—Autonomous Church, 238-41, 244-6; and Banderist terror 239-40, 243-4; and monasticism 242, 244-5; and religious revival 241-7; seminaries 245, 247; and Soviet terror 246
Orthodox Church, in Poland—and autocephaly 303, 305; and Jesuits 303; and Polish nationalism 305; persecution of 266, 307; in WWII 224, 233, 236-8
Orthodox Church, under Romanian occupation 247-8
Orthodox Church in America (OCA) 271, 272, 279-300, 307, 361, 489-90; Cleveland Sobor (1934) 290; Cleveland Sobor (1946) 295-7; and conversion of Uniates 281; Detroit Sobor 287; and émigré Synod 276-7; and English-language services 281-2; and Karlovci Synod 284, 286-97, 489-90; and Moscow Patriarchate 287-99, 445; New York Sobor (1937) 291, 489-90; South Canaan Sobor (1907) 281; Statute 297; theological schools of 281, 299
Osipov, Alexander 332
Osipov, Vladimir 375, 439, 447, 460
Ostapov, Daniil 387, 388, 391
Overprocurator of Holy Synod 45-6; modern comparisons to 485

paganism, revival of 350, 406
Pallady, Metropolitan of Orel 412, 416, 419
Panteleimon, Belorussian metropolitan 233
Papadopoulos, George 445
parishes—"amalgamation" of 342; clergy of 328, 336-7, 341; executive troika 338, 395; finances of 337; rural, life of 465; rural, oppression and closures of 342, 465; Soviet laws on 341-2; Statute (1961) 336-8; "twenties" 62-3, 213, 341, 446
pastoral preparation, extraseminary 320-2
Paul (Popov), North American bishop 280
Pavel (Golyshev), Archbishop of Vologda 393-4, 422
Pavel, Bishop of Narva 229
Payne, Ernest 448
peace conferences 313, 396; and attacks on US 313; and the Church 333-8; Kremlin Conference of the Soviet Public for Disarmament 333-5; Prague Peace Con-

ference 361; World Christian Peace Congress 336
Peace Fund, as tax on churches 217, 325, 466
persecutions 173, 333-5, 339-40, 346, 347, 349, 356, 358, 418, 432-3, 435, 441, 443, 477-81; tacit admission and assessment of 355, 375, 450; see also "believers," clergy," "bishops," "parishes"
Peter, Bishop 180
Peter the Great 30, 43, 45, 269, 484
Peter (Polyansky), Metropolitan 107, 109, 111, 143, 153, 188; death of 189, 269, 274; and Grigorians 66, 70-2, 125; inspirer of Tikhon's last testament 63-4, 125, 127; and Karlovcians 124-5, 138, 289; letter to Sergii (1930) 186, 187; as locum tenens 65-6, 104, 105, 108, 122, 124-5, 150, 151, 154, 158; and Renovationists 64-5
Petlyura regime 73, 133, 239, 240, 241
Petrov, Grigory 35, 128
Petukhov, Georgy 389
Philaret, Metropolitan 256, 274-7, 278
Photios II, Ecumenical Patriarch 167, 168, 259, 262, 263
pilgrimages and processions—ban on 344-5; persecutions of 344-5, 442-4
Pimen, Ukrainian Renovationist 77
Pimen (Izvekov), Patriarch 111, 379, 382, 416; biography 176, 391-2; and CRA 408, 410, 428, 449, 453, 470; criticized by Furov 415; and dissident believers 389; Dudko's letter to 437; and Ecumenical Patriarchate 445; election as patriarch 212, 390, 391, 394-5; and émigrés 273-5, 387, 444-5; fear of authorities 112, 424; investigation of corruption of 394; Lenten message and Solzhenitsyn 445, 461; new gains under 405, 425; as pastor 393; at UN 453; and WCC 446, 449
Pitirim (Nechaev), Archbishop of Volokolamsk 394-5, 410, 419, 430, 432, 451, 453
Platon (Rozhdestvensky), Metropolitan of North America 88, 123; appointed to administer Church in America 130, 134, 282; death of 290; elected metropolitan by American sobor 283-4; first tenure in US 282; opposition from Karlovcians 265, 286-7, 289; opposition to Karlovcians 132, 138, 287, 288; opposition to Renovationists in US 285-6; suspended by Sergii 289-90
Platonov, Nikolai, Renovationist metropolitan 54, 63, 90
Plekhanov, A. 112, 388, 421, 431
Pobedonostsev, Konstantin 46, 128
Pochaev Monastery 343-5; harassment of monks 443; police attacks on pilgrims 442-4
Pokrovsky, A.I. 26, 28
Polsky, Mikhail 105, 114, 187, 286, 287, 483-4
Polykarp (Sikorsky), Archbishop of Lutsk 198, 237
Popovsky, Mark 174, 183, 202
Poresh, Vladimir 434
post-Karlovci Synod—see "émigré Synod" and "Russian Orthodox Church Abroad"
Potter, Philip 446, 449-50, 464, 469
Preconciliar Commission (1905-6) 24, 44, 281-2
Preconciliar Commission (1944-5) 210
Preconciliar Commission (Council of Bishops, 1971) 389-95; critique of ecumenism and theological revisionism 389; discussion of 1961 Statute 395; petitions to 388-9; request for right to teach and preach religion 389; and revolutionary (social) Christianity 389
Prokhanov, Ivan 40, 41

Radkey, Oliver 96
Raiser, Konrad 450
Rasputin 24, 185, 186
Regelson, Lev 109, 142, 155, 156, 161, 162, 189, 389, 435, 447, 448, 449, 450, 484
religion Soviet studies on—see "Soviet studies on religion"
religiophilosophic seminars 433-4; *samizdat* publications of 433
religiosity, growth and revitalization of—in 1920s 67-8, 99-102; in 1950s and 1960s 351-8; in 1970s and 1980s 457
religious associations—and Council of Ministers 494, 497, 499; legislation on 164, 170, 341-3, 399, 425, 493-500; and monetary collections 499; and Permanent Committee for Religious Matters 494-5, 499-500; and prayer houses 495, 497-9; and religious congresses 496; and religious functions 499-500; registration of 165, 493-8
religious instruction 217, 496; ban on 32, 342; of children 164; under German occupation 230; of groups 164; request for right of 389; under Romanian occupation 247
Renovationist movement, prerevolutionary 51-2; All-Russian League of Democratic Orthodox Clergy and Laity 49-50; Group of Thirty-two 45, 47, 49, 53, 55, 69
Renovationist schism 52-60, 68-70; in America 282-3, 285; arrests of clergy of 168; in Central Asia and Siberia 68; as church party 484; and eastern patriarchs 64-5; and émigré churches 65; failure of 63, 67-8; Higher Church Council (VTsS) of 57, 60; leaders of 53-4; and Lenin 51; as Soviet subversion of Church 53, 54-7, 62, 66-7; statistics 61-2; strategy and tactics 52; support for Soviet government 56; talks with Tikhon 60-1; in Ukraine 70, 72; see also next entry
Renovationist schism, factions of—Living Church 54-5, 58, 83, 89; Union of Church Renovation 55, 58, 80-2; Union of Communities of Ancient Apostolic Churches 55, 58, 82-6; see also next entry
Renovationist schism, sobors and conferences—Conference (August 1923) 60; First Sobor (1923) 56-9; Moscow Clergy Conference (June 1923) 60; Second Sobor (1925) 64-5
Rodzyanko, Mikhail V. 116, 117, 127
Roman, Bishop of Tallin 319
Rosenberg, Alfred 221-2, 224-6, 232, 234, 239
Rostislavov, D.I. 45
Rudkevich, Lev 433
Russian émigrés—and Hitler 221; monarchists 221, 255; and Moscow Patriarchate 255, 445; and Soviets 255
Russian nationalism 68, 333-5, 457, 461; and national bolshevism ("change of signposts") 87-9; and Soviets 423
Russian Orthodox Church, prerevolutionary—Edict of Toleration 22; and intelligentsia 20-1, 46-7, 49, 68; missionary congresses 49; and Provisional Government 25-7, 29; and revolution 24-5; as state religion 20-4, 27, 46; statistics 20
Russian Orthodox Church, after Tikhon 209-16, 336, 339, 341-2, 388; "concordat" with Soviets 52, 164, 302; Council of Bishops 209-10, 212, 336-7, 338-40; Department of External Ecclesiastical Relations 202, 218-9, 360, 410, 439, 451; diocesan conferences 321; faithful of 384; Fund for Defense of the Country 200, 207; growth of 171; legal position of 72, 165, 398; and patriotism 197-200; repression in 1960s, Eshliman-Yakunin report 393; request for full legalization 399; role in society 361; status after 1975 399; Synod of Bishops 167, 211, 336, 338, 393, 408-9

Russian Orthodox Church, publications of 301-2, 427; request for increase of 467; *Theological Endeavors* (*Bogoslovskie Trudy*) 265-7; as threat to atheism 330, 421; see also "*Journal of the Moscow Patriarchate*"
Russian Orthodox Church Abroad, First Sobor (Karlovci Laity-Clergy Conference) 116-7; appeal to Genoa conference 118-9; legitimacy of 117; monarchists role in 116-7; resolutions of 119; and Tikhon 118-9
Russian Orthodox Church Abroad, Second Sobor 430; and anti-Semitism 266; *.Deyaniya* (Acts) 257-8
Russian Orthodox diaspora 114, 168, 276-8; in Austria 304; in Bulgaria 304; in China 304-6; in Czechoslovakia 303; in Finland 304; in Romania 304; and Sergii 262-5; in Yugoslavia 304
Russian Orthodox West European Exarchate of Ecumenical Patriarchate 265, 270; and émigré Synod's Third Sobor 276
Rybalkin, Fedor 367

Sabler 186
Sagan, Dimitry 449
Sakharov, Andrei 388
samizdat, religious 438; *Community* (*Obshchina*) 433; *In the Light of the Trans-figuration* (of Dudko) 438, 439, 460; *Veche* 461
Savva (Kolchugin) 376, 462
Sawatsky, Walter 398, 399
Schmemann, Fr. Alexander 270, 284, 299
Science and Religion (*Nauk i religii*), atheist monthly 330
Sebastian (Dabovich) Archimandrite 281
sects and sectarians—Baptists 424-5, 448; Dukhobors 69; extremists 368; Jehovah's Witnesses 406; Molokans 69; increase of, under Khrushchev 352
seminaries and theological academies—control over by CRA 407; postwar revival of 302, 323, 325, 327-8; prerevolutionary 44; prewar 31, 41, 104, 110; Renovationist 77, 86; student body, statistics 323, 407; under German occupation 230, 234, 245, 247
Seminary and Academy, Leningrad—Afro-Asian students 361; buildings added to 403-4; exchange students 361, 452; life of 463-4; and new clergy 390; student body 458
Seminary and Academy, Moscow 384
Seminary, Odessa 407
Serafim, Synodal bishop in US 297
Serafim, Metropolitan of Krutitsy 416-7, 418, 438, 463
Serafim (Aleksandrov), Metropolitan 155, 286
Serafim (Chichagov), Bishop 24
Serafim (Lade), German Synodal bishop 223-4, 231, 238, 255, 257, 262
Serafim (Lukyanov), Metropolitan 256, 270
Serafim (Samoilovich), Bishop of Uglich 107, 108, 153, 186
Serafim (Sobolev), Synodal archbishop in Bulgaria 256, 304
Serapion (Mashkin) 48
Sergii, Bishop of Odessa 410
Sergii, Bishop of Serpukhov 156
Sergii (Labuntsev) 78
Sergii (Stragorodsky), Bishop, Metropolitan, Patriarch 57, 70-2, 164, 166-8, 183-91, 194-204, 314, 390, 411, 485; administration of 167, 186-90, 213-4, 485; arrests of 105, 107, 186, 485; attitude of sects toward 180-1, 365-70; church

statistics of 62, 172, 175; conflict with other locum tenentes 107, 150-7, 158-9, 162, 269; and Declaration of Loyalty 67, 77, 108-11, 124, 146-50, 154, 163-4, 169, 264, 274, 341, 368, 379, 484-5; and German occupation 228-33, 238; labeled a heretic 487; named deputy locum tenens by Peter 104; petitions for seminaries and press 41, 106; and Renovationists 66-7, 107-8, 167; and his Synod 147, 193, 273, 485; as theologian 148, 184-5, 205; threatened by GPU 67; and WWII 194-203, 207; and 1905-6 Preconciliar Commission 28, 210; see also "All-Russian Sobor, 1943" and next entry

Sergii (Stragorodsky), relations with Orthodox *oikoumene*—with Ecumenical Patriarchate 64, 259, 262; with Russian émigré churches 106-7, 122, 125-7, 133, 139-42, 265, 289-90; with Serbian Church 263-4

Sergii (Voskresensky), Metropolitan 116, 147, 187, 190, 377; appointed exarch for Baltic region 193, 227; assassination of 232; cooperation with Germans 195; official criticism of 198; policies under Germans 228-32; and Pskov mission 229-32; support from patriarchate 197-8, 231

sermons and preaching 169-70, 354; decree on 32; sobor resolution on 34-5

Shafarevich, Igor 174

Sharaevsky, Nestor 473, 476

Shavelsky, Georgy 24, 88, 286

Shchegolev, V. 436

Shchipkova, Tatyana 434

Sheptytsky, Metropolitan 308, 309

Shishkin 205

Shpiller, Vsevolod 328-9, 339, 360-1, 399

Simeon (Du), Bishop of Peking 305

Sinyavsky, Andrei 375

Skoropadsky, Ukrainian hetman 73, 222

Skvortsov-Stepanov, I.I. 91

Smidovich 107

sobornost' 185, 337, 339

sobors of Russian Orthodox Church—see "All-Russian Sobors"

social Christianity—and Christian communes 47-8, 51, 434; Christian Fraternity of Struggle 46; Christian socialism 46-9, 51; Social-Christian Workers Party 50; and western secularism 451

"socialist legality"—and Church 341, 343

Socialist-Revolutionary Party (SRs) 49-50

Sofrino church articles plant 427, 431

Sokolov, N.M. 21

Solovei, Nikolai, Renovationist bishop 65-6, 99, 143

Soloviev, Vladimir 20

Solzhenitsyn, Alexander 457, 460; and émigrés 275, 276-7; expulsion of and church reaction to 418; Lenten letter of 445-6, 456, 461

Soviet decrees and laws on religion—All Russian Central Executive Committee Presidium's Permanent Committee on Religious Cults, Instruction of 216; anti-monastic decree (1958) 344, 345, 353; on church closures 32, 39; on finances and taxes 172-3, 431; instructions of NKVD (1929) 164; on relics 39; on separation of Church from schools and state 477; see also "religious associations"

Soviet foreign policy and the Church 302, 311, 314-5, 469-70; attacks on US 313, 360; see also "Aleksii (Simansky)," "Pimen (Izvekov)," "Nikodim (Rotov)," "Nikolai (Yarushevich)"

Soviet policies on religions—and Evangelicals 40-1; importance of antireligious

struggle 52; and Jews 40; and Moslems 40; and Orthodox Church 63, 65-6; and Roman Catholics 40-1
Soviet studies on religion 355-7; categorization of believers 370; surveys and statistics 172, 454-6
Spassky, Nikolai 332
Spinka, Matthew 107, 185
Stalin 169, 190, 208, 256, 301, 312, 320, 409; cult of and impact on society 341, 350-1; death of and affect on Church 51, 102, 327, 330; "Dizziness from Success" article 166; limited toleration of Church after WWII 215, 218-9, 302, 388; and liquidation of Church 141, 160, 175; meeting with metropolitans (1943) 201-2, 203; persecution of Uniates 306, 309; and purges 177, 195, 246, 274, 350-1; recognition of Church in 1943 107, 111, 201-2; Soviet criticism of 330, 341; Te Deums for 315, 319; thanks Church for war efforts 200, 216; wartime church policies of 159-61, 194, 196
Stavrou, Theofanis 221, 228, 232, 239, 244, 245, 246
Stefan, Bulgarian exarch 304
Stefan (Dzubai), Bishop of Pittsburgh 287
Stratonov, Irinarkh 108, 121, 127, 134, 260
Struve, Nikita 341, 347, 438
Suslov 332
Sventsitsky 46, 48
Sylvester (Bratanovsky), Archbishop 155

Talantov, Boris 340-1, 346, 348, 354, 432
Talberg, N. 124, 132, 266
Tarnavsky, Petro 473
Tavrion (Batozsky) 460
taxation, on Church and clergy—Church as private enterprise 165, 347-8, 431-2; under German occupation 230-1; 1981 reform 431
Telnikov, Vladimir 375
Temporary Church Administration, Crimea 115
Temporary (Provisional) Higher Church Administration of South Russia 113-5; Novocherkassk sobor 115; Stavropol council and administration 115
Teodorovich, Ioann 75, 76
Theofan (Noli) 282
Theophilus, Metropolitan of North America 261, 271, 290-1, 296-8
Tikhomirov, Lev 54
Tikhon, Synodal bishop in US 489
Tikhon, Synodal bishop in Berlin 140, 223, 262
Tikhon, Archbishop of Urals 122
Tikhon (Agrikov), Archimandrite 407
Tikhon (Belavin), Patriarch 30, 66, 71, 88, 104, 141, 156, 163, 168, 181, 266, 290, 447, 483; administration, decrees, encyclicals of 38-9, 57, 78, 158, 332, 368; and America 33, 281-3, 285-7, 289; appoints locum tenentes 103, 107-8, 136-7, 150, 189; and Civil War 113-5; death and testament of 63, 103, 123-4, 142, 150; and Ecumenical Patriarchate 60, 64, 258; elected Metropolitan of Moscow 26; elected patriarch 31, 129, 387; and famine 93; and Georgian Church 205; imprisonments and releases 52, 55-6, 59, 72, 99, 119, 147-8; and modernization of services 83-4; petitions for seminaries and press 41; and Renovationists 53, 57, 59-61, 81, 148, 258; and Russian Church administration abroad 65, 114, 118-9, 120-1, 125, 131, 134, 146, 257, 277, 285; status of among faithful 67,

116, 127, 197, 276; and "True Orthodox" 150, 368; and Ukrainian Church 73, 75, 237, 473-4
Timashev, N. 291
Titlinov 28, 50, 54, 56, 59, 81
Tito 256, 295, 315
Tivetsky, Konstantin 218, 325, 331, 348, 401, 408, 420
Tolgsky, Alexander 63
Tolstoi, Dmitry A. 45, 46
Tolstoy, Leo 49
Toth, Alexis 281
Troitsky, Sergei 118, 258, 290, 328
Trotsky 107
Trubetskoi, Prince E. 27
Trubetskoi, Nikolai 232
Trubnikova, Alla 356
"True Orthodox Church" (IPTs) and "True Orthodox Christians" (IPKh) 365-70, 372, 373-5, 378, 382; and celibacy 371-2; and female clergy 373-4; and Soviet power 372; and youth 371; see also "catacomb Church" and "Old Believers"
Trushin, CRA official 401
Tuchkov, Evgeny 63, 150; attempts to cause schisms 66, 70, 107; offer to Illarion 72, 483; offer to Kirill 105-6, 213; and Renovationists 52, 59-61, 84; as "overprocurator" 485
"twenties"—see "parishes" and "religious associations"

Ukraine, Western (Galicia) 307; see also "Uniate Church, Ukraine"
Ukrainian Autocephalists (Lypkivskyites) 70, 473-6; and All-Ukrainian Orthodox Council 473-4; bishops and leaders of 476; confiscations of churches by 474-6; and 1921 *rada* 476
Ukrainian Autocephalous Church, revival under German occupation 236; and Banderist partisans 239-40, 243-4; bishops of 327, 239-41, 246; and German policy 239-40; and Lypkivsky clergy 237-8; and monasticism 242-5; and nationalism 236-46; and Orthodox *oikoumene* 237; and Poland 236-7; and religious revival 242; and Soviet terror 239; and West Ukraine 236-7
Ukrainian Orthodox (Patriarchal) Exarchate, Kiev—raided by KGB 432; youth choir harassed 432
Uniate Church, Romania 307
Uniate Church, Slovakia 307—see also "Carpathian Ukraine"
Uniate Church, Ukraine (Galicia) 306, 476; and liquidation council (St. Iur's Cathedral) 307; as national Church 309; Soviet persecution of 306, 308-9; and Ukrainian nationalism 306, 309; and WWII 245, 308
Ustasi regime, Yugoslavia 256

Vakhitov, Nur 40
Valentinov, A.A. 477
Varfolomei (Remov) 41, 181
Varnava, Serbian Patriarch 188-9, 261, 263-5, 290
Varsonofy (Khaibulin), Hieromonk 389, 435
Vasilevskaya, V.Ya. 161-2, 179
Vasilios III, Ecumenical Patriarch 64, 129, 259

Vasily (Basil Krivocheine), Archbishop of Brussels 393, 395-6, 410, 418-9, 437, 440
Vatican 308-9
Vedernikov, A.V. 202
Venedikt, Bishop of Ivanovo and Kineshma 321
Venyamin, Metropolitan of Petrograd 99, 134; cooperation on church valuables issue 97; election of 26; trial and execution of 55, 98, 117, 119, 155
Venyamin (Fedchenkov), Archbishop 115, 256, 289
Venyamin (Novitsky), Archbishop 246, 388, 395, 399, 422
Veryuzhsky, V. 157-8
Viktor, Archbishop of Peking 264, 305
Vitaly (Maximov) 259, 291, 294, 296, 489
Vladimir, Archbishop of Nice 141; succeeds Evlogy as Metropolitan of Western Europe 142, 270
Vladimir (Putyata) 88, 168
Vladimir Kirillovich, Grand Duke 222
Vlasov army 224-5
Vostokov, Vladimir 115
Voznesenskaya, Yu. 460
VTsS—see "Renovationist schism"
Vvedensky, Alexander 53, 68, 79, 88, 97, 155; active collaboration with GPU 52, 59, 65-6, 98; head of Union of Communities of Ancient Apostolic Churches 58, 82; ideas of 82-3, 85, 89; prerevolutionary activities 20, 82; visits Tikhon 55

West European (Evlogian) parishes 167; and Moscow Patriarchate 303
Witte, Sergei 22
World Council of Churches 361-2, 470; appeals to 435, 447-9; criticizes Soviet church policy 450; and Moscow Patriarchate 337, 447-8, 450; and Russian Baptists 448; and Soviet propaganda 316
Wrangel, General 115

Xenia of Petersburg 272

Yakimov, Nikon 442
Yakov, Abbot 443
Yakunin, Gleb 399, 400, 417, 418, 425, 431, 467, 471; and human rights movement 435-6, 440; letter, with Regelson, to WCC (1975) 447-8; letter, with Regelson, to WCC (1976) 449; memorandum, with Eshliman (1965) 346, 393, 421, 422, 464; petition for reinstatement 389; support from patriarchate 440
Yaroslavsky 172
Youth, and Church—choirs and their persecution 432-3; revitalization of 352-3; state prevention from attending and serving in church 342
Yuvenaly, Metropolitan of Krutitsy 451, 452, 453; administration of own diocese 410; and foreign policy work for Soviets 410, 448, 450; retirement of 451; on Solzhenitsyn letter 445-6; support of Dudko 438, 450; support of Yakunin 440

Zenkovsky, Vasily 132

Zheludkov, Sergei 354, 461
Zilberberg 431
Zinoviev, Grigory 52
Znanie society 316-7
Zubatov, Sergei 54
Zubov, P. 291